NAVAL TERMS DICTIONARY

Third Edition

NAVAL TERMS DICTIONARY

Third Edition

by

John V. Noel, Jr.
Captain, U.S. Navy (Retired)

and

Edward L. Beach
Captain, U.S. Navy (Retired)

Naval Institute Press, Annapolis, Maryland

Copyright © 1971, 1966
by the United States Naval Institute
Annapolis, Maryland

4th Printing, 1977

First edition copyright © 1952
by D. Van Nostrand Company, Inc.
Princeton, New Jersey, New York, N.Y.
Library of Congress Catalog Card Number: 77-151229
ISBN: 0-87021-481-0

Printed in the United States of America

TO MARY
AND
INGRID

Preface to the Third Edition

As in the previous editions, the primary consideration in selecting terms for inclusion in this edition of *Naval Terms Dictionary* has been current usage. A number of Old Navy expressions have, however, been included in recognition of the fact that old sailors never die and the lore of the sea by which they are living is being perpetuated even in these modern days of nuclear power and guided missiles. Old terms sometimes appear in current naval literature and their definition should be useful.

One of the other important considerations for this edition has been the ever-growing relationship between science, industry, and business on the one hand, and contracting, budgeting, appropriations, and the government on the other. Their composite effect on the Navy has, of course, been massive, as these pages reflect.

The U.S. Naval Institute has recently published the *Dictionary of Naval Abbreviations* (DICNAVAB), wherein will be found the acronyms, code names, and abbreviations not included in this edition of *Naval Terms Dictionary*. This book and DICNAVAB provide comprehensive coverage of terms and abbreviations in use in today's Navy.

In using this dictionary, it is helpful to know that words or phrases in italics indicate terms that are cross-referenced elsewhere in the book. Five appendices also add to the usefulness of this new edition.

Appendix A lists all ship types in the Navy. Appendix B explains the enlisted rating structure, lists the various rates, and shows the relationship of the several petty officer designations. As with ships, only those enlisted ratings presumed to be of greatest interest to the greatest number of persons have been defined in the body of the text.

The letters for classification, modified mission, basic mission, and series, as well as design number, are explained in Appendix C, Aircraft Designation System. A listing of popular names for aircraft is also found, with model designation and cognizant service. An individual aircraft is listed in the body of the dictionary under its popular name instead of its basic designation.

The missile designation system is treated in the same manner in Appendix D. The electronics nomenclature system, often referred to as the AN system, is covered in Appendix E. The kind of installation, the type of equipment, and its purpose are presented.

Because of the wide interest shown in the compilation of this dictionary, the list of contributors has grown to the point where they must be unnamed and unnumbered — but certainly not unappreciated. Our thanks to the many patient people who have helped.

The Authors

CONTENTS

NAVAL TERMS DICTIONARY

Third Edition

TERMS

A

Abaft:
To the rear of.

Abandon ship:
To leave the ship in an emergency such as sinking.

ABC Air Standardization Agreement (ABCAIRSTD):
Agreement among the American, British and Canadian governments for standardization of aircraft equipment and fittings.

Abeam:
In approximately the same horizontal plane of the observing ship or aircraft, *Bearing* 90° away from its heading or course.

ABLE:
Alfa.

Able Seaman (AB):
Merchant and civil service marine rating above an ordinary seaman. Also known as able-bodied seaman, from which the colloquial term "AB" is derived.

Aboard:
In a ship or on any activity such as a naval station. See *Close Aboard.*

Abort:
Failure to accomplish a mission for any reason other than enemy action.

Abreast:
By the side of; side by side. See *Abeam.*

Absence indicator:
Pennant flown by a ship to indicate absence of Commanding Officer or embarked flag or staff officer. Also called *Absentee.*

Absence without leave (AWOL):
See *Unauthorized absentee.*

Absentee:
Man missing at a muster. Slang for *Absence Indicator.*

Abyssal-benthic zone:
Subdivision of the deep-sea system of the *Benthic division* including waters deeper than 1000 meters.

ACADEME:
Model designation: TC-4C; cognizant service: Navy.
A commercial Grumman (Gulfstream I) aircraft modified as a bombardier/navigator trainer. Prop-jet.

Accepting authority:
The officer designated to accept a ship for the government, usually a Naval District Commandant or his representative.

Access, classified material:
The ability and opportunity of an individual to gain knowledge or possession of classified material.

Accommodation ladder:
Portable steps from the gangway down to the waterline. Sometimes incorrectly called *Gangway.*

Accountability:
The responsibility and obligation imposed by law on military personnel for keeping accurate records of property or funds and for submitting periodic reports thereon. See *Responsibility.*

Accountable officer:
One detailed to duty involving personal pecuniary responsibility for government funds.

Ace:
Pilot who has shot down 5 or more enemy aircraft.

Ace High:
Tropospheric forward scatter communications system.

Acey-deucy:
Nautical version of backgammon.

Acknowledge:
To inform originator by special message that his message has been understood.

ACORN:
Unit of administrative personnel and material needed to establish and operate an advanced naval air base.

Acoustic Data Analysis Center (ADAC):
Computerized library of data on underwater sound characteristics maintained at Naval Research and Development Center, Carderock, Maryland.

Acoustic dispersion:
Sound speed changes caused by frequency changes.

Acoustic mine:
One detonated by sound. See *Mine.*

Acoustics:
The science of sound dealing with its propagation, transmission, and effects.

Acoustic scattering:
Dispersion of sound waves caused by irregular reflection, refraction, etc.

Acoustic torpedo:
: Torpedo guided by sound. Active versions emit sounds and home on their echo, passive types home on sound emanations of target itself. See *Torpedo, Mark* 37.

Action Data Automation System:
: British version of Naval Tactical Data System, NTDS.

Action port (starboard):
: Command to gun and missile crews to indicate direction of enemy attack.

Action report:
: Detailed report of combat with the enemy.

Activation:
: The process, work and fitting out required to prepare a ship of the reserve fleet for transfer to the active fleet.

Active acoustic torpedo:
: Torpedo which homes on reflected sound which it emits. See *Acoustic torpedo.*

Active duty:
: Full-time service as distinct from inactive, retired, or reserve duty.

Active sonar:
: Equipment which provides information on distant underwater objects by evaluation of reflections of its own sound emissions. See *Passive sonar.*

Activity:
: Organizational unit of the Navy established under an officer-in-charge or a commanding officer.

Adapter:
: Coupling or similar device that permits joining fittings of different size.

Addressee:
: Activity or individual to whom a naval message is directed for action or information.

Adiabatic phenomena:
: Changes in material state (volume or pressure) occurring without a gain or loss of heat.

Administration:
: The management of all phases of naval operations not directly concerned with strategy or tactics.

Administrative Command:
: Command without operational functions; only concerned with logistics, maintenance, etc.

Administrative Contracting Officer (ACO):
: Contracting officer assigned to administer a contract at the contract administration office.

Administrative lead time:
: Interval between start of a procurement action and the actual contracting or ordering.

Admiral:
> The highest rank in the Navy, equivalent to General. An officer of four-star rank. A Rear Admiral wears two stars, a Vice Admiral three. Fleet Admiral, a special rank bestowed by Congress on WW II naval leaders, had five stars; but no officers of this rank survive. Sometimes called "full Admiral" to distinguish from other admirals, inasmuch as the title of "Admiral" is loosely used to refer to all. A *Commodore* wears a single star and is equivalent to a Brigadier General, but this rank is not used in the Navy in peacetime. Commodores and Admirals are *Flag Officers* since they are authorized to fly a flag with stars to denote their rank. The corresponding Army and Air Force term is General.

Admiral's March:
> Ceremonial music for flag officers and officials of equivalent rank. The number of ruffles and flourishes preceding the ceremonial tune denotes the number of stars authorized for the individual honored.

Admiralty law:
> Body of law that deals with maritime cases.

Adrift:
> Loose from towline or moorings; scattered about; not in proper stowage.

Advance:
> Distance gained in the direction of the original course when turning a ship, measured from the point at which the rudder is put over to the point where the ship has changed heading 90°. See *Transfer.*

Advanced Development Objective (ADO):
> Prepared by CNO outlining an experimental system of still untested military usefulness, technical feasibility and financial acceptability prior to preparation of a Specific Operational Requirement.

Advanced Sea Based Deterrent (ASBD):
> CNM program to develop follow-on to the *POLARIS POSEIDON* missile system for use in the late 1970-80 era.

Advanced Surface Missile System (ASMS):
> CNM development effort to produce a successor to the *TARTAR, TALOS* and *TERRIER* missiles for use in the 1970s.

Advance force:
> Task force preceding the *Attack Force* in an amphibious assault, conducting preparatory minesweeping, bombardment, and reconnaissance.

Advance Material Requirements (AMR):
> List of materials requisitioned in advance of actual shipbuilding construction, conversion or repair.

Advancement in rating:
> Promotion of an enlisted man to a higher *Rate.*

Advection fog:
> Fog formed when warm air passes over cold water.

AEOLUS:
> Small meteorological sounding rocket.

Aerial mine:
> See *Mine.*

AEROBEE:
Research Rocket.

AERO COMMANDER:
Model designation: U-4 or U-9; cognizant service: Air Force.
High-wing cantilever monoplane for administrative use. 2-crew, 4-passengers.
Propeller-driven.

Aerographer:
Warrant officer advanced from *Aerographer's Mate.*

Aerographer's mate (AG):
Petty officer trained in weather forecasting. See Appendix B.

AEROSCAR:
Experimental rocket under study for the HYDRA program.

Affirmative:
Communications term meaning: Yes; permission granted; authorized;
approved; recommended approve; etc.

Afloat:
Supported by the water. Also, at sea, as in "forces afloat."

Aft (after):
Pertaining to the stern or towards the stern of a ship or aircraft.

After body:
The section of a ship or boat hull abaft the center. The detachable portion
of a torpedo, immediately abaft the energy storage compartment (air flask
or battery compartment), which contains the propulsive and guidance
mechanisms.

After bow (quarter) spring:
Mooring line leading aft from the bow (quarter) of a ship to the pier.

Afterburner (AB):
Part of a jet engine into which fuel is injected and ignited by exhaust, to
increase thrust for short periods.

Afterburning:
The process of fuel injection and combustion in the exhaust jet.

Afterleech:
The downwind *Leech* of a *Fore-and-aft* sail. The edge opposite the *Luff,* or
Fore Leech.
Aftermost:
Nearest the stern.

Afternoon effect:
Thermal gradient caused by sun's warming of the sea's surface. Effect is a
possible reduction in sonar effectiveness.

Afternoon watch:
1200-1600 watch.

Agency:
Any independent portion of the Executive Branch of the government, including corporations wholly or partially owned which are government instrumentalities but excluding the District of Columbia. Loosely used, however, to designate subordinate organizational parts of the Defense Department and the military departments.

Aground:
Fast to the bottom. A ship runs aground or goes aground.

Ahead:
Forward of the bow.

Ahead-thrown weapon:
Missile projected by rocket power or fired from a launcher ahead of a ship, used against submarines.

Ahoy:
A distinct nautical hail. Supposedly once the dread war cry of the Vikings.

Aide:
Officer assigned as administrative or personal assistant to a flag officer or senior civilian official. An aide wears *Aiguillettes.*

Aids to navigation:
Buoys, markers, lights, bells, fog horns, radio and loran stations, any similar device to assist navigators. Most aids to navigation are in fact piloting aids, as distinguished from aids to navigation offshore such as Loran.

Aiguillette:
The badge of office of a personal aide to an officer entitled to an aide. The aides to the President of the United States wear their aiguillettes on the right shoulder. Aides to all other senior officers and dignitaries wear them on the left shoulder. Dress aiguillettes are extremely ornate— braided loops terminating in two devices resembling pencils and, in fact, so called. Service aiguillettes are merely simple loops pinned over the shoulder, but distinguish the rank of the officer aided: e.g., four loops for officers of four star rank and above, otherwise a number of loops equal to the number of his stars. Presidential aides wear aiguillettes of solid gold. Aides to other officers wear blue and gold braid if Navy, or red and gold if Marine Corps or Army.
One theory of the origin of aiguillettes is that the aide-de-camp of a superior officer carried the rope and pegs for tethering his superior's horse, and generally, for convenience, carried them around his shoulder. Thus the rope and pegs became a distinguishing mark. A variant theory is that the pegs were indeed pencils intended to write the leader's orders.
Slang: *loafers loops, chicken guts.*

Aileron:
Movable control surface of an aircraft wing, used to impart rolling motion to the aircraft.

Air and Naval Gunfire Liaison Company (ANGLICO):
An organization composed of Marine and Navy personnel specially qualified for shore control of naval gunfire and close air support.

Air bedding:
Aboard ship, to bring bedding topside for exposure to sun and fresh air.

Airborne early warning (AEW):
The extension of radar detection range by means of airborne search radar and relay equipment to provide early warning.

Airborne Radiation Thermometer (ART):
A device used to measure ocean surface temperature by radiation.

Air bunting:
Hoisting signal flags to dry them.

Air cock:
Valve placed at the highest point of a boiler to release entrapped air.

Air control center:
A space that is set aside for control of aircraft.

Air controller:
One who directs aircraft by means of radar, radio, electronic plot, etc.

Air controlman:
A petty officer who stands watches in air-control stations ashore and afloat.

Air control ship:
A ship detailed responsibility for air defense.

Air corridors:
Restricted air routes of travel specified for use by aircraft.

Aircraft (AC):
Vehicle designed to travel through the atmosphere supported by its own buoyancy or by lift developed by an airfoil.

Aircraft Accident Report (AAR):
Required on the occurrence of any type of aircraft accident.

Aircraft antisubmarine attack:
Classified by submarine position at time ordnance is launched: blind, submarine fully submerged not visible; early, submarine surfaced or diving with part exposed; late, submarine submerged from 10 to 20 minutes; tardy, submarine in dive less than 10 seconds; visible, submarine submerged or snorkeling, but visible.

Aircraft carrier:
Major offensive ship of the fleet whose chief weapon is its aircraft. See Appendix A.

Aircraft designation system:
See Appendix C.

Aircraft division:
Two sections of aircraft of same type.

Aircraft Equipment Requirement Schedule (AERS):
Delivery schedule for government furnished equipment in the Master Configuration List.

Aircraft Maintenance Delayed for Parts (AMDP):
Code to indicate reason an aircraft is not operational (parts unavailable).

Aircraft Not Fully Equipped (ANFE)
: Code used to indicate that restrictions are placed on aircraft for lack of equipment.

Aircraft Out-of-Commission for Parts (AOCP):
: Code used to indicate reason for aircraft not being operational.

Aircraft section:
: Basic tactical unit of 2 aircraft of same type.

Aircraft squadron:
: Two or more divisions of aircraft.

Aircraft system:
: Any aircraft, including its airframe, propulsion machinery, armament, electrical, electronic, and mechanical equipment. See *System*.

Aircrew Survival Equipmentman:
: Petty officer who tests and repairs parachutes, survival gear, and flight clothing.

Airdale:
: Jocular term for a naval aviator.

Air defense:
: All measures designed to nullify or reduce effectiveness of hostile aircraft or guided missiles after they are airborne.

Air Defense Identification Zone (ADIZ):
: Airspace above specified area in which ready recognition and control of aircraft are required.

Air defense warning conditions:
: Degree of air raid probability: air defense warning yellow—attack probable; air defense warning red—attack imminent or is taking place; air defense warning white—attack is improbable.

Air ejector:
: Device using the suction created by steam flowing through a nozzle to remove air and other noncondensable gases from a condenser or other part of the return-feed system. The purpose is to enable the condenser to maintain a better vacuum, thus promoting efficiency of the steam cycle, and to reduce corrosion by reducing oxygen content.

Airfoil:
: Surface designed to produce lift from the air through which it passes. See *Foil*.

Airframe:
: Generic term including all parts of an airplane except power plant, armament, and electronic gear.

Air group:
: The aircraft of an ASW carrier, made up of squadrons. See *Air Wing*.

Air intelligence (AI):
: Activity formerly known as Air Combat Intelligence. Deals with intelligence aspects of naval air operations.

Air lock:
A double door giving access to and preserving air pressure in a fireroom or similar space under pressure.

Airman (AN):
An enlisted man in paygrade E-3 who performs aviation duties. See Appendix B.

Air officer:
Officer responsible for aviation matters in an aircraft carrier. Heads the Air Department.

Air operations (air plot):
Air operations control center aboard a carrier.

Air Pilots:
Printed guides similar to *Coast Pilots* but of interest mainly to aviators, published by the U.S. Navy.

Air port:
A round window in a ship's side, fitted with a lens frame and a metal cover called a *Battle Port. Air Scoops,* screens and ventilating *Deadlights* are an airport's removable fixtures. Commonly called "porthole." See *Port.*

Air Refueling
Process of refueling aircraft in the air.

Air register:
A device in the casing of a boiler for regulating the amount of air for combustion.

Air scoop:
A sheet metal device fitted into an *Air port* for catching a breeze.

Air Search Attack Team (ASAT):
Aircraft ASW team consisting of a search aircraft and one or more attack aircraft.

Air Search Attack Unit (ASAU):
Tactical designation given one or more ASW aircraft assigned to locate and destroy submarines.

Air speed:
Speed of aircraft through and relative to the air, distinct from *Ground speed.* Indicated air speed is an uncorrected reading of the air-speed indicator. Calibrated air speed is the indicated air speed corrected for instrument errors. True air speed is corrected for altitude and temperature.

Air stabilizer:
A parachute-type tail stabilizer for aerial torpedoes to slow them down before impact with the water.

Air Strike:
Fighter attack aircraft assigned an offensive mission against specific objectives. It may consist of several tactical organizations under a single command in the air.

Air support:
See *Close Air Support.*

Air surface zone:
  Restricted ocean area for antisubmarine operations.

Air Systems Command:
  Functional command replacing Bureau of Naval Weapons in 1966 Navy
  Department reorganization. Component of *Naval Material Command.*

Air-to-Surface Missile (ASM):
  Former designation of missile launched from an aircraft against a surface
  target. See Appendix D for new designations.

Air-to-Underwater Missile (AUM):
  Former designation of missile launched from aircraft against underwater
  targets. See Appendix D for new designations.

Air Traffic Control Radar Beacon System (AIMS):
  Chief of Naval Material project in cooperation with civilian agencies to
  permit positive identification of every plane airborne over the United
  States at any time.

Air Transportable Sonar (ATS):
  Sonar Equipment designed for aircraft use.

Air Transport Group:
  A task organization of transport aircraft units organized to transport
  amphibious troops to the objective area, or for logistic support.

Air wing:
  The aircraft of an attack carrier, made up of squadrons.
  See *Air group.*

ALBACORE:
  Experimental submarine developed in connection with high-speed hull
  design.

ALBATROSS:
  Model designation: HU-16; cognizant services: Navy, Coast Guard, and
  Air Force. High-wing, all-metal amphibious aircraft with fixed-wing
  floats. For search and rescue missions. 4-crew, 10-passengers. Propeller-
  driven.

Aldis lamp:
  A portable signal light used in ships and aircraft.

Alert, dusk or dawn:
  Special precautions, normally all hands to *Battle stations,* at time when
  attack is most likely prior to first light and at sunset.

ALFA:
  RUR-4A rocket-boosted depth charge formerly known as Weapon Able. Also
  phonetic word for letter A, formerly *Able.*

Algae:
  A group of marine plants ranging in size from single cell varieties to the
  large kelps.

Alidade:
  A telescopic device used with a gyro repeater for taking bearings.

Align:
 Electronics: to adjust two or more resonant circuits. Gunnery, to adjust guns and the fire control equipment that controls them to the same plane of reference, and to line up all aiming devices and bearing transmitters.

All hands:
 All those aboard ship (except, under certain circumstances, those on watch). Name of a call on *Boatswain's Pipe.*

All hands parade:
 A designated assembly place for all hands on board ship. Used for such events as change of command ceremony.

Allied Administrative Publication (AAP):
 Group name used to identify administrative publications written for use by the U.S. and its allies. Normally followed by a specific identification number.

All night in:
 A full night's sleep with no watch.

Allotment:
 Portion of a man's pay or of an appropriation or fund, regularly assigned to a specific account.

Allowance:
 Authorized personnel on a peacetime level, reduced from the wartime *Complement,* based on peacetime operations, habitability, budgetary considerations, and upkeep requirements. See *Complement,* also *Manning level.*

Allowance list:
 A listing of repair parts, equipage, and consumable supplies authorized and required to be on board a ship or in a naval activity.

Alluvium:
 Silt, sand, gravel or other material deposited by running water.

All-weather air stations:
 Designated air station to which single pilot aircraft may be cleared under IFR.

Almanac (nautical and air):
 Naval Observatory publications providing astronomical data needed for navigation.

Aloft:
 Up high, as on a mast, or, "strong winds aloft."

Alongside:
 Near the side of the ship.

Altars:
 Steps in the side of a *Graving dock.*

Alteration:
 Any change in equipment or machinery which involves a change in design, materials, number, location, or relationship of the component parts of an assembly.

Alternating light:
   Navigational light showing color variations. May be flashing, group
   flashing, occulting, or fixed.

Altimeter:
   An *Aneroid barometer* which measures in feet, yards, or meters an
   aircraft's elevation above a given reference plane, such as sea level.
   Must constantly be corrected for barometric pressure on the ground.

Altitude:
   The height of an aircraft above a reference point. True altitude is
   height above sea level, corrected for temperature. Absolute altitude
   is height above ground.

ALUMINAUT:
   Aluminum submarine developed privately for deep ocean research.

ALUSNA:
   U.S. Naval Attache, normally followed by name of city, or nation in which
   stationed--AL in communication serves only to differentiate from USNA
   (U.S. Naval Academy.) See *Naval Attache.*

ALVIN:
   Deep-submergence vehicle for oceanographic research.

Ambient noise:
   Sound produced in water by sources external to the measuring equipment.

American British Canadian Standardization Agreement (ABC):
   Joint agreement by these nations for the standardization of military equipment to make it useable in material of each nation.

Amidships:
   In or toward the middle of a ship.

Ammo:
   Slang: *Ammunition.*

Ammunition:
   Shells, powder, missiles, rockets, etc., designed for firing from guns or
   launchers.

Amphibian:
   An airplane designed to operate from land or water.

Amphibious:
   Capable of operating on land and sea.

Amphibious assault ship (LPH):
   Ship designed to transport and land troops, equipments, and supplies by
   means of embarked helicopters.

Amphibious Construction Battalion (ACB):
   Naval unit organized to provide and operate ship-to-shore fuel systems,
   pontoon causeways, transfer barges and tugs, and to provide salvage and
   beach improvement capability to a Naval Beach group.

Amphibious control group:
   Personnel, ships and craft designated to control the water-borne ship-to-
   shore movement in an amphibious operation.

Amphibious force:
>Naval force and landing force, together with supporting forces that are trained, organized, and equipped for amphibious operations. Also; administrative title of the amphibious type command of a fleet.

Amphibious group:
>Command within the amphibious force, consisting of the commander and his staff, designed to exercise operational command of assigned units in executing all phases of a division-size amphibious operation.

Amphibious lift:
>See *Lift.*

Amphibious operation:
>Attack launched from the sea by naval and landing forces, embarked in ships or craft, including the following stages: planning, embarkation, rehearsal, movement and assault.

Amphibious squadron:
>Tactical and administrative organization composed of amphibious assault shipping to transport troops and equipment for an amphibious assault operation.

Amphibious transport dock (LPD):
>Ship designed to transport and land troops, equipment, and supplies by means of embarked landing craft, amphibious vehicles and helicopters.

Amphibious Troops:
>Troop components, ground and airborne, assigned to land in an amphibious operation. Synonomous with "Landing Forces" as defined in the National Security Act of 1947.

Amphibious vessel:
>A ship designed to participate in amphibious operations. See Appendix A.

AN/:
>The standard prefix for an item of electronic equipment listed in the Joint Electronics Type Designation System. Pronounced as two letters: A—N. See *Electronics nomenclature system,* Appendix E.

Anadramous fish:
>Fish which lay their eggs in fresh water where they hatch but which spend their adult life at sea, returning to fresh water to spawn.

Analytical Studies of Surface Effects of Submerged Submarines (ASSESS):
>A system for detection of submarines independent of acoustic phenomena.

Anchor (n):
>A device used to hold a ship or boat fast to the bottom. Old-fashioned anchors were in the form of the traditional hook, and weight for weight such anchors still have the best holding power. They are however so difficult to rig for sea that, as ships became bigger and required heavier anchors, the currently familiar stockless type was developed. Such anchors can very simply be hoisted snugly into their hawsepipes when the ship gets underway, in contrast to the old-fashioned ones which require fishing, catting, and placement on the billboard and then must be strongly secured— all very hazardous in a seaway.
>Anchors may be: *Bower, Stream, Stern, Kedge, Boat,* and *Sheet.*

Anchor (v.i.):
> The process of dropping the anchor, of veering chain to the prescribed scope, i.e. six to ten times the depth of water, and of securing so that the ship can ride to the anchor in its designated berth. In nautical terms the maneuver is called "bringing a ship to an anchor."

Anchorage:
> Area assigned for anchoring ships. Also any stationary object that acts as a stop or anchor for bracing or shoring.

Anchorage buoy:
> Buoy marking limit of an anchorage area; not to be confused with a *Mooring buoy* or an *Anchor buoy.*

Anchor at short stay:
> Anchor chain at minimum length with anchor still down. Anchor is "hove short."

Anchor ball:
> A black, circular shape hoisted to indicate that the ship is anchored.

Anchor buoy:
> Small float attached to the anchor to facilitate recovery if the chain is slipped or is parted.

Anchor cable:
> Wire or line running between anchor and small vessel.

Anchor chain:
> Heavy stud-linked chain used for anchoring large ships.

Anchor detail:
> Men on forecastle assigned to handle the *Ground tackle.*

Anchor engine:
> The driving mechanism for the *Windlass* or *Capstan* by which the anchor may be raised. Usually a steam engine, though hydraulics are sometimes used. Located under the *Forecastle.*

Anchor ice:
> All submerged ice that is attached to bottom.

Anchor in sight:
> A report made by anchor detail on forecastle to the bridge when the anchor itself has been sighted; followed by "clear anchor" or "foul anchor" depending on whether or not the anchor has become tangled.

Anchor lights:
> Lights required by *Rules of the Road* indicating that vessel is anchored. Also called *Riding lights.*

Anchor man:
> Last man of a list or of a group. The "anchor man" of a U.S. Naval Academy class is the last in academic standing and consequently ranks junior to all his classmates.

Anchor watch:
Seamen on deck (or turned in topside on cots) available during the night when ship is moored or anchored to assist the *OOD*, particularly with *Ground tackle.*

Anchor's aweigh:
Expression used to report that anchor has just been lifted clear of bottom. The ship now bears the weight of her anchor and is considered to be *Underway,* (not "underweigh").

Anemometer:
Instrument for measuring wind velocity.

Aneroid barometer:
Instrument using a bellows device to measure atmospheric pressure, thereby indicating changes in weather.

A-NEW:
Navy management program directed at assembly of an integrated airborne electronics system for anti-submarine warfare. "A new" approach because the design accommodates the equipment rather than building equipment to fit a pre-designed plane. Program begun in 1960.

ANFE:
Aircraft not fully equipped.

Angle, drift:
Horizontal angle between the fore and aft axis of an aircraft and its path relative to the ground.

Angle of attack:
Angle between a fixed *Airframe* reference line and the apparent relative flow line of the air.

Angle on the bow:
Angle between fore and aft axis of target and the line of sight, measured from target's bow to port or to starboard through 180°. Estimated angle on the bow is one of the critical observations made through a submarine periscope during an approach to a torpedo firing position. See *Target angle.*

ANNA:
Joint Army, Navy, Air Force, NASA geodetic satellite program, formerly known as *FIREFLY.*

Appropriation, annual:
An appropriation available only during the fiscal year specified in the appropriation act.

Annunciator:
Signal device on a ship's bridge to deliver orders to engine room. See *Engine-order telegraph.*

AN system:
Colloquial term for the electronics nomenclature system. Pronounced as two letters: A—N. See Appendix E.

Antiaircraft Projectile (AA):
   General term applied to projectiles for antiaircraft ammunition.

Anti-Air Warfare (AAW):
   Warfare directed against airborne vehicles.

Anti-Air Warfare Area:
   An area to be kept under surveillance and where protective measures are
   to be started. Associated terms are: *Anti-Air Warfare Axis, Cross-
   over Point, Destruction Area, Surveillance Area,* and *Vital Area.*

Anti-Air Warfare Axis:
   The true bearing from the center of the area to be protected, or the task
   group position, in the most probable direction of attack.

Antiblackout suit:
   Pilot's suit which, when inflated, helps a pilot resist centrifugal force.
   Also called G-suit and pressure suit.

Anticorrosive paint:
   A composition applied to prevent rust.

Antifouling paint:
   A composition applied over the anticorrosive paint on a ship's bottom
   to prevent attachment of marine growth.

Antirecovery device:
   Device incorporated into mine to explode it if disturbed.

Antisubmarine support aircraft carrier (CVS):
   An aircraft carrier equipped for sustained antisubmarine warfare and for
   protection of convoys. It also may be used to provide close air support.

Antisubmarine Warfare (ASW):
   All-inclusive term embracing all techniques employed against enemy
   submarines.

Antisubmarine warfare (ASW) screen:
   Formation of ships and aircraft in advance of a Navy force designed to
   protect against submarine attack.

Antisubmarine Warfare Systems Analysis Group (ASWAG):
   Staff of the Undersea Warfare Research and Development Planning
   Council established at *NOL* to continually review R&D programs.

APACHE:
   Meteorological and radiation research rocket based on an improved
   INJUN.

Apogee:
   The point at which a missile trajectory or a satellite orbit is farthest
   from the center of the gravitational field of the controlling body or
   bodies.

Applied research:
   Research conducted in support of some fleet need.

Apportionment:
> The determination by the Bureau of the Budget as to the amount of obligations or expenditures which may be incurred or authorized during a specified period.

Apportionment estimate:
> The repricing of individual programs in terms of appropriations expected.

Apportionment request:
> Navy request, via the Navy Comptroller, justifying its apportionment from each appropriation.

Appraisal:
> Analysis at each management level to determine progress or effectiveness of approved programs in order to measure and evaluate them and determine if changes are necessary.

Apprehension:
> Taking a person into custody. See *Arrest.*

Appropriation:
> Congressional authorization to spend government funds for specific purposes. May be continuing or annual.

Appropriation, continuing:
> An appropriation available until exhausted for the purpose made without any time limit.

Appropriation title:
> The descriptive name assigned to an appropriation account. It does not include a fiscal year, hence could include money available from several fiscal year's accounts.

Approved circuit:
> A communication channel or frequency approved for transmission of classified traffic in the clear.

Approved program:
> Individual program element or component of the Five-Year Defense Program approved by the Secretary of Defense.

Apron:
> Area of a pier or wharf upon which cargo is unloaded. Also edge of airfield short of runway.

AQM 35A, B:
> Jet-powered drone for training of *TALOS* crews.

AQM 36A:
> Target drone.

AQM 37A:
> Supersonic target missile, speed Mach 3.5, ceiling 90,000 feet.

AQM 38A, B:
> Supersonic rocket powered target drone for use with air-to-air and surface-to-air missiles.

AQS 10:
Helicopter borne dipping sonar for ASW use.

Arbor, depth charge:
Device holding a depth charge on its projector. See *K-gun, Y-gun.*

ARCHER:
Sounding rocket.

Archibenthic zone:
Subdivision of the deep-sea system of the benthic division including
waters of 200 to 1000 meters in depth.

Arc of visibility:
Portion of the horizon, expressed in degrees, through which a navigational
light is visible from seaward.

ARCON:
Sounding rocket developed with NASA.

Arctic Research Laboratory (ARL):
Located at Pt. Barrow Alaska, operated by the University of Alaska for
ONR.

Area, forward:
Geographical: combat zone.

Area, mounting:
Where forces are assembled prior to an amphibious operation.

Area, objective:
Definite geographical area containing a military objective.

ARGUS ISLAND:
Oceanographic Research Laboratory located on Plantagenet Bank near
Bermuda.

Arm:
To make a weapon ready to fire or explode. To equip a ship or aircraft
with weapons. To fill cavity at bottom of sounding lead with soap or
tallow to obtain a bottom sample.

Armament:
Weapons of a ship or aircraft.

Armed forces of the U.S.:
Collective term for all the components of the Army, Navy, Air Force,
and Coast Guard, when part of the U.S. Navy, as during time of war.
See *United States Armed Forces.*

Armed guard:
Naval gun crews on merchant ships during wartime.

Armed Services Procurement Planning Officer (ASPPO):
Staff member of a military field office assigned to coordinate all production
planning for DOD in specified plants.

Armed Services Procurement Regulations (ASPR):
The body of regulations governing writing of all contracts for supplies
or services to DOD.

Arming crew:
    Men who provide weapons and ammunition to carrier aircraft.

Armor:
    Steel or other protection against projectiles, in ships, aircraft, or
    special uniform.

Armored rope:
    Wire rope with hemp core and a flat wire wound around outside of each
    strand; used chiefly in salvage or similar work.

Armor Piercing (AP):
    Ammunition specially designed to penetrate armor.

Armor Piercing Incendiary (API):
    Armor piercing projectiles specially designed to set fires after piercing
    armor.

Armor Piercing Tracer (APT):
    An armor piercing projectile fitted with tracer for spotting.

Armory:
    Compartment aboard ship where small arms and light machine guns are
    stowed and serviced.

Array:
    Two or more hydrophones feeding into a common receiver.

Arrest:
    Restraint of a person by competent authority. See *Apprehension.* Involves
    relief from military duties. See *Restriction.*

Arresting gear:
    Arrangement of wires on carrier flight deck that stops an airplane after
    airplane's tailhook has engaged it.

Articles for the Government of the Navy:
    No longer effective, replaced by the *Uniform Code of Military Justice.*
    See *Rocks* and *Shoals.*

Artificial horizon:
    An instrument indicating the attitude of an aircraft by simulating the
    appearance of a natural horizon with reference to a miniature airplane.
    Also a simulated horizon in a navigating instrument. A pool of mercury
    used for a mirror. Since the mercury will lie absolutely horizontally,
    a sight may be taken using the heavenly body's own reflection in place
    of a horizon, and dividing the observed angle by two.

Asbestos kit:
    Fire-resistant clothing for firefighting. Also called a "hot suit"
    worn by a *Hot suitman.*

A-Scope:
    Cathode ray indicator used to measure target ranges and size through
    vertical deflections on a horizontal scale.

ASDIC:
Echo ranging equipment, the British equivalent of *Sonar.*

Ashcan:
Slang: *Depth Charge.*

Ashore:
On the beach or shore. A man may go ashore on *Liberty,* but if a ship goes ashore, she is *Aground.*

ASPECT:
Short-pulse ASW classification device designed for destroyer use but now used in the *SEA KING* helicopter.

Aspect ratio:
For an aircraft wing—its span divided by its width. For a rudder—its depth divided by its width. Thus: the length of any moving surface, measured across the direction of motion, divided by its length in the direction of motion. A long thin wing therefore has a higher aspect ratio than a short stubby one.

ASROC:
Model designation: RUR-5; cognizant service: Navy. Anti-submarine rocket, fired from a trainable mount in a surface ship.

Assault craft:
Landing craft used in amphibious operations.

Assault shipping:
Amphibious vessels carrying assault troops and equipment for a landing operation.

Assault waves:
Scheduled, leading waves of boats and amphibious vehicles of an amphibious landing.

Astern:
Towards the back or after end of a ship or formation. Generally used in the sense of "behind." Thus, a fast ship leaves a slower one *astern.*

Astro compass:
Optical device for solving the astronomical triangle mechanically. Used by aircraft for determining true heading.

Asymmetry factor:
Ratio of length to width of a sea target.

As you were:
Command meaning: "Resume former activity or formation."

Athwart, athwartships:
At right angles to the fore and aft centerline of a ship or boat. Sometimes pronounced "thwartships." *Thwarts* are always athwartships.

Atlantic Ridge:
Undersea ridge which runs from Iceland to Bouvet Island and separates the Atlantic Ocean into two large basins.

Atlantic Undersea Test and Evaluation Center (AUTEC):
Located in Tongue of the Ocean, in the Bahamas. Environmental laboratory for calibration of sonar, measurement of sounds emanating from ship and testing of weapons undersea, on the surface or in the air. Instrumentation area; five miles wide by approximately 50 miles.

ATLANTIS:
Long-range study of feasibility of large ocean surveillance systems.

ATLAS:
Model designation: CGM-16; Cognizant service: Air Force. Inertial guided surface-to-surface ICBM.

Atoll:
A ring-shaped coral reef usually found in the Pacific and Indian Oceans, often carrying low sand islands. The body of water enclosed by the reef is a lagoon.

Atomizer:
Device feeding fuel oil into a boiler as a fine spray. Together with the *Air register* it forms the *Burner.*

Attack aircraft carrier (CVA, CVAN):
Warship designed to support and operate aircraft in attacks on targets afloat or ashore, and engage in sustained operations in support of other forces. See Appendix A.

Attack director:
Computing element of a fire-control system.

Attack force:
All ships, troops, and aircraft used in the attack phase of an amphibious assault.

Attack group:
Subordinate task organization of the Navy forces of an attack force, e.g., an amphibious attack group is composed of assault shipping and supporting naval units designated to transport, protect, land, and initially support a landing group.

Attack plane:
Multi-weapon carrier aircraft which can carry bombs, torpedoes, and rockets.

Attack plotter:
Device displaying movement of ship and target, part of fire-control system.

Attack teacher:
Training device for simulation of actual tactics involved in submarine or antisubmarine combat. Originally devised to train submarine commanders in attacking ships. Subsequently a modification was developed for ASW attacks on submarines.

Attend the side:
To be on the quarterdeck to meet important persons.

Attention to port, starboard:
Command given to topside personnel when ship is rendering *Passing Honors*. Personnel in view of the honored ship are required to come to attention facing the designated side, prepared to salute if ordered.

Augmentor:
Device for increasing the efficiency of an air pump in a steam power plant.

AURORA:
Concept for a submarine-launched satellite interceptor.

Aurora Australis:
Equivalent of Aurora Borealis, southern hemisphere.

Aurora Borealis:
Phenomenon, called commonly, "Northern Lights" appearing as streamers of light in upper atmosphere, northern hemisphere.

Auroral zones:
Areas in the higher latitudes where polar lights occur.

Authentication:
Communication security measure designed to prevent fraudulent transmissions.

Authorized Data List (ADL):
Master list of technical data and information from which data requirements must be selected.

Auto cat:
Airplane used to relay radio messages automatically.

Automatic Carrier Landing System (ACLS):
Designated project of CNO for development of a system to automatically control planes landing on carrier decks.

Automatic Merchant Vessel Report (AMVER):
The U.S. Coast Guard's computerized worldwide merchant ship plotting system that provides search and rescue information.

Auxiliary Landing Field (ALF):
Landing facility normally used for special purposes, or emergencies, but normally regarded as a part of or an air station complex.

Auxiliary machinery:
All machinery other than the main engines aboard ship. Examples are condensers, feed pumps, anchor engine, evaporators, ice machine, etc.

Auxiliary Power Plant (APP):
Applied to aircraft, usually refers to the model of afterburner used in jets.

Availability:
Period assigned a ship for accomplishment of work at a repair activity. May be restricted, technical, regular overhaul, voyage repairs, or up-keep period availability.

Availability factor:
Percentage of aircraft that are operational or *On the Line.*

Avast:
Order to "stop" or "cease."

Average depth:
Of water, based on soundings reduced to low water datum, on a chart.

Average limit of ice:
The average seaward extent of ice during a normal winter.

Aviation boatswain's mate:
Petty officer who operates airplane handling and fueling gear of all types.

Aviation electrician's mate (AE):
Petty officer who tests, maintains, and repairs all types of aviation electrical equipment.

Aviation electronicsman (AL):
Petty officer who operates electronic gear in flight.

Aviation electronics technician (AT):
Petty officer who maintains aircraft electronics equipment.

Aviation machinist's mate (AD):
Petty officer who maintains and repairs airplane engines and accessories.

Aviation ordnanceman (AO):
Petty officer who operates, installs, and maintains aviation ordnance.

Aviation storekeeper (AK):
Petty officer who receives, stores, and issues aviation supplies and spare parts.

Aviation structural mechanic (AM):
Petty officer who maintains and repairs aircraft structures and hydraulic equipment.

Awaiting Aircraft Availability (AAA):
Term applied to indicate that aircraft is due for overhaul.

Awash:
So low that water washes over.

Away:
Term used in passing the word aboard ship. e.g.: "Call away the gig." "Away rescue and assistance party, away." Refers to prospective departure from the ship on a mission or errand.

Aweigh:
Said of an anchor when clear of the bottom. See *Anchor's aweigh*.

Axis:
Reference line for stationing ships, originating at the formation center.

Aye Aye:
A seamanlike response to an order or instruction signifying that the order is heard, is understood, and will be carried out. "Aye" is Old English for "yes."

Azimuth:
   Angle measured clockwise between the direction north and the other
   direction being described. Usually the bearing of a celestial body.

Azimuth circle:
   Compass bowl fitting used to measure bearings or azimuths.

AZTEC:
   Model designation: U-11; cognizant service: Navy.
   Light, low-wing monoplane used for light logistic support at naval bases
   in continental United States. Same as commercial Piper Aztec. 1-crew,
   4-passenger. Propeller-driven.

B

Babbitt metal:
Soft, white antifriction alloy of copper, tin, and antimony used for
bearing surfaces.

Back:
To reverse engines so that ship may be stopped or made to go astern.

Background noise:
Noise which limits echo detection. At sea it may interfere with sonar
and can be caused by sea life, sea action, or the system itself.

Back pressure:
Pressure on the exhaust side of a steam or reciprocating engine.

Backrush:
The flow of water down the foreshore after the uprush of incoming waves.
Also called backwash.

Back to battery:
Return of a gun after recoil to firing position. Also, slang for personal
recovery from shock, injury, or illness.

Backs:
The wind backs when it changes direction counterclockwise. See *Haul*.
(Note: the direction of the wind is the direction *from* which it is blowing.)

Backstay:
A stay supporting a mast from aft.

Backwash:
Water thrown aft by turning of ship's propeller.

Backwater:
Command given to oarsmen to reverse usual rowing motion.

Bad Conduct Discharge (BCD):
A punitive discharge awarded to an enlisted man for severe infractions
of regulations. The only type of discharge which carries greater
prejudice is the "dishonorable discharge."

Baffle:
Plate used to deflect fluids, gases, or sound waves.

Baffle area:
An area roughly 30 degrees either side of the stern of a ship in which
maintenance of a sonar contact is most difficult. Because of the noise
from own propellers, sonar equipment is frequently designed with a baffle
area astern.

Bail:
To dip water out of a boat. The spreader to which the *Accommodation
ladder* topping lift is secured.

Bail out:
To jump from or eject from aircraft. Slang: to rescue one from an
administrative predicament.

Baiting:
>   Tactic designed to lull an enemy, especially a submarine, into a false
>   sense of security and inducing it to take action making it liable to
>   detection or attack.

Balanced rudder:
>   Rudder in which part of the blade surface is forward of the axis to
>   counterbalance water pressure on after part.

Balancing:
>   In submarines, the maintenance of depth with no way on by riding on
>   top of a density layer. Also called *hovering.*

Ballast:
>   The weight added in a ship or boat to insure stability; to pump sea
>   water into empty fuel tanks.

Ballast tanks:
>   Tanks used to surface or submerge a submarine. These tanks are lightly
>   constructed, are always open to the sea, and are always carried either
>   fully flooded or fully dry. (During World War II submarines running on
>   the surface at slow speed, as on patrol off the enemy coast, sometimes
>   reduced silhouette by leaving ballast tanks partially flooded and thus
>   radically reduced surface buoyancy.) Distinguished from "variable"
>   tanks or "trimming" tanks, which control trim so that the submarine
>   will be neutrally buoyant when submerged. In a surface ship, tanks used
>   to vary trim and buoyancy are sometimes called "ballast tanks" despite
>   the conflict with the specific submarine usage.

Ballistic correction:
>   Correction in aiming a gun, necessary because of variation in powder
>   temperature, gun erosion, or the motion of the target, wind, or gun itself.

Ballistics:
>   The science of projectile motion. Interior ballistics deals with inside
>   of a gun, exterior ballistics deals with action of projectiles in flight.

Ballonet:
>   Gastight fabric compartment within an airship.

Bank:
>   Relatively flat subsurface elevation which is comparatively shallow but
>   whose depth is sufficient for surface navigation. Also, to incline an
>   aircraft about its longitudinal axis.

Bank effect:
>   Lateral motion of a ship in a narrow channel where the bank tends to
>   attract the stern—(bank suction)—and repel the bow—(bank cushion).

Bar:
>   Shallow-water feature, an obstruction to navigation, usually at a harbor
>   entrance, either exposed or submerged, made up of sand, gravel, and other
>   sediment. Also, a unit of pressure equal to 10^6 dynes per square
>   centimeter.

Barbette:
>   Nonrotating armor protecting the rotating part of a ship's *Turret* below
>   the gun house.

Bare boat charter:
Lease of a ship without equipment or crew.

Barge:
Boat for personal use of a *Flag Officer.* A vessel that carries liquids, as a fuel barge, usually towed.

Bark or Barque:
A three-masted sailing ship with the first two masts *Square-rigged* and the third *Fore-and-aft* rigged.

Barkentine:
A three-masted sailing ship with the first mast *Square-rigged* and the second and third *Fore-and-aft* rigged.

Barnacles:
Marine crustaceans which attach to and grow on hard objects at or below the surface, particularly on the hulls of ships. A growth of barnacles will have a noticeable effect on a ship's speed.

Barometer:
Instrument that measures atmospheric pressure.

Barricade:
Aircraft barrier on a carrier flight deck.

Barrier:
Collapsible fences on a carrier flight deck to stop airplanes which miss the arresting gear.

Barrier Combat Air Patrol (BARCAP):
One or more divisions of fighter aircraft deployed between an objective area and an enemy force as a defensive barrier across the most probable direction of attack.

Barrier (ice):
Edge of shelf ice.

Barrier Line:
See, *Barrier patrol.*

Barrier patrol:
Ship or aircraft patrol designated to detect passage of enemy ships or aircraft, especially submarines through a particular ocean area or across a designated barrier line.

Barrier reef:
Name given to reefs separated from land by channels or lagoons.

Basegram:
A message delivered by radio to delivery authorities, such as port directors, who give them by hand upon request to forces afloat. Used for *General Messages.*

Base line (extension):
The arc of a great circle passing through two *loran* stations. A ship on or near this line cannot use readings from these two stations to obtain a position.

Base loading:
>   Loading of a ship intended for delivery to a base or a replenishment group. Distinguished from *Combat loading.*

Base, Naval:
>   A shore command providing administrative logistic support to the operating forces.

Base speed:
>   Resultant speed along a base course when evasive steering, such as zigzagging is being carried out.

Basic Naval Establishment Plan (BNEP):
>   Outline of the Naval Establishment for the current year including force level, deployment of forces, personnel strengths, state of training and degree of readiness, etc., to be maintained on a peacetime basis, prepared in OpNav for SecNav approval.

Basic research:
>   Research solely for the purpose of increasing man's knowledge.

Basic test battery:
>   Series of tests designed to measure intelligence, aptitudes, and potential skills of recruits.

Basin:
>   Submarine bottom feature of large size and roughly circular shape where the depth is greater than depths on its perimeter.

Bathyconductograph (BC):
>   Device to measure the conductivity of sea water at various depths while a ship is underway.

Bathymetric chart:
>   One showing depths of water by use of contour lines and color shading. See *Bottom contour chart.*

Bathymetry:
>   Measurement of water depths, temperature, salinity, etc.

Bathythermograph (BT):
>   Temperature and depth sensing device used to obtain water temperatures at various depths while a ship is at anchor or underway.

Battalion landing team (BLT):
>   Battalion of troops specially organized for an amphibious landing.

Batten:
>   Strip of wood or steel used in securing tarpaulins in place over a hatch; locking device for aircraft control surfaces. A strip of wood or plastic used to stiffen the *Leech* of a sail.

Batten down:
>   To cover and fasten down; to close off a hatch or watertight door. To make secure, as in "Batten down for heavy weather."

Battery:
>   Ship's guns of the same caliber or used for the same purpose; e.g., main, secondary, and antiaircraft batteries. In submarines, the main (electrical) storage battery.

Battery Control:
Direction of use of all mounts or turrets of a similar caliber or purpose.
Types of control—collective, dispersed, divided, and sector—determine
how battery command is exercised.

Battery Record Book:
Charge and discharge data and data on capacity of a submarine's main
storage battery.

Battle Bill:
List of battle assignments based on ship's armament and ship's
Complement. See *Watch Quarter and Station Bill.*

Battle dress:
Flash and splinter protective clothing worn in battle by Navy men on
surface ships.

Battle efficiency award:
An award to ships and aircraft squadrons of active fleet.
See *Prize Money* and *E Award.*

Battle efficiency pennant:
Red pennant with a black ball flown by a ship winning that award.
Also called the *Meat Ball.*

Battle lantern:
Electric lanterns, battery powered, for emergency use.

Battle lights:
Dim red lights below decks for minimum illumination. Since red has the
least effect on the retina of the eye, dim red lights permit quick dark
adaptation for those who must go topside during darkness.

Battle line:
Two or more *Battleships* formed into a "line of battle" with purpose to
engage an enemy in surface gun action. In World War I some especially
heavy *Cruisers* were considered marginally capable of standing in the
battle line, but the Battle of Jutland, 1 June 1916 proved otherwise.
In World War II a battle line was employed by U.S. forces at the Battle
of Surigao Strait, but this is considered an anachronism of that war.
At present "battle line" is a figure of speech which might be used
to refer to almost any assembly of fighting ships.

Battle pin:
Marine term for collar pin.

Battle port:
Hinged metal cover for an *Air port.*

Battle problem:
Simulated battle exercise.

Battleship (BB):
Derived from "line of battle ship" or "ship of the battle line."
The battleship, whether of wood or steel, was originally the largest
and most powerful man-of-war that could be built. Development of the
airplane produced the *Aircraft carrier* which in World War II decisively
replaced the battleship as the primary capital ship of navies. The biggest
battleships ever built were the 80,000-ton *Yamatos* of Japan. The only
ones now in existence and potentially usable are the four 65,000-ton
Iowa class (nine 16-inch guns, 30 knots speed) of the United States. USS
New Jersey of this class was put in commission for shore bombardment
in the Vietnam War but is now back in the reserve fleet. USS *Missouri*
was the site of the surrender of Japan in World War II; the others are the
USS *Iowa* and USS *Wisconsin.*

Battle stations:
See *Watch Quarter and Station Bill.*

Battle wagon:
Slang: battleship.

Baxter bolt:
Fitting that screws flush into deck, used to fasten down aircraft.

Beach:
As used in amphibious operations, portion of shoreline required for
landing of one *Battalion Landing Team.* To run a ship or boat ashore
is to beach it. Slang: the shore. In oceanography, area extending from
shoreline inland to a marked change in physiographic form, or to line
of permanent vegetation. *Coastline.*

Beach capacity:
An estimate, in tons, of the cargo that may be unloaded daily on a strip
of beach during an amphibious operation.

Beachcomber:
A tramp of the sea. An unreliable drifter, a species of man found in
seacoast towns haunting the waterfront, occasionally begging a handout
or working for a short time to get enough money to buy more drink. More
frequently encountered in ports in the warm seas, such as the Caribbean
or Central Pacific.

Beach dump:
Temporary storage for supplies landed in amphibious operation.

Beach exit:
Route for movement of material and personnel inland from the beach.

Beach gear:
Generic term for all equipment meant to be used on the beach during an
amphibious landing. Beach gear would include all material intended to
remain under the command and disposition of the *Beachmaster,* as distinct
from that intended for the troops which have been or are to be landed.

Beach group, naval:
Naval unit to provide personnel, boats, and equipment to supplement
the shore party of the landing force in an amphibious operation.

Beachhead:
> The initial objective of an assault landing. A section of enemy coast which, after capture, will be used for continuous landing of men and equipment in an amphibious operation. After consolidation of the beachhead, the next move will be to break out of same, and at this point the operation takes on the characteristics of regular land warfare, except that, until capture of a suitable harbor or port, the beachhead remains the support base, under the charge of a *Beachmaster.*

Beaching gear:
> Cradles on wheels used for hauling boats and seaplanes out of the water and up onto a ramp or beach.

Beach marker:
> Colored panel or other device marking limit of specific landing beaches for assault craft in an amphibious landing.

Beachmaster:
> In amphibious operations, the officer designated to take charge of logistic activities on the beach once the assault phase of the landing has been concluded.

Beachmaster unit:
> Personnel assigned to the *Beachmaster.*

Beach matting:
> Steel netting or mesh laid on soft sand to improve traction of vehicles.

Beach party (amphibious):
> Naval shore party to control boats, survey channels, salvage landing craft, etc.

Beach patrol:
> A patrol along the beach to warn vessels away from danger and, in time of war, to prevent sabotage and landing of contraband.

Beach wagon:
> A cart used to carry a surfboat along the beach.

Beacon:
> A navigational aid for establishing position of ship or aircraft. May be lighted, aerial, radar, radio, radio-marker, radio range, 2-marker, or infrared.

Beacon, fan marker:
> Aircraft radio marker beacon transmitting signals in a vertical, fan-shaped pattern.

Beam:
> Extreme width of a ship or boat. In wooden ship construction, the heavy horizontal *athwartships* timbers upon which the deck planking was laid were called "beams." The longest such beam spanned the maximum width of a ship, external planking excepted, giving rise to the term "beam" to denote this measurement. A ship heeled over 90 degrees was said to be "on her beam ends." Any other ship or object reasonably nearby in the direction that the beams normally pointed was said to be *abeam,* or *on the beam.*

Beam rider:
> Guided missile that follows a radar beam to the target.

Beam width:
Critical characteristic of a radar transmission governing accuracy of the bearings measured by radar.

Bean rag:
Slang for flag flown in port to indicate that the crew is at mess and that other than routine honors should not be expected.

Bear:
To lie in a certain direction, e.g., the target bears 170 degrees.

Bear a hand:
Hurry up; expedite.

Bearing:
The direction of an object from the observer, expressed in three figures from 000 clockwise through 360 degrees. True bearing is measured from true north. Magnetic bearing is measured from the magnetic north and is now rarely used except internally for boats or aircraft equipped only with a magnetic compass. Relative bearing is measured from the bow of own ship or aircraft.

Beaufort scale:
Standard, graduated table of wind velocities.

BEAVER:
Model designation: U-6; cognizant service: Army/Navy/Air Force. A high-wing general utility aircraft. 1-crew, 5-passengers. Propeller-driven.

Becket:
An eye for securing one end of a line to a block. A rope eye as on a cargo net.

Beef boat:
Slang: supply ship or cargo ship.

Beep:
To control a drone or pilotless plane. The man who does the controlling is known as a beeper.

Beer muster:
Slang: beer party ashore.

Belay:
To make fast or secure, as "belay the line." To cancel, as "belay the last word."

Belaying pin:
A long, round metal rod used for securing lines. Most common use today is in the pin rail of a *Flag Bag* for securing signal halyards. In the hands of an angry sailor of the old school, a belaying pin was a lethal instrument.

Bell book, engineer's:
Official record of the engine orders received in the engineroom from the bridge.

Bell, ship's:
Used for sounding fog or distress signals, as fire signal, and to denote time. See *Ship's bell.*

Below:
Downward; below decks; downstairs.

Bench mark:
A permanently fixed point of known position used for reference in survey or alignment, as in aligning a gun.

Bend on:
To secure one thing to another, as to bend a flag on to a halyard. To "bend on ten turns" is a term meaning to increase propeller speed by 10 rpm.

Bends:
Affliction caused by formation of nitrogen bubbles in the blood, resulting in paralysis, vertigo, cerebral shock, blindness, etc. Experienced by divers after excessive exposure to pressure or too rapid decompression. Pilots also sometimes experience too rapid a decrease in pressure and resulting discomfort. This is popularly known also as the bends, but cannot compare in severity with the bends experienced by divers.

Bent:
Attached. To *bend on* means to attach. Also, slang for a victim of the bends.

Benthic Division:
Primary division of the sea, including its floor. Subdivisions are: *Littoral System,* including waters between high water and depths of 200 meters or the continental shelf edge; and *Deep-sea System,* including all other waters. Other divisions are: *Eulittoral, Sublittoral, Archibenthic,* and *Abbyssal-benthic* zones.

Benthos:
Collective term used to describe all plants and animals living on the ocean bottom.

Berg:
See *Iceberg.*

Bergy-bit:
Medium-sized piece of glacial ice floating in the sea. Smaller pieces are *Growlers.*

Berm:
Nearly horizontal portion of a beach or backshore having an abrupt fall, formed by materials deposited by wave action.

Berne list:
Volume listing international call signs, radio stations, etc., published by International Union of Telecommunications, Geneva, Switzerland.

Berth:
Anchorage or mooring space assigned a vessel. Sleeping place assigned a man on board ship. A margin in passing something, as a wide berth. To inhabit, as "he is berthing in the forward compartment."

Between wind and water or Betwixt wind and water:
Refers to that part of a ship just at the waterline which is alternately
exposed and underwater as the ship heels and rolls. To receive a shot
between wind and water means that the ship has been hit in a very
vulnerable place. Hence the reference has come to mean the vulnerable
part of anything.

Bight:
Loop of rope, line, or chain. An indentation in the coast; a small
cove. Slang: caught in a blight: entangled in some sort of difficulty.

BIKINI:
A lightweight helicopter transportable reconnaissance drone.

Bilge or Bilges:
The inside bottom of a ship or boat. The "turn of the bilge" refers
to the curved plating where a ship's side joins the bottom. A ship is
said to be "bilged" if her bottom has been damaged sufficiently to take
on water, as when running aground, but the expression is almost never
used to refer to battle damage—even though torpedo damage could technically be so described. To "bilge" an examination is a slang term
meaning to receive an unsatisfactory grade. To "bilge" another person
is to fail him, if one is an instructor or otherwise his superior, or
to get a higher grade if a peer.

Bilge blocks:
Wooden supports under a vessel's bilge in drydock.

Bilge keels (chocks):
Fins at the turn of the bilge which reduce rolling of a ship.

Bilge pump:
Pump used to clear the bilge of water.

Bill:
Assignments, with names, for training, administrative or emergency
activities, e.g., rescue and assistance bill. Also, the end of the arm
of an old-fashioned anchor.

Billboard:
The inclined platform near the bows of a ship upon which the old-
fashioned anchor is stowed, ready to be dropped.

Billet:
Duties, tasks, and responsibilities performed by one person. Also,
a specific assignment in a ship or station organization.

Billet slip:
Printed form, giving a man his duty and living assignments aboard ship.

Billet specification:
See *Job Analysis.*

Bill of lading (blading):
Shipping document showing the name and address of shipper and
consignee and list of cargo with weights and dimensions.

Bill of material:
Descriptive and quantitative list of materials, supplies, parts and components needed for specific end-items or assemblys, for overhaul and repair of items, or for construction or repair of structures or facilities. May include cost estimates.

Binnacle:
The stand or support for a magnetic compass. Originally spelled "bittacle." In the old navy this was a wooden structure mounted in a location convenient to the helmsman. In later years it took on a characteristic shape and was made of brass because of the nonmagnetic properties of that metal. The wooden binnacles, being of various designs, were frequently fitted with small cupboard-like compartments for stowage of accoutrements for the watch on deck, such as the log book, candles, or any nonmagnetic gear. Because of the effect on the compass, placing magnetic material in the binnacle was of course an offense. See *Binnacle list*.

Binnacle list:
A list of men excused from duty because of illness or injury, customarily placed in the *Binnacle* for the information of the officer of the watch. Although the binnacle list survives with the same meaning, it is of course no longer placed in the binnacle.

Binoculars:
Telescopic instrument used for distant seeing. Actually a pair of telescopes, attached in such a way that a single view is presented to both eyes in a manner as near as possible to normal vision.

Bioluminescence:
The emission of visible light by living organisms.

Bird cage:
Air Control Officer's station in the island of an *aircraft carrier*.

BIRD DOG:
Model designation: O-1; Cognizant services: Army/Navy/Air Force. High-wing observation aircraft of conventional design. 2-crew. Propeller-driven.

Birdfarm:
Slang for *aircraft carrier*.

Bitter end:
The absolute end of a piece of line or cable.

Bitts:
Pair of short steel posts or horns on board ship used to secure lines. See *Bollard*.

Black gang:
Slang for Engineering Department of a ship. Now generally obsolete because the basic reference was to coal and the coal dust with which all old-time engineers had to contend.

BLACKHAWK:
A Sikorsky helicopter.

Black shoe:
Slang: line officer who is not an aviator or submariner. See *Brown shoe*.

Blading:
See *Bill of Lading.*

Blast:
Signal on a ship's whistle: short (1 second), prolonged (4-6 seconds), long (10-12 seconds).

Bleeding a buoy:
To let the water out.

Blind bombing zones:
Areas restricted to air operations. Bombing permitted without any restrictions.

Blind zone:
Electronic Countermeasures term meaning an area in which echoes cannot be received.

Blinker tube (gun):
Directional, low-powered, visual signaling device used aboard ship.

Blinker, yardarm:
Signal lights at end of yardarms keyed from signal bridge.

Blinking:
Distinctive loran signal used to indicate unusable impulses.

Blip:
Echo as recorded on a radar or sonar screen. Also *Pip.*

Blister:
Bulge in fuselage or wing of airplane enclosing equipment such as machine guns. Also, a built-in bulge in hull of man-of-war to protect against mines, bombs, and torpedoes.

Block:
Device consisting of a pulley encased in a *Shell,* over which a line or wire rope can run freely. A *Snatch block* is one in which the shell opens to take the bight of a line or wire.

Blockade:
Naval operation barring merchant ships from certain ports or ocean areas. Although many different types of blockade have been proclaimed including "paper" blockades, international law has generally held that a blockade, to be meaningful, must be physically enforced at the spot, i.e., a blockade runner is not subject to capture merely because she had, sometime previously, run a blockade.

Block coefficient:
The ratio of a ship's immersed volume divided by the product of the ship's length, beam, and draft. Serves as a measure of the vessel's fullness.

Blocking:
Arrangement of keel and bilge blocks in a drydock in accordance with the *Docking Plan.*

Blockship:
Ship sunk to block off a channel or harbor entrance.

Bloomer:
    See *Buckler*. Also loosely used for any canvas cover topside.

Blow:
    To expel water from a tank by use of compressed air. Also, a gale or
    storm.

Blower:
    Motor-driven fan in ventilating and exhaust systems.

Blowerman:
    Man in fireroom who controls blowers which force air through boilers.

Blow tubes:
    To inject steam into fireside of boilers for purpose of removing soot
    from tubes.

Blue Angels:
    A team of naval aviators who specialize in precision formation acrobatics.

Bluejacket:
    Navy enlisted man below the rate of CPO. Also, in slang: white hat,
    tar, swabbie.

Bluenose:
    One who has crossed the Arctic Circle.

Blues:
    Blue uniform worn by naval personnel.

BOAR:
    Air-to-surface rocket-boosted bomb.

Boarders:
    Also called "Boarding party." Men and officers detailed to go aboard
    an enemy ship in order to capture or destroy it. The term Boarders
    is more generally applied to those who spontaneously board an enemy when
    the opportunity presents itself, as when the two antagonists foul each
    other as occurred in the battles between *Constitution* and *Guerriere*
    and *Chesapeake* and *Shannon,* in 1812 /1813. A boarding party,
    having been detailed and organized, may board the enemy ship directly,
    but is more frequently sent by boat or other secondary means. One of
    the most famous boarding parties in history was Stephen Decatur's in
    the *Intrepid* when he boarded and burned the *Philadelphia* in 1804.
    See *Boarding party* for use in social sense.

Boarding call:
    Official visit by a naval boarding officer to another ship of war or
    public vessel of importance. Generally made to foreign ships when they
    call in U.S. ports, but may be made in foreign ports also, and in such
    cases may be made to U.S. ships as well. The visit is initiated by the
    senior officer in port to ships arriving, with purpose of exchanging
    courtesies and information leading to mutual beneficial cooperation.
    The boarding officer should be as senior as possible, but always certainly
    junior in rank to the senior officer of the ships upon which the call is
    made. The call is always returned in kind, as soon as possible, again by
    an officer junior to both seniors. Such calls do not take the place of
    official calls between the seniors themselves, to which they are prelim-
    inaries.

Boarding party:
> See *Boarders.* Also, a group of men who make a boarding call or other
> official visit afloat. Sometimes, following an official boarding call
> and exchange of calls between the commanders of ships, there will be
> visits exchanged between wardrooms and even between enlisted groups.
> Occasionally, especially during time of war, incoming merchant ships
> of a belligerent nation will be visited by a boarding officer and a
> party of men to determine nationality, destination, cargo, and other
> facts relating to the war. Such a visiting group of persons can loosely
> be termed a "boarding party."

Board of Inspection and Survey (INSURV):
> Legally constituted group of experienced officers representing Office
> of the Chief of Naval Operations (OPNAV) who make periodic inspections
> of naval ships to evaluate their material and operational readiness.

Boat:
> A small craft usually capable of being hoisted aboard a ship. Submarines
> have traditionally been called "boats," but modern subs are really
> ships and are now so called.

Boat ahoy:
> Used to hail a boat; one of the *Boat hails.*

Boat Anchor:
> A very light *Anchor* with extra large flukes for use in small boats.
> Generally small and light enough to be handled by hand and stowed in
> the bottom of the boat or in a locker. Part of the necessary
> equipment of every boat.

Boat boom:
> A spar swung out from ship's side from which boats can be *hauled out* or
> *made fast.* Also called a boat spar or riding boom. Permits boats to
> ride safely alongside a ship while at anchor.

Boat box:
> First-aid kit for use in a boat.

Boat call:
> Flag signal used to establish communication with a boat. Recall is
> a signal used to direct boats to return.

Boat chock:
> A strong deck fitting that supports one end of a boat that is resting
> on deck.

Boat cloak:
> Officer's cloak; now an optional article of uniform.

Boat deck:
> Partial deck above the main deck, usually fitted with boat davits.
> See *Deck.*

Boat falls:
> The lines used in hoisting or lowering a boat.

Boat gong:
> Signal used to indicate departure of officer's boats and the arrival or
> departure of various officers.

Boat hails:
> Ships at anchor hail approaching boats at night with "Boat ahoy." Responses depend on passengers; e.g., if commanding officer, response is the name of his ship; if a commissioned officer, response is "Aye, aye;" if an enlisted man, "Hello," etc.

Boat hook:
> Wooden staff with combined hook and pushing surface usually made of brass to reduce danger of sparks, employed to engage rings, lines, or buoys from deck of a small craft, or to push away from any object or surface.

Boat painter:
> Rope attached to the bow or stern of a boat, used to tow it or to secure it. Not to be confused with the *Sea-painter,* which is a much longer rope used exclusively for towing alongside, hence must be on the near bow but never on the *Stem.*

Boat plug:
> Threaded drain plug fitted in the bilge of a boat.

Boat pool:
> Group of boats available for general use at a harbor, port, or base.

Boat skids:
> Deck fittings designed to hold and support a boat.

Boat sling:
> Rope or chain for hoisting or lowering larger size boats with a single davit or crane.

Boat station:
> Allotted place of each person when boat is being lowered.

Boatswain:
> *Warrant officer,* pronounced "BO-sun," whose major duties are related to deck and boat seamanship.

Boatswain's call:
> See *Boatswain's pipe.*

Boatswain's chair:
> Seat sent aloft or over the side on a line to facilitate repairs or painting.

Boatswain's locker:
> Compartment where deck gear is stowed.

Boatswain's Mate (BM):
> Petty officer who supervises the deck force in seamanship duties.

Boatswain's pipe:
> Whistle used to call attention before passing the word, to render honors *Piping the side,* and to give orders to winchmen, crane operators, etc. A call is the notes played on the pipe, but sometimes the pipe itself is referred to as a "BO-sun's call."

Boehme equipment:
> An automatic code-sending and code-receiving device.

Bogey:
  Unidentified aircraft.

Bogie wire (cable):
  Wire that pulls bogie car, holding mine, along track of minelayers.

Boiler:
  Metal chamber in which steam is generated. Consists of components such
  as firebox or furnace, tubes, steam drum, etc. according to type
  and design.

Boiler central control station:
  Centrally located station in a multi-fireroom ship for directing the
  control of all boilers at boiler operating stations.

Boiler emergency station:
  Station for a chief water tender from which he can quickly reach any
  fireroom, boiler room, or boiler operating station.

Boiler full-power capacity:
  Total quantity of steam in pounds per hour at the contract-specified
  pressure and temperature that the boiler can produce.

Boilermaker:
  A petty officer who maintains marine boilers and heat exchangers.

Boilerman (BT):
  Petty officer who operates and repairs boilers and fireroom machinery.

Boiler operating station:
  Location from which boilers are operated.

Boiler pick:
  See *Chipping hammer.*

Boiler room:
  Compartment containing boilers.

Bollard:
  Steel or iron post on a dock, pier, or wharf, used in securing ship's
  lines. See *Bitts, Cleat, Dolphin.*

Bolo line:
  A nylon shot line with a padded lead weight or a weighted *monkey fist*
  heaved by a boatswain mate from ship to ship or from ship to pier in
  underway replenishments and mooring.

Bolt rope:
  Line sewn around the edge to strengthen a sail, tarpaulin, or awning.

BOMARC:
  Model designation: CIM-10; Cognizant service: Air Force.
  A surface-to-air, long-range area-defense guided missile designed to
  intercept and destroy enemy aircraft. Ground-controlled by SAGE air
  defense system, switching to target-homing system as terminal guidance.

Bomb:
  Explosive dropped from aircraft other than guided missile, torpedo, or mine.

Bomb farm:
 Slang for topside stockpile of bombs used for rearming carrier aircraft.

Bombing, Types of:
 Glide bombing; attack at angles of 30-55 degrees without brakes or flaps.
 Dive bombing; high angle attack (60-70 degrees) using dive brakes.
 Masthead or skip bombing; level flight or shallow glide (under 30 degrees).
 Horizontal bombing; attack from steady, level flight at high or medium
 altitude.

Booking (cargo):
 Advance agreement between shipper and carrier as to details of transportation.

Booklet of General Plans:
 Set of ship's plans including list of ship's dimensions.

Boom:
 A horizontal spar, hinged at the forward end to a mast a few feet above
 the deck, to which the Foot of a *Fore-and-aft* sail would be *Bent.* With
 the sail removed and a suitable *Topping lift* attached, the boom could be
 used as a lifting device, or *Derrick,* and from this has developed the cargo
 booms seen commonly on cargo ships. *Boat booms* are hinged to ship's
 side and are rigged out for the purpose of securing ship's boats when
 ship is moored or anchored.

Boondocks:
 The "sticks"; a long way from the center of activity. Boondockers:
 Marine slang for field boots.

Boost:
 To supply an aircraft engine with additional air or mixture of fuel and
 air. As a noun, manifold pressure.

Boot:
 Slang: recruit. A newly enlisted Marine or sailor.

Boot camp:
 Slang: recruit training center.

Boot topping:
 Paint for ship's waterline.

Boot-topping paint:
 Special paint applied to boot-topping area; both anticorrosive and antifouling. Generally applied at the waterline, and on hatch coamings where
 foot scuff marks are likely.

Bore:
 The abrupt front of churning water, waves or series of waves produced
 as a rising tide proceeds upstream. Also: the interior of a gun, from
 after end of rifling to muzzle.

Bore sight:
 To align the axis of a gun with its sights. In slang usage, to "bore-
 sight" an object or to bore sight on it is to prepare to give it a
 quick accurate attack.

Bottom blow (valve):
Valve at the bottom of the boiler (*water drum*) for blowing out the sediment.

Bottom bounce:
Technique which employs sonar impulses reflected off the ocean bottom in the location of targets.

Bottom contour chart:
See *Bathymetric chart*.

Bottom reverberation:
Reverberation of sound from the sea bottom.

Bottom sediments:
Materials of varying size and origin which remain unconsolidated on the sea bottom.

Bounce field:
Slang for simulated carrier deck ashore.

Bouncer line:
In night *Underwater Demolition Unit* operations, the point off the enemy beach at which rubber boats are launched.

Boundary layer:
Any object moving in water drags along adjacent to its surface a relatively thin layer of water called a boundary layer. Movement in other liquids results in the same phenomenon with the thickness of the boundary layer being dependent upon the viscosity of the fluid.

Bourrelet:
Bands around a projectile, machined to provide support for the projectile in the bore. Made of soft metal, such as copper, so as to engage the rifling.

Bow:
The front or forward part of a ship. Sometimes referred to as bows, since every ship has a starboard bow and a port bow.

Bow door:
See *Ramp*.

Bower anchor:
Generally, an anchor carried on a ship's bows. When ships began to be built of steel and became of much greater size than before, the custom grew of carrying the *Sheet anchor* also on the bow which because of steel construction could now be made strong enough to hold this additional weight, instead of in the waist. In the new position, the sheet anchor came also to be called the "best bower" or sometimes simply "the bower," in distinction from the port or starboard anchors. Some U.S. battleships and aircraft carriers built between the two World Wars had a pronounced clipper bow with an anchor right in the *Stem* which, though the same size as the others, for this reason became the bower.

Bow hook:
Member of a boat's crew who mans the *Boathook* forward and who handles lines. See also *Stern hook.*

Bow insignia:
Stars, pennants, or arrows displayed on bow of boat assigned to an officer for his regular use.

Bowline:
A classic knot that forms a loop that will not slip and become tighter under tension.

Bow number:
Type identification and serial number of a ship, e.g., CA-125, painted on bow.

Bow painter:
See *Boat painter.* A rope attached to the stem of a boat.
See *Stern fast, Sea painter.*

Bowser boat:
Boat used to refuel boats, aircraft, or vehicles.

Box:
In convoy operations, the three rear stations in the commodore's column and in the columns adjacent on either side are left vacant for air operations when a carrier is stationed in the convoy. This vacant space is known as the box.

Box the compass:
To name all points of compass in succession.

Bracket:
A succession of two salvos; one over and one short; or one left of target and one right. Thus the target has been bracketed, and a correction approximately half the previous one, in the opposite direction, should produce a *Straddle.*

Brackish water:
Slightly salty water, specifically water with a salinity roughly between 0.5 and 17 parts per thousand.

Brash ice:
Small fragments of sea or river ice with a diameter of less than six feet.

Brassard:
Arm band, e.g., *Shore Patrol* brassard.

Brass hat:
Slang: Officer in rank of commander or above. Refers to gold cap visor. Originally this was a term of mild disrespect, but this inference is now obsolete.

Bravo:
Phonetic word for letter B.

Bravo pattern:
> The sound-range pattern obtained by bathythermograph reading in water
> less than 100 fathoms. The term bravo means bottom effect.

Bread and water:
> Reduced rations authorized with confinement as punishment. Slang:
> cake and wine.

Break:
> To unfurl a flag with a quick motion. In ship construction, an abrupt
> change in the fore and aft contour of ship's main deck.

Breakbulk cargo:
> General cargo handled item by item as distinct from containerized cargo.

Breakdown lights:
> Two vertical red lights on foremast which denote "not under command."
> Also denote "man overboard."

Breaker:
> A small container for stowing drinking water carried by boats or
> rafts. A wave that breaks into foam against the shore.

Breaker height:
> Vertical distance from crest of a breaker to preceding trough.

Breaker, plunging:
> A surf wave that builds up rapidly and then crashes forward violently,
> indicating a rapidly shoaling bottom.

Breaker, spilling:
> A surf wave that breaks gradually with the top spilling over forward with
> little violence, indicating a gradually shoaling bottom.

Break ground:
> Come loose from the bottom, as an anchor does when hoisted.

Break-off position:
> Position at which a unit or units of a convoy break off in order to
> proceed to a terminal port different from that of the main convoy.

Break out:
> Take out of stock or storage. To prepare for use.

Breakwater:
> Structure that shelters a port or anchorage from the sea. Also, a low
> bulkhead forward that prevents solid water from sweeping the deck of
> a ship.

Breasting float:
> See *Camel.*

Breast line:
> A mooring line from ship to pier, perpendicular to the fore-and-aft
> axis of the ship. See *Spring* or *Spring line.*

Breech:
> Opposite end from muzzle of a gun. Generally used to refer to large guns.

Breech block:
Device which closes firing chamber of a large gun after loading.
For a rifle, the same device is called the bolt.

Breeches buoy:
A device for transferring personnel from a stranded ship to the shore
or, at sea, between ships. Derived from the early design: a life buoy
fitted with a strong canvas bottom with leg holes. Thus, if the buoy
fell into the water, even a sick or disabled person could be supported
by it.

Breech mechanism:
Device for closing the breech of a gun; the moving parts which insert
the *breech block* (or plug) and lock or unlock it.

Breeze:
General term for winds: 22-27 knots (strong); 17-21 knots (fresh);
11-16 knots (moderate); 7-10 knots (gentle); 4-6 knots (slight).

BRICK-BAT:
Urgency designator established by *JCS* to show the relative priority
between end-products destined for *DOD*. BRICK-BAT has higher priority
than *CUE-CAP*.

Bridge:
Ship's structure, topside and usually forward, that contains control
and visual communication stations.

Bridge deck:
On merchant-type ships, a partial deck above main deck, usually
amidships.

Bridge gauge:
A machinery tool or instrument used to determine the drop of a journal
in any type of sleeve bearing which is made in halves. It bridges between
the two sides of the lower bearing half, thus the term.

Bridle:
A span of rope, chain, or wire with both ends secured and the strain
taken on the midpart, as in towing a ship or pulling an aircraft on
a *Catapult*.

Brief:
To instruct people for a specific mission or operation. Debriefing, thus,
means a verbal report back after the operation has been completed.

Briefing:
Conference or meeting held to give instruction for a specific operation.

Brig:
A place of confinement. A prison. A type of small, fast sailing vessel
popular 150 years ago. A two-masted *Square-rigged* sailing ship.

Brigantine:
Sailing vessel with two masts, the foremast *Square-rigged* and the
mainmast *Fore-and-aft* rigged. Same as a *Hermaphrodite brig,* except
that a square topsail might be carried on the mainmast, well above the
normal position for a topsail.

Brightwork:
  Unpainted and uncovered metal, generally brass or chromium, which is
  kept bright by polishing.

Bring home:
  To move a piece of gear to its proper or stowed position, as a boom
  being rigged in is brought home.

Broach:
  To be thrown broadside to a surf or heavy sea. To break surface partially,
  either deliberately or accidentally, as with a submarine, but not coming
  fully to the surface.

Broadcast:
  Originally a naval term meaning to transmit radio messages to the fleet.

Broad command pennant:
  Blue and white pennant flown by an officer, not a flag officer, who
  commands a major unit of ships or aircraft. See *Burgee command pennant.*

Broad on the port (starboard) bow:
  Said of something having a relative bearing midway between the beam and
  dead ahead, on the port (starboard) side.

Broad on the port (starboard) quarter:
  Bearing midway between the beam and the stern, on the port (starboard) side.

Broadside:
  Simultaneous firing of all main battery guns on one side of a warship,
  except that in the British Navy half the guns are fired in alternate
  salvoes at half the interval.

Broken deck:
  A weather deck of a ship which is not continuous from bow to stern.
  Thus a ship with a raised forecastle would have a broken deck. Different
  classes of Destroyers are frequently referred to as "broken deckers" or
  "Flush deckers."

Broken stowage:
  Wasted space in a ship's hold. Small packages used to fill such hold
  space.

Broken water:
  An area of small waves and eddies in otherwise calm water.

BRONCO:
  Model designation: OV-10; Cognizant services: Navy/Air Force.
  A two-place tandem, lightweight, multipurpose, armed reconnaissance
  aircraft. Prop-jet.

BRONCO BUSTER:
  Hydrofoil anti-submarine-launched-ballistic-missile vehicle.

Brow:
  Portable wooden bridge or ramp between the ship and a wharf, pier, or
  dock. Usually fitted with wheels at the shore end. Also; *Gangplank.*

Brown bagger:
  Slang: a married man, one who carries his lunch to work.

Brown shoe:
> Slang: naval aviator or submariner. The Brown Shoe officer is entitled to extra hazardous duty pay for flight or submarine duty. The term originally referred to uniforms; only aviators and submariners wore khakis and the brown shoes that went with them. See *Black shoe.*

Bryozoans:
> Minute animals which usually form into plantlike colonies and attach to submerged objects at most depths.

B-Scope:
> Cathode ray indicator which presents plot of target range versus bearing.

Bubble pulse:
> Echo caused by collapse of the bubble resulting from an underwater explosion.

Bubble sextant (octant):
> Sextant (Octant) which determines the horizontal plane by a bubble instead of the horizon and is used to measure the altitude of a celestial body. Less accurate than a regular sextant, hence used only in aircraft, or when horizon is otherwise not usable.

Buccaneer:
> A pirate. The term was first given to early Frenchmen in Haiti. The word boucan was of Caribbean origin, meaning a dealer in smoked or dried meats. In the Caribbean area, hunters placed meat to dry on wooden lattice work known as boucans. Some "boucanners" took to privateering and general lawlessness, and ultimately "buccaneer" became a synonym for pirate.

Buck:
> Small object placed on the wardroom table to mark the place of the officer who is to be served first.

Bucket of steam:
> Nonexistent item, often requested of new men aboard ship.

BUCKEYE:
> Model designation: T-2A; cognizant service: Navy. Basic carrier trainer aircraft. 2-crew. Jet.

Buckled:
> Bent or distorted; misshapen.

Buckler:
> Flexible cover attached externally to a turret's front armor plate so that the guns are free to train or elevate, yet water cannot enter the *Gunport*. Slang term is *Bloomer.* Also, the metal plate over a hawse hole to keep water from squirting up on deck through it when the ship plunges into a sea. In general, any device used for a similar purpose anywhere.

Bug:
> *Speed Key.*

Bug battery:
> Concept developing from the fact that some micro-organisms act as super-catalysts in promoting electrochemical reactions. Bacteria filled fuel cells are referred to as bug batteries.

Bugle:
> A horn with limited notes, all controlled by the player's lips, used for martial purposes to broadcast a general order to all hands within hearing range, such as Taps, Reveille, Retreat, Liberty Call, Torpedo Defense, General Quarters. The first bugle calls were supposedly written by Joseph Haydn, the celebrated musician, in about 1793, but of course the bugle has been used for military purposes since antiquity. The first bugles were made from the horns of wild oxen. The Horn of Roland was one of these.

Builder (BU):
> Petty officer who constructs and repairs wood and concrete structures.

Builder's trials:
> Trials conducted at sea or at a dock by the builder to prove readiness of a ship for preliminary acceptance trials.

Build-up:
> The reinforcement and maintenance of an expeditionary force or of a base.

Bulkhead:
> Walls or partitions within a ship, generally referring to those with structural functions such as strength or water-tightness. Light partitions are sometimes referred to as partition bulkheads.

Bulkheading:
> Slang: complaining or grumbling with the intention of being overheard by seniors.

BULLFROG:
> Command and control system study.

Bull horn:
> High-powered, directional, electric megaphone.

Bullnose:
> Closed chock at the bow of a vessel. Has the appearance of a large flared nostril.

BULLPUP:
> Model designation: AGM-12; cognizant services: Air Force/Navy. A short-range air-to-surface guided missile used against comparatively small defended surface targets. Radio-link command guidance.

Bull rope:
> Line used in cargo handling or in connection with a topping lift.

BULLSEYE:
> Tactical communications system.

Bulwark:
> Section of ship's side continued above the main deck as a protection against heavy weather.

BUMBLEBEE:
> Program which led to development of the TERRIER, TALOS and TARTAR missiles.

Bumblebee:
> Noise-making device for sweeping acoustic mines.

Bumboat:
> A civilian boat selling supplies, provisions, and other articles to
> the crews of ships. Supposedly derived from "boomboat" signifying
> a boat permitted to lie at the ships' booms. Bumboats and bumboatsmen
> had a bad reputation in the Navy because they frequently were the
> source of a great deal of trouble among a ship's crew.

Bumwad:
> Slang: a newspaper or a magazine. Also, toilet paper.

Bungee:
> Securing line for the control stick of an airplane; part of the parking
> harness used when the airplane is on deck.

Bunk:
> Bed.

Bunk bottom:
> Canvas laced to bunk frame, used instead of springs to support a
> mattress.

Bunk covers:
> Flameproof covers for bedding aboard ship.

Bunker:
> Compartment or tank used for the stowage of fuel.

Bunting:
> Cloth from which signal flags are made. Also, the flags themselves, as
> in the order, *Air bunting.*

Buoy:
> Floating object, anchored to the bottom, to indicate a position on the
> water or to provide a mooring for a vessel. May be can, nun, spar,
> lighted, mooring, *Dan,* etc.

Buoy tender:
> Vessel designed for and engaged in servicing aids to navigation,
> especially buoys.

Burdened vessel:
> The vessel required to take action to avoid collision under the *Rules
> of the Road.* Other vessel is the *Privileged vessel* which must
> maintain course and speed.

Bureau:
> Major organizational unit of the Navy Department, established by law.
> Some now replaced by "Systems Commands."

Bureau of Medicine and Surgery (BuMed):
> Generally responsible for medical and dental care of Navy, Marine
> Corps, dependents, and retired personnel; for training of medical
> personnel, operation of Naval Hospitals.

Bureau of Naval Personnel (BuPers):
> Generally concerned with the procurement, training, promotion, assign-
> ment and discipline of officer and enlisted personnel of the Navy.

Bureau of Naval Weapons (BuWeps):
Dissolved May 1966. Was responsible for design, development, procurement, production, testing, fitting out, maintenance, alteration and
repair of all Navy weapons and aircraft. Replaced May 1966 by *Air
Systems Command, Ordnance Systems Command.*

Bureau of Navigation (BuNav):
Name changed to Bureau of Naval Personnel (BuPers) in 1942.

Bureau of Ships (BuShips):
Was responsible for design, procurement and maintenance of all types
of ships for the Navy and other Military services. Replaced May 1966
by *Electronics Systems Command; Ships Systems Command.*

Bureau of Supplies and Accounts (BuSandA):
Dissolved May 1966. Was responsible for supervision of procurement,
warehousing, transportation and issuance of Navy supplies and materials
(except ammunition) and for the supervision of food service installations
ashore and afloat. Replaced by *Supply Systems Command.*

Bureau of Yards and Docks (BuDocks):
Was responsible for design, construction and maintenance of shore
facilities of the Navy, real estate management; and procurement and
maintenance of railroad equipment, heavy lifting gear, automotive
equipment. Duties in general assumed May 1966 by *Facilities
Engineering Command.*

Bureau Planned Procurement Guide (BPPG):
Publication by the former BuWeps listing planned procurements.

Burgee:
A swallow-tailed pennant.

Burgee command pennant:
Red and white or blue and white burgee flown by an officer who commands
a division or squadron of ships, such as submarines or destroyers.
Such officer has the courtesy title of *commodore* while so serving.
If he held the rank of commodore, he would be a *flag officer* and
would fly a blue flag with a single white star.

Burn bag or basket:
Receptacle for classified matter that is to be destroyed.

Burnerman:
Man in fireroom who tends the burners in the boilers.

Burnout:
Point in time or in the missile trajectory when combustion of fuels
in the rocket engine is terminated by other than programmed cutoff.

Burton:
Small tackle formed by two blocks with a hook block in the bight of the
running part. Generally used for setting up or tightening rigging, for
shifting weights, or for use in other purposes.
For transferring supplies during replenishment at sea, a burton rig
might be set up between ships, in which case the gear used might be
quite heavy.

Bury:
To hide or conceal certain words or phrases in the text of a message.

Bushing:
   Metal liners serving as a bearing for a shaft.

Bust:
   Slang: to reduce in rate. Also, to fail or make a mistake.

BUTCHER BIRD:
   Study program for an advanced anti-radar missile.

Butt bucket, butt kit:
   Slang: ash tray.

Butts:
   That part of a rifle range in which targets are tended.

Butterworth:
   Method of cleaning and gas-freeing oil tanks by use of seawater
   under pressure.

By-pass:
   To divert the flow of a gas or liquid. Also, the line that diverts the
   flow.

By the board:
   Overboard, as to go by the board.

By the head:
   Ship's attitude with a greater draft forward than aft.
   "Down by the head."

By the stern:
   Opposite of *By the head.*

C

Cabin:
Quarters aboard ship for *captain* or *admiral.*

Cable:
Any heavy wire or rope such as towing cable or degaussing cable. A unit of length, 120 fathoms or 720 ft.; 100 fathoms in British Navy.

Cable jack:
Device for lifting anchor chain off the deck to insert a slip hook. Sometimes shortened to *Jack.*

Cable-laid rope:
Three or four plain-laid, three-stranded ropes twisted in the opposite direction to the twists in each rope; used for ropes much exposed to water.

Cable markings:
Turns of wire and stripes of paint on anchor chain links to show scope of chain out.

Caduceus:
Symbol of Medical Corps, a staff entwined by two snakes, topped by a pair of wings.

Caisson:
Any temporary structure of wood or metal built to hold-back water for repairs or construction. Also, the floating gate of a drydock.

Cake and wine:
Slang: *bread and water* (as a punishment).

Calacerous algae:
Marine plants having a hard covering of calcium compounds which are found in all oceans. They frequently form reefs.

CALEB:
Vehicle for ship or aircraft launch of satellites and space probes.

Caliber:
Diameter of a gun's bore measured in inches: 3"/50 gun is 3" in bore diameter and 50 calibers (150") long. A 50-caliber machine gun is one whose bore is one-half inch or 0.50 caliber.

Call:
> Formal social visit by an officer and his wife to the home of another.
> Involves leaving calling cards and was once rigidly prescribed and care-
> fully followed, including return calls. Now largely passé as a custom,
> although large stations may have an annual party with the understanding
> that it also constitutes "all calls made and returned." An informal
> visit of courtesy to another ship just arrived. Made by an officer
> junior to the commanders of the arriving unit and the visiting unit,
> and requires no special ceremonies, other than *Piping the side.*
> See *Official visit* and *Boarding call.* If made by a principal,
> the call is termed an official call or official visit.

Call away:
> To order a ship's boat or vehicle manned and made ready for a trip.

Call book:
> See *Morning callbook.*

Call Contract:
> *Indefinite Delivery Contract.*

Call sign (communications):
> A group of letters and/or numerals that identifies a station, command,
> or activity.

Calving:
> The breaking away of ice from a berg, a glacier, or from shelf ice.

Camber:
> Convex curvature athwartships of the deck of a ship.

Camel:
> Float used as a fender between two ships or a ship and a pier. Also
> called *Breasting Float.*

Canada balsam:
> Optical cement, used in binoculars, periscopes, etc.

CANBERRA:
> Model designation: B-57; cognizant service: Air Force.
> A small twin-jet bomber aircraft. Two-crew.

Can buoy:
> Cylindrical, flat-topped metal buoy.

Can-do:
> Slang: efficient, capable and willing. e.g., a repair ship might be
> praised as a can-do ship.

Canister:
> A large number of bullets, or balls, similar to *Grape,* made up in a
> can of the proper diameter to fit the bore of the gun for which designed.
> The can would burst when the gun was fired, resulting in a shotgun effect.
> An antipersonnel weapon. The same as grape, except that the canister
> was more easily loaded, gave a more uniform load, and, because it fitted
> the bore of the gun better, gave more accuracy. In historical accounts
> of 17th, 18th, and early 19th century actions, the phrase "grape and
> canister" is frequently encountered. See also *Langridge, Dismantling
> shot,* and *Double-shotted.*

Cannibalize:
To remove serviceable parts from one item of equipment for use in another.

Canopy:
Canvas or metal cover fitted over part of a boat.

Canopy, parachute:
Main supporting surface of a parachute.

Cant:
The inclination of an object from the perpendicular.

Canyon:
A deep, steep-walled trench perpendicular to a coast which cuts both the shelf and the slope.

Capillary waves:
Small waves, less than about 0.5 centimeters in length, with rounded crests and v-shaped troughs whose characteristics are a function of surface tension.

Capsize:
To turn over; to upset.

Capstan:
The rotating mechanism which actually raises the anchor or other heavy weight. In sailing days it was turned by wooden bars inserted into the capstan head itself, thus giving it a characteristic look. Small ships built in the 1920's still used capstan bars as a standby in case of failure of the *Anchor engine.* Development of engines to do this heavy work resulted in various other power take-offs for lesser jobs involving heaving in lines, called *Gipsy* or *Warping* heads. The term niggerhead, once also used in this context, has been abandoned by general consent. If the mechanism has no connection with the anchor it is called a *Winch.* See *Windlass.*

Captain:
Commanding officer of any naval unit or activity. The rank next above commander. Equivalent to colonel.

Captain of the head:
Man responsible for cleaning washrooms and toilets. Known to Marines as the head orderly.

Captain of the port:
The Coast Guard officer responsible for port security.

CAPTOR:
Encapsulated torpedo.

Captured Air Bubble (CAB):
Boat which rides on air bubble to increase speed by reducing hull drag.

CARDINAL:
Model designation: MQM-61A; cognizant service: Army.
A propeller-driven, target guided missile.

Cardinal point:
   One of the four principal points of the compass—north, east, south,
   and west.

Caretaker status:
   Condition in which a non-operational activity, such as an air station,
   is preserved and guarded.

Cargo:
   Material carried in ships or aircraft. Classified as dry, bulk, general,
   heavy lift, deck, dangerous, liquid, refrigerated, etc. May be palletized,
   breakbulk, or containerized.

Cargo classification:
   The division of military cargo for combat loading.

Cargo cluster:
   Cluster of lamps used for lighting when working cargo at night.

Cargo documentation:
   Papers required for a ship to enter or leave a port. Includes manifest,
   crew list, stores list, bills of lading, tonnage certificates, and other
   marine certificates as required.

CARGO MASTER:
   Model designation: C-133; cognizant service: Air Force.
   A high-wing monoplane with facilities for truck-bed height loading,
   an aft loading door with integral ramp, and a forward side-loading
   door. 4-crew plus 3 relief crew. Prop-jet.

Cargo net:
   Square net of heavy line used to lift cargo in loading or unloading
   operations.

Cargo papers:
   Documents to assist in cargo handling, including bills of lading,
   manifests, stowage plans, and hatch lists.

Cargo plan:
   Plan showing capacity of each of a ship's holds.

Cargo port:
   Opening in a vessel's side through which cargo can be loaded.

Cargo whip:
   Rope or chain used with a *derrick* and *winch* for handling cargo.
   One end has a heavy hook; the other end is rove through the derrick
   and taken to the winch. Also called cargo hoist, cargo rope.

CARIBOU:
   Model designation: C-7A; cognizant service; Air Force.
   Light cargo/transport aircraft. 2-crew, 30-passengers.
   Propeller-driven.

Carling:
   Short fore-and-aft timber or girder placed under a deck to stiffen
   it; for example, under mooring bitts, winches, masts, etc.

Carpenter stopper:
   Holding and quick-release device for wire rope.

Carriage:
>That part of a gun mount which supports the slide.

Carrick bend:
>Most usually seen as a double carrick bend, a much-used knot for bending two lines or hawsers together.

Carrier:
>*Aircraft carrier.* Also any unit of men and equipment which operates ships for ocean transport. By general usage the term is now extended to include transporters of freight on land as well (e.g., railroads).

Carrier Controlled Approach (CCA):
>Landing approach to an *aircraft carrier* during which the pilot is guided in speed, heading and altitude by a controller aboard the carrier.

Carrier (logistic):
>Any unit of men and equipment which operates vessels for ocean transport.

Carrier-on-deck delivery (COD):
>System of delivering support items and mail from shore to *aircraft carrier* underway.

Carrier Qualification (CARQUAL):
>Material or pilots qualified for use or landings aboard carriers.

Carrier task force:
>*Aircraft carriers* and supporting heavy ships and *destroyers.*

Carrier wave (CW):
>Radio transmission in code, in contrast to voice.

Carry away:
>Tear or break loose; break; part; wash away.

Carry on:
>An order to resume or continue previous activity, usually after men have come to attention.

Carry rudder:
>To require constant right or left rudder in order to maintain course.

Case depth:
>The vertical distance from the surface of the water to a planted mine case.

Cast:
>Act of heaving the lead into the sea to determine depth of water; to direct the ship's bow in one direction or another when getting underway.

Castaway:
>A man from a wrecked ship. Generally, but not exclusively, refers to a survivor in a primitive area.

Cast loose:
>To let go a line or lines.

Cast off:
Order given to let go or throw off mooring lines.

Casualty board:
A visual display of ship's compartment and systems. Used by damage control personnel.

Casualty control book, engineering:
Maintained by ships to assist in control of engineering damage. Contains machinery readiness bills and examples of casualties and how to correct or repair them.

Casualty Report (CASREP):
Report required when casualties of a specified nature occur either to personnel or material.

Catapult:
A device for launching aircraft from a ship's deck at flying speed.

Catenary:
The dip in a length of chain or cable because of its own weight. The catenary provides spring or elastic effect in towing, anchoring, or in securing to a buoy.

Cathead:
A projection on the bow for rigging *Tackle* to hoist an anchor aboard. There would of course be one cathead on each bow. In the old days a cat's head would be carved on the wooden timber for good luck, hence the name.

Cat-of-nine-tails:
A short piece of rope fashioned into an instrument for flogging. Traditionally the victim who was to be punished was required to make his own "cat" by unlaying a portion of the three-strand line, separating each of the strands into three parts, then tarring and braiding the parts into nine "tails." Through tradition and pride the cat was often made as fearsome as the maker could, by knotting the tails and even including small nails or other metal objects in the knots. A poorly made or soft cat was considered a mark of the craven, and in any case, if it did not pass muster, it would be replaced contemptuously by one that did. See *Room to swing a cat.*

Cat's-paw:
A light puff of wind. See *Flaw.*

Catwalk:
A walkway constructed over or around obstructions on a ship for convenience of the crew.

Caulking, calking:
Burring or driving up the edges of iron or steel plates along riveted seams to make them watertight; forcing a quantity of caulking material into the seams of a ship's deck or sides to make them watertight. Pronounced "Kawking."

Caulk off:
Slang: To take a nap; to doze. Also to "cork off."

Cavitation:
>   Disturbance around revolving propeller blades struts, etc., caused by collapse of transient pressure disturbances resulting from flow of water over their surfaces.

CAYUSE:
>   Model designation: OH-6A; cognizant service: Army.
>   Light observation helicopter with dual flight controls, with secondary control element easily removable. Four-place cargo area contains troop-type seats which are easily stowable.

Ceiling:
>   The minimum height above the ground at which all clouds, at and below that height, cover more than one half the sky. Also, a lining inside hull of ship to keep cargo off the side plating.

Ceilometer:
>   Instrument for measuring cloud ceiling.

Celestial equator:
>   A great circle on the *celestial sphere* everywhere 90° from the celestial poles. The plane of the equator extended to the celestial sphere.

Celestial meridian:
>   A great circle on the *celestial sphere* passing through the North and South celestial poles.

Celestial navigation:
>   Determination of position by observation of celestial bodies.

Celestial sphere:
>   An imaginary sphere of infinite radius concentric with the earth on which all celestial bodies, except the earth, are imagined to be projected.

Centerline:
>   An imaginary line down the middle of the ship from bow to stern.

Center of buoyancy:
>   The geometric center of gravity of the volume of a ship's displacement taken so that in computations for *Metacentric height* the entire buoyant effect of the sea upon the hull floating in it may be considered as being applied at a single point. Used in combination with *Center of gravity* for this calculation.

Center of gravity:
>   Point in a ship where the sum of all moments of weight is zero. With the ship at rest the center of gravity and the center of buoyancy are always in a direct vertical line. For surface ships center of buoyancy is usually below center of gravity, and the ship is prevented from capsizing by the additional displacement on the low side during a roll. Thus the point at which the deck edge enters the water is critical because from here onward increased roll will not produce corresponding increased righting force. In a submerged submarine, center of buoyancy of the submerged hull is always above the center of gravity and the ship remains upright because of the pendulum effect, which is equally important fore and aft as it is athwartships.

Centralized Electronic Control (CEC):
   Concept of the Naval Electronics Laboratory for centralized electronic
   control of all systems within ships.

Chad tape:
   A 5-unit code tape used in teletypewriter operation with perforations
   not completely severed.

Chafe:
   Wearing away the surface of a line, spars, or chock by rubbing.

Chaff:
   General name for radar confusion reflectors. Includes *Rope,* a long
   roll of metallic foil or wire for broad, low-frequency response; and
   rope-chaff which contains one or more rope elements.

Chafing gear:
   Material used to prevent chafing or wearing of sails, line, etc.

Chain cable:
   See *Anchor cable.*

Chain grab:
   See *Windlass.*

Chain hook:
   Hand tool for handling anchor chain.

Chain locker:
   Compartment where anchor chain is stowed.

Chain of command:
   The succession of officers through which command is exercised.

Chain pipe:
   Heavy steel pipe to lead the anchor chain through the deck to the
   chain locker.

Chains:
   The platform or position in the bows from which the *Leadsman* heaves
   the *Lead.* In the sailing navy, the masts were braced by *Standing
   rigging,* much of which was secured to platforms jutting out from the
   sides of the ship, outboard of her bulwarks. To prevent the pull of the
   rigging from snapping off the platforms, short sections of chain were
   led from their outboard edges to points lower on the side of the ship.
   Leadsmen customarily used these platforms to stand upon when heaving
   the lead, and hence their nautical designation, "the chains," has
   persisted.

Chain stopper:
   Short length of chain fitted with a slip hook secured to an eyebolt on
   the forecastle: used for quickly releasing anchor and chain upon anchor-
   ing and for securing anchor and chain, in the hoisted *(Housed)* position.
   Also secures the chain after anchoring when the proper *Scope* is out.
   See *Stopper.*

Chalk test:
   A test of the tightness of a watertight fitting by rubbing chalk on the
   Knife Edge. The resultant imprint on the gasket indicates whether
   or not the knife edge is bearing against the gasket.

Challenge:
A demand for identification or authentification. Can be as simple as the flashing light "AA" signal which internationally requires the recipient to respond with name and destination (warships need only identify themselves). May be a coded signal, transmitted by any of a number of means which must be properly replied to, such as in *IFF*.

Chamber:
The enlarged rear interior of a gun which holds the explosive charge.

Chandelle:
An abrupt climbing turn to nearly a stall in which the momentum of the airplane is used to obtain a higher rate of climb.

Change order:
Written order directing a contractor to make changes in a contract.

Channel:
The frequencies within which a radio transmitter must maintain its modulated carrier signal. Also, the deeper or marked portion of a harbor or waterway through which ship traffic is directed.

Channel Conditioning:
Surveying of areas normally travelled by shipping to detect and locate any minelike objects. Purpose is to facilitate location, avoidance and clearance of enemy minefields and other explosive weapons.

Channel (tape relay):
One electrical path over which transmissions can be made from one station to another.

Chantey, chanty:
A sailor's song of simple lyrics and tune. Pronounced "shanty." Traditionally sung by men walking the capstan around, and became something of a ceremony if they were heaving in the anchor to get underway. If the ship was lucky enough to have a fiddler on board, he might perch on top of the capstan, sawing away on his violin as his shipmates did their best to make him dizzy.

Chaplain:
Minister, rabbi, or priest of a recognized religious order, commissioned in the Navy. Slang term is *sky pilot.*

Charlie:
Phonetic word for letter C.

Charlie Noble:
Sailors' nautical name for the galley smokepipe. Derived from the British merchant service captain, Charlie Noble, who required a high polish on the galley funnel of his ship. His funnel was of copper and its brightness became known in all ports his ship visited.

Chart:
Map. Hydrographic chart shows depths of water, nature of bottom, and aids to navigation. Aeronautical chart shows terrain features and other information for air operations.

Chart, bathymetric:
Chart showing depth of water by labeled contour lines.

Chart correction card:
Record of *Notice to Mariners* changes for a particular chart.

Chart datum:
The plane to which soundings on a chart are referred, in the U.S. usually
Mean low water or *Mean lower low water.* Navigators in shallow
water must always check their charts for this. Datum is always specified
on harbor charts.

Charter party:
The formal, written agreement under which a vessel is leased (chartered).

Charthouse or chartroom:
Compartment on or near the *bridge* for handling and stowage of navigational
equipment. Usually contains a chart table and stowage for charts.

Chart, sonar:
Chart containing oceanographic data useful in echo ranging under water.

Chase:
The sloping part of the outside of a gun between the muzzle and the slide.

Chaser:
In sailing days of broadside fire, a gun so placed that it could fire
ahead or astern and be used for pursuit or when pursued. Also modern
slang for *Sentry* or guard, i.e., "Brig Chaser."

Check:
To keep a strain on a line but to ease it out to prevent parting.

Checkman:
Man in fireroom who controls water level in boilers.
See *Water Tender.*

Check valve:
One that permits a flow of liquid in one direction only.

Chemical alarm:
Distinctive signal used only on board ship to warn of impending gas or
atomic attack.

Chevron:
V-shaped mark that denotes *Rate* located beneath the *Specialty
Mark* of a *Rating Badge.*

CHEYENNE:
Model designation: AH-56A; Cognizant service: Army.
Compound helicopter, designed for high performance and ground attack.
Incorporates rigid rotor for stability and high control power, plus
pusher propeller. Carries pilot, copilot or gunner, 3500 lbs. of
weapons and ammunition. Highly controversial because of large cost
over-run, and because of rotor failures. Performance has not been up
to specifications and the contract has been cancelled.

CHICKASAW:
Model designation: H-19; Cognizant services: Army/Navy/Air Force.
Sikorsky helicopter equipped for search and rescue missions.
2-crew, 10-passengers.

Chicken guts:
Slang for *Aiguilettes.* Also called *Loafers' loops.*

Chief of Naval Operations (CNO):
The senior active duty officer in the Navy.

Chief of Staff:
The captain or admiral who assists an admiral, as his second in command,
especially in supervising his staff. The senior assistant to a commodore
or below is a Chief Staff Officer.

Chief of the Boat or Ship (COB, COS):
Senior chief petty officer in a submarine; the executive officer's
righthand man in the administration of the crew. Now that submarines
have become much larger and more important craft than previously,
the tendency has grown to refer to them as ships instead of boats.
The term boat referring to a submarine is therefore obsolescent, and
the title Chief of the Boat is slowly giving way to Chief of the Ship.
Like all such changes, it will be some time before it is fully effective.

Chief petty officer (CPO):
An enlisted man in paygrade 7. Until recently, this was the highest
rank attainable by an enlisted man while still in the enlisted category. For further promotion he had to look to the *Warrant* grade.
Now, however, two superior grades have been established: Senior
Chief Petty Officer, paygrade 8, and Master Chief Petty Officer,
paygrade 9.

Chief police petty officer:
See *Chief Master-At-Arms.*

Chief staff officer:
See *Chief of Staff.*

Chinese landing:
Bringing a boat or ship alongside another bow to stern. Bringing a
ship alongside down-current or landing an aircraft down-wind. Anything
done "Chinese" style is done backward, or the reverse of normal.

CHINOOK:
Model designation: CH-47; cognizant service: Army.
Tandem rotor passenger/cargo helicopter with all-weather flight
capabilities and rear-loading ramp. 3-crew. 33-passengers.

Chipping hammer:
Small hammer with a sharp peen and face set at right angles to each
other; used for chipping and scaling metal surfaces. Also called
Scaling hammer or *Boiler pick.*

Chips:
Slang: ship's carpenter.

Chit:
Letter, note, voucher, or receipt probably derived from the old East India Company, and the Hindu word "chitti." The word gained wide acceptance in the Far East and was used throughout the British Army and Navy, and the American Navy as well.

Chlorinity:
Total grams of chlorine, bromine and iodine contained in one kilogram of seawater. For computation the assumption is made that the bromine and iodine have been replaced by chlorine.

Chock:
Metal fitting through which hawsers and lines are passed. May be open or closed. Blocks used to prevent aircraft or vehicles from rolling. Also, blocks used to support a boat under repair. See *Roller Chock.*

Chock-a-block:
Two-blocked; full, *close up.*

Chockmen:
Men who handle chocks under wheels of aircraft on carrier.

CHOCTAW:
Model designation: CH-34; cognizant services: Army/Air Force. Large helicopter with a four-bladed main rotor. Equipped to carry external sling loads. 2-crew, 18-passenger or 8-litters.

Chop:
Change of operational control. The date and time at which the responsibility for operational control of a ship or convoy passes from one *Operational Control Authority* to another. Used as verb: "To chop to - - -."

Chopline:
A boundary expressed in longitude and latitude, at which ships change operational control.

Chopper:
Slang: helicopter.

Chow:
Slang; food. Chow line is the mess line. "Chow down" means "mess call" or "dinner is served."

Christmas tree:
Any control panel featuring red and green indicator lights; such as used in submarines and magnetic minesweepers. Now falling into disuse because of conflict with requirements for night vision.

Chronometer:
An accurate navigational clock.

Chuffing:
The characteristic of some rockets to burn intermittently and with an irregular noise.

Church pennant:
> A blue and white pennant flown during church service. By tradition, the only flag or pennant flown on the same hoist and above the national colors, and then only during services aboard ship.

Cigar mess:
> A cooperative within the wardroom mess that sells cigars, cigarettes, candy, etc., for the convenience of the officers.

Cigarette deck:
> Open deck abaft the bridge of a submarine. Now obsolete because of streamlining. The term developed because in the early submarines it was the only place where personnel were permitted to smoke.

Cipher:
> Any system in which arbitrary symbols represent units of plain text of regular length (usually single letters).

Cipher device:
> Hand-operated enciphering and deciphering apparatus.

Cipher machine:
> A mechanical or electrical cipher apparatus.

Ciphony:
> Term applied to equipment or transmission pertaining to enciphered messages.

Circuit:
> Communication link between two or more points capable or providing one or more communication *Channels.*

Circuit discipline:
> Proper use of equipment, radio communications, adherence to prescribed frequencies and operating procedures, remedial action, net control, monitoring, and training.

Circular Error Probable (CEP):
> Estimate of the accuracy of a weapon used to determine the probable damage to a target. Developed during advent of electronically or inertially guided missiles, now applied also to bombing, esp. area bombing. Seldom used for gunfire, except shore bombardment.

Clamp down:
> To sprinkle with water and dry with a moist or dry mop. Distinguished from swabbing which utilizes a wet mop frequently doused and wrung out in buckets of water.

Clap on:
> To clap on a rope means to catch hold in order to haul on it; to clap on a stopper or tackle means to put on a stopper or tackle; to clap on canvas means to put on more sail.

Clapoits:
> Standing waves produced by the reflection of a wave train from a breakwater, bulkhead, or steep beach.

Class I Property:
> Real property in lands, buildings, structures and various appurtenances.

Class II Property:
>   Plant equipment personal property of a capital nature such as
>   machinery, equipment, furniture, vehicles, machine tools, excluding
>   special tooling.

Class III Property:
>   Minor plant equipment items having a unit value of less than $200,
>   and other equipment of higher value specifically designated as Class III.

Class IV Property:
>   Material or items which may be incorporated into an end-item through
>   the manufacturing process and consumable tools and supplies required
>   in the production.

Class V Property:
>   Special toolings; special jigs, dies, molds, etc., of such specialized
>   nature that they are useable only on production of specific items unless
>   they are substantially modified.

Classification (personnel):
>   Collection of information regarding education, abilities, pre-Navy
>   training, performance, and experience of men and officer. See *Job
>   Classification.*

Classified contract:
>   Any contract that will require access to classified information by the
>   contractor or his employees. A contract may be classified even though
>   the contract document itself is unclassified.

Classified information:
>   Any information whose revelation must be controlled in the interest of
>   national security.

Classified matter:
>   Information or material which must be safeguarded in the manner and to
>   extent required by its importance. See *Top Secret, Secret,
>   Confidential.*

Class Improvement Plan (CIP):
>   Plan for similar improvements to any ship class for improvement of
>   military characteristics.

Clean Nonmilitary Vessel Category:
>   Vessel of the United States, her allies or neutral nation for which
>   movement information for the past six months is available and about
>   which there is no question, or close examination raises no questions.

Clean Vessel:
>   Subdivision of *Nonmilitary Vessel Categories.*

Clear:
>   To remove stoppages or fouled gear. To remove ammunition from a gun.
>   To pass a point, cape, or other landmark or object. Not enciphered or
>   coded. To approve or obtain approval for.

Clearance:
>   Determination that an individual is eligible to have access to classified
>   information of a specific category. Also: an aspect of *Mine Counter-
>   measures.* Permission for a ship to enter or leave harbor; clearance
>   through quarantine, etc.

Clearance, mine:
General term embracing specific procedures which rid an area of the danger of mines, including sweeping, disposal and explosive clearance.

Clearance Minesweeping:
Primary objective of making an area as safe as possible for all classes of shipping.

Clear anchor:
Report made to commanding officer that the anchor (as it appears) is observed to be free of any entanglement, particularly its own chain. Opposite of *Foul anchor*.

Clear for running:
Ready to run out without fouling.

Clear hawse pendants:
Short length of chain and wire used in clearing hawse.

Clear (open) hawse:
No turns in chain with two anchors down.

Clear ship:
Prepare a ship for action by removing items such as jackstaffs, stowing paint and other inflammables below, opening ready service ammunition boxes, etc. See *Strip Ship*.

Cleat:
An anvil-shaped deck fitting for securing or *Belaying* lines. *Wedge Cleats* are used in yachting to hold *Sheets* ready for instant release. All sailors of small boats are enjoined "never *belay* a sheet" because it cannot then be quickly relased in event of a sudden squall.

Clew:
The after, lower corner of a triangular, fore-and-aft sail.

Clinker:
Noncombustible matter blocking passage of air through the grate of a coal-fired boiler.

CLINKER:
ASW system for sensing heat from submarine water trails.

Clinometer:
Device for measuring amount of roll aboard ship. Same as *Inclinometer*.

Close:
To close means for a ship to go near to, take position on.

Close aboard:
Near; within 600 yards for ship, 400 yards for boat.

Close air support:
Aircraft action against targets so close to own forces as to require detailed integration with the fire and movement of own forces.

Close covering group:
Naval vessels formed to protect ships or shore facilities against enemy surface attack.

Close up:
> Hoisted all the way up, as signal flags; *Two blocked.*

Clothes stop:
> Small cotton lanyard used for fastening clothes to a line after washing them, or for securing clothes that are rolled up.

Clothing:
> Insulating material wrapped around pipes; covered by *Lagging.*

Clothing and small stores:
> A government operated shop on a base or in a large ship which stocks standard articles of uniforms for officers and enlisted men with such related articles as buttons, brushes, etc.

Clove hitch:
> A knot much used for fastening a line to a spar or stanchion.

Clump:
> Fitting welded to ship's stem for *Paravane* chain.

Clutter:
> Interference on radar scope tending to obscure targets. May be due to waves, rain, snow, or other extraneous signals.

Coaling bag:
> Large (4'x4') canvas bag used in transporting material between ships during underway replenishment. Originally designed for use when cooling ship.

Coaming:
> Raised framework around deck or bulkhead openings and cockpits of open boats to prevent entry of water.

Coastal currents:
> Same as *Nearshore Currents.*

Coast pilot:
> Directions for piloting in inland and coastal waters of the U.S. and possessions. Issued by the Coast and Geodetic Survey of the Department of Commerce.

COCHISE:
> Model designation: T-42A; cognizant service: Army.
> An all-metal, four-place, fixed-wing, instrument flight trainer, having dual instrumentation, side-by-side seating for student pilot and instructor, plus seats for two additional students. Propeller-driven. 2-crew. 2-passengers.

Cockbilled:
> Slanted; uneven in appearance; cockeyed; drunk. The yards of a square-rigged man-of-war were traditionally cockbilled as a sign of mourning analogous to soldiers marching with rifles reversed, or a horse with boots reversed in the stirrups.

Cockpit:
> The pilot's compartment in an aircraft; a well, or sunken place in the deck of a boat, almost always protected with a *Coaming,* for use of the crew or passengers.

Code word:
Word which conveys a special prearranged meaning.

Coding delay:
Time interval between transmissions of the *Loran* master and slave stations.

Coding room:
Compartment aboard ship in which coding and ciphering are done.

Codress:
Message having the address buried in the encrypted text.

Cofferdam:
Void space between compartments of a ship; waterproof wall built around a damaged area of a ship's hull.

Cognizant technical bureau:
Navy bureau responsible for all technical and engineering matters pertaining to a particular contract.

Coil down:
To lay out a line in a circle with coils loosely on top of one another. See *Fake, Flemish.*

Cold-iron watch:
Security patrol in the engineering spaces of a ship whose machinery is not in use nor tended.

Cold ship:
One without fires lighted, thus having no source of power. Also called *Dead Ship.*

Collier:
Vessel specially designed to carry coal.

Collision bulkhead:
Watertight athwartships bulkhead of a ship, usually near the bow.

Collision mat:
A mat of canvas and fiber designed to be hauled down over the hole in a ship's hull caused by a collision or grounding. See *thrum, thrumming.*

Colors:
The national flag. The ceremony of raising the flag at 0800 and lowering at sunset aboard a ship not underway, or at a shore station.

Column:
Formation of ships or aircraft in single file, one astern of the other.

Column, open order:
Line of ships in column having alternate ships staggered a few degrees to the right and to the left of the *guide,* even-numbered ships to the left.

COM:
Prefix used with short title of a command indicating reference to the commander rather than the command—i.e. COMCRUDESLANT, indicates Commander, Cruiser-Destroyer Force, Atlantic Fleet, not the force CRUDESLANT.

Combat aircrewmen:
Aviation enlisted men, wearing winged insignia, who comprise the crews of combat aircraft.

Combat air patrol (CAP):
Fighter aircraft over task force or objective area to provide protection against hostile aircraft.

Combatant vessel or ship:
One whose primary mission is combat with the enemy. See *Ship.*

Combat distinguishing device:
A small metal V worn on the Legion of Merit, Bronze Star, and Commendation Ribbon to indicate the medal was awarded for actual combat operations.

Combat Information Center (CIC):
The section of a ship or aircraft manned and equipped to collect and collate tactical information. the embarked flag officer, commanding officer and certain control agencies.

Combat loading:
Loading assault troops and equipment for rapid debarkation in predetermined priority during amphibious assault. See *Base loading* and *Commercial loading.*

Combination lantern:
Light divided into red and green sections, used on a small craft instead of side lights.

Combined Acceptance Trials (CAT):
A single trial combining preliminary and final acceptance trials.

Combined operation:
Operation conducted by forces of two or more allied nations. See *Joint.*

Combined publications:
Those designed for use with allied forces. Compare with *Joint.*

Combustion chamber:
In a steam torpedo, the chamber in which air, fuel, and water are mixed and ignited to produce steam to power the torpedo turbine.

Come along:
Fitting flush with the deck, covering a pad-eye or cleat used for securing vehicles, aircraft, cargo, etc. Also a seaplane anchor cable clamp.

Come home:
Said of an anchor when it drags toward the ship while heaving in, or of anything as it approaches its normal stowed position.

Command:
Authority vested in an individual for the direction, coordination, and control of military forces. Order directing a particular action in a specific way. Unit, activity, or area under the command of one individual. See Order.

Command Active Sonobuoy System (CASS):
Airborne ASW detection and classification device.

Command Channel:
Same as Chain of Command.

Commander:
An officer who commands. Also the rank below captain and above that of lieutenant commander. Equivalent to lieutenant colonel.

Commanding officer (CO):
Officer in command of ship, squadron of aircraft, or naval activity with duties and responsibilities as specified in U.S. Navy Regulations. May be a staff officer in special cases, as the doctor who commands a hospital.

COMMANDO:
Model designation: C-46; cognizant service: Air Force. Paratroop transport. 2-crew, 42-passenger. Propeller driven.

Commendatory mast:
Ceremony at which the commanding officer commends, congratulates, or decorates members of his command.

Commercial loading:
Loading of troop and equipment for maximum utilization of space, rather than for military purposes. See *Combat loading.*

Commissaryman (CS):
Petty officer who performs cooking, baking, and butcher duties. Slang: bellyrobber, stewburner.

Commissary store:
Food store for military personnel. The lower prices at such stores are among the fringe benefits taken into account when military pay scales are established.

Commission:
To put a ship in active service under a commissioned commanding officer, who breaks his pennant and sets the watch.

Commissioned officer:
One who derives his authority from a commission under authority of the President confirmed by the Congress.

Commission pennant:
Narrow red, white, and blue pennant with seven stars, flown at the main truck of ship in commission, under command of commissioned officer. See *Distinctive mark.*

Commitment position:
The point in a depth-charge attack at which the ASW ship must be committed to the attack course and speed in order to reach the correct firing point.

Commodore:
> A naval rank, not used in peacetime, below rear admiral and above captain. Corresponds to brigadier general. A captain commanding two or more small ships, such as destroyers, is addressed as commodore. A convoy commodore, assisted by a rear and a vice commodore, is the merchant marine or naval officer in command of the convoy.

Common servicing:
> System whereby functions are performed by one activity for another, not necessarily of the same service, without reimbursement from the unit receiving the service.

Communication countermeasures:
> Any measures, generally highly classified as to techniques, intent, and results, designed to detect, locate, interfere with, confuse, or misinform enemy communications or communications equipment. Includes intercept search, jamming, or any other ingenious techniques which may be useful.

Communications link:
> A ship or aircraft stationed between two or more units, thereby extending the communications range for a given condition of radio security.

Communications satellite:
> An orbiting vehicle, either active or passive, which relays signals between communications stations.

Communications technician (CT):
> Petty officer who performs special communications duty of a confidential nature.

Commutation of quarters:
> Rental allowance.

Commuted rations (Comrats):
> Credit for rations an enlisted man does not receive in a general mess. See *Subsistence Allowance.*

Companionway:
> Set of steps leading from one deck to another. Also called a *Ladder.*

Company, ship's:
> Everyone assigned to a ship or station; all hands.

Compartment:
> Room or space on board ship. Usually lettered and numbered according to location and utilization.

Compartment check-off list:
> A list of fittings, their location, and function in a compartment for a specific purpose, such as damage control.

Compass:
> Instrument for determining direction: magnetic, depending on the earth's magnetic field for its force; gyroscopic, depending on the tendency of a free spinning body to seek to align its axis with that of the earth.

Compass card:
A circular card in a compass which is marked with the *Cardinal points, Intercardinal points,* and the others in between. The compass card appears to rotate, but it is the ship which rotates around the card, which always points to the North. The *Lubber's line* is marked on the fixed portion of the compass, and thus the heading of the ship can be ascertained by reading the direction marked on the compass card which lies at the lubber's line. In days of sail, of course, a proud helmsman would steer by the wind and would only refer to the lubber's line to check that the wind had not shifted.

Compass error:
Total difference between compass heading and true heading. Is composed of *Variation* and *Deviation.*

Compass rose:
Diagram of a compass card in a chart, assists navigator in laying out courses and directions on chart.

Compensate:
To adjust water in trim tanks to attain desired buoyancy in a submarine. Also, to correct the magnetic compass.

Competitive year:
That on which Battle Efficiency Competition is based; the fiscal year.

Complement:
Authorized personnel for full combatant manning, designed for full operational effectiveness considering the inherent capabilities of the unit and the possible requirements of war. See *Allowance* and *Manning level.*

Comply:
In any naval message means "You are to comply."

Composite squadron:
Two or more divisions of ships or aircraft which are of different types.

Compound:
Area set aside for temporary storage at an advanced base.

Compound formation:
An arrangement of two or more simple formations of ships.

Compressor:
Device or brake, actuated by hand, in a chain pipe that governs the movement of the anchor chain.

Compromise:
Loss of security resulting from revelation of classified information to an unauthorized individual. May include possible compromise, as when a classified document is lost.

Concentrate:
Join up, as ships or aircraft concentrate to make an attack.

Condenser:
Low-pressure heat-transfer device in which steam is condensed to water for further use in a closed cycle system.

Conditions of readiness:
See *Readiness.*

CONDOR:
Model designation: AGM-53; cognizant service: Navy.
Air-to-surface missile.

Cone:
Said of a helicopter's rotor blade tips when they flutter and tend to point upward.

Cone of silence:
Space directly over radio range station in which signals are not heard or are greatly reduced in volume.

Confidential:
Class of information and material whose disclosure would be prejudicial to the national interests or prestige. A lower classification than *Secret* or *Top Secret.*

Confusion reflectors:
General term for nonelectronic mechanical devices and materials used in countermeasures against radar. Examples are *Chaff, Gull, Kite* and *Corner reflector.*

Conn:
Control of ship's movements; the officer in control has the conn. To guide or pilot a ship is spoken of as conning.

Conning tower:
Armored control station in any armored ship. The Captain's station in battle. Also, submerged control station in a submarine, if separate from the *Control room.* U.S. WW II submarines were built with conning towers to permit greater periscope-height extension. Most post-World War II submarines have been built without conning towers, and the conning station is an area set aside in the control room.

Consolidated pack ice:
Large area of drift ice driven closely together to produce total coverage.

Consolidation of oilers:
Transfer of fuel among oilers to enable some to return to base to reload.

Constant helm plan:
An evasive maneuver used by a ship which suspects the presence of a submarine in the vicinity. Although the ship appears to be changing course constantly, it will not get very far off its base track. Similar to *Sinuating.*

CONSTELLATION:
Model designation: C-121; congizant services: Navy/Air Force. Transport aircraft similar to commercial Constellation or "Connie" with unusual "droop" airfoil-shaped fuselage and triple rudders. 8-crew, 92-passengers. Propeller-driven.

Construction battalion, naval *SeaBees*:
Specially qualified men and officers organized to do military construction work. May be amphibious (ACB), mobile (MCB', or maintenance units (CBMU).

Construction Electrician's Mate (CE):
   Petty officer who installs and repairs construction electrical equipment.

Constructionman (CN):
   Enlisted man in paygrade E-3 who performs construction duties.

Construction mechanic (CM):
   A petty officer who maintains and repairs automotive and construction
   equipment.

Consul:
   An official in the diplomatic service representing the U.S. Government
   in foreign places. The consul is concerned with all U.S. shipping at
   the port which he resides. He assists sailors in distress and undertakes
   the repatriation of shipwrecked or stranded American citizens.

Consular Shipping Advisor (CONSA):
   Naval Officer appointed to the staff of a consular authority in a neutral
   country for naval control of shipping duties.

Consumables:
   Materials expended or used.

Contact:
   Indications of the presence of a target made by sight, sound, or
   electronic means.

Contact mine:
   Explosive designed to detonate upon contact with ship's hull.

Contact report:
   Report of first sighting or knowledge of enemy forces.

Containerization:
   The shipping of general cargo in sealed van-type boxes, which are carried
   aboard ships, trains, and trucks.

Continental shelf:
   The sea bottom from shore to a depth of 200 meters. Width varies from
   nearly zero to 800 miles. Generally speaking, the depth increases very
   gradually to about 100 fathoms (200 meters) at which point it increases
   more rapidly, at a steeper slope.

Continental slope:
   The sea bottom slope from the 200 meter line to great depths; varies
   between 3.5 and 6 percent.

Contract administration:
   Management of the entire contract to be sure the government and the
   contractor fulfill all provisions.

Contract change notification:
   Written order of the contracting officer directing changes in supplies
   or services, usually contains an estimated price or cost of such changes;
   firm price or cost changes are made by a supplemental agreement.

Contract clause book:
   Publication containing a variety of standard clauses required in government
   contracts. These clauses may be incorporated into a contract by
   referencing the clause book and need not be written out in each contract.

Contract management:
>Field actions on behalf of the government necessary to performance of a contract or in support of the buying organization.

Contract modification:
>Any written alteration of contract provisions by unilateral or mutual action including change orders, terminations or exercises of contract options.

Contractor:
>Individuals or organizations having accepted agreements or orders to provide supplies and services to DOD under procedures of ASPR.

Contractor Data Requirements List (CDRL):
>Listing (on DOD Form 1423) of all technical data and information required to be delivered to the Government by a contractor.

Contractor Independent Technical Effort (CITE):
>Program for contractors for independent research and development efforts performed in connection with contracts.

Contractor Performance Evaluation (CPE):
>Reports filed at intervals detailing the manner in which major contractors are meeting commitments.

Contractor-Responsible Items (KRA):
>Deficiencies or omissions noted at time of original acceptance or during guarantee period which are contractors responsibility. Term "KRA" (Contractor Responsible, Authorized) is applied when they are authorized for accomplishment at a post-delivery availability.

Contractor support:
>An interim arrangement during initial development or production requiring a contractor to furnish hardware support items before this resonsibility is assumed by the Government.

Contractor Weighted Average Share (CWAS):
>Program to give contractors who take high-risk contracts special consideration in judging allowable costs on contracts.

Contract termination:
>As applied in DOD procurement, refers to ending (in whole or in part) work under a prime contract or subcontract for convenience of, or at the option of, the government.

Controlled mine:
>An underwater explosive whose detonation is controlled from a shore station.

Controlled net:
>A communication circuit on which activity is governed by one station.

Controlled port:
>Harbor or anchorage in which entry departure, berthing and traffic are controlled by military authorities.

Control, operational:
>Authority over combat, service, or training operations, in contrast to administrative control.

Control room:
Control center of a submarine containing most of the valves, switches, gauges, and other instruments for surfacing and submerging, steering, and general operational control. May include conning station and torpedo fire-control station, but does not include torpedo tubes, torpedo-firing apparatus, engineering plant or engineering control equipment. The control room is, however, the central station from which emanates the basic direction of all these outlying activities. See *Conning tower.*

Control ship:
One that controls and directs the boats in an amphibious assault, usually stationed on the line of departure.

Convening authority:
The command legally empowered to organize *Courts-martial, Courts of inquiry,* and *Boards of investigation.*

Conversion, ship:
The changing of a ship in design or characteristics resulting in a major change in its mission or assignment to a different class.

Convoy:
A number of merchant ships or naval auxiliaries, or both, usually escorted by warships and aircraft. A single merchant ship or naval auxiliary under surface escort.

Convoy commodore:
Officer (naval or merchant) designated to command convoy. He is subordinate to the escort commander.

Convoy escort:
Naval ships or aircraft in company with a convoy and responsible for its protection.

Convoy routing:
The assignment of specific ocean paths for convoys to follow.

Cook-off:
Explosion of a projectile due to heat in firing chamber alone.

COPPER QUEEN:
Checkout and test equipment for the E-2A.

Coppers:
Large cooking kettles in galley.

Copy:
To maintain a continuous radio receiver watch, recording all transmissions. See *Guard, Cover, Listen.*

Corange lines:
Lines on a map or chart passing through all points having the same tidal range. See *Cotidal Lines.*

Cordage:
General term for rope and line of all kinds.

CORE:
Project to use waste products of reactor cores for conversion of gamma rays directly into electrical energy and for the direct conversion of nuclear energy to electricity.

Coriolis force:
Effect of the earth's rotation on all moving bodies, including air and water masses.

Corner reflector:
Reflector formed of mutually perpendicular surfaces or planes. It increases the radar reflection from any object to which it is attached.

Correction for datum:
Conversion factor in tidal prediction to resolve *Chart datum* of the reference and secondary station.

CORSAIR II:
Model designation: A-7; cognizant services: Navy/Air Force. A single-place carrier-based light attack aircraft. Used primarily for tactical strike, close support, and interdiction-type missions. Jet.

Cost and Economic Information System (CEIS):
System administered by DOD for the collection of data from contractors on past production experience and its use in establishing costs of future weapons systems.

Cost contract:
Contract providing for payment to the contractor of costs allowed by contract provisions and required for performance of the contract; also a cost-reimbursement type contract under which the contractor receives no fee.

Cost effectiveness analysis:
Method for evaluating alternate methods of accomplishing military missions to determine which forces and weapons will produce the greatest effectiveness for the least cost.

Cost-plus Incentive Fee Contract (CPIF):
Cost reimbursement contract providing for a fee adjusted by formula related to ratio of total allowable costs to target costs thus giving the contractor an incentive to keep costs down.

Cost-plus percentage-of-cost contract:
Now illegal for military departments but formerly used and permitting payment of actual costs plus a fixed percentage for accomplishment of work.

Cost reimbursement type contract:
Provides for payment of allowable costs in performance of contract within limits prescribed and establishes an estimated total cost for purpose of funds obligation and contract price ceiling; includes cost contracts, cost-plus-fixed-fee-contracts, cost-plus-incentive fee contracts and cost sharing contracts.

Cost sharing contract:
Provides for reimbursement without fee to the contractor for agreed portion of allowable contract costs.

Cotidal Lines:
Lines on a map or chart passing through all points at which high waters occur at the same time. See *Corange Lines.*

COUGAR:
Model designation: F-9; cognizant service: Navy.
Carrier-based fighter aircraft. 1-crew. Jet.

Counter:
Overhang at the stern of a ship.

Counterbattery fire:
Fire delivered against active enemy weapons and/or fire control stations.

Counter Countermeasures (CCM):
Warfare or equipment designed to impair or reduce the effectiveness of enemy countermeasures.

Counter current:
A secondary ocean current adjacent to and setting in a direction opposite to the main current as on both sides of the *Gulf Stream.*

Counter flood:
To take water into a ship's tanks or compartments to reduce list or inclination by bow or stern. Must be done with care, for total buoyancy is also reduced.

Countermeasures (CM):
A form of warfare carried on to eliminate or reduce the threat from or effectiveness of enemy equipment.

Countermining:
The explosion, either accidental or deliberate, of mines by nearby explosions.

Countermining distance:
The limiting distance between mines which will avoid chain countermining. Recommended minimum spacing for each type of mine is prescribed from statistical results of experiments. Also called countermining radius.

Country:
Definite area of ship such as admiral's country, wardroom country, chief's country. Rarely used alone.

Coupling:
Metal fitting at the ends of a length of fire hose or fuel hose.

Course:
A rhumb line direction. The horizontal intended direction of travel. Often designated as true, magnetic, compass, or grid, e.g., "steer course 000^0 pgc" (per gyro compass). In aviation, because of high winds aloft, the course to steer may be quite different from the intended course to travel, referred to as "course made good" by navigators everywhere.

Course recorder:
Device which graphically records the path of a ship.

Court of inquiry:
A body of three or more officers, to investigate any matter, convened by any person authorized to convene a general court-martial.

Courts-martial:
Military courts of law for military personnel.

Cover:
To maintain a continuous radio receiver watch with transmitter calibrated and available. See *Guard, Copy, Listen.* Also command to don hats.

Covert:
In intelligence work: secret and clandestine. Opposite of *Overt.*

Cowl:
Bell-shaped air funnel or scoop, projecting above the deck or deckhouse of a vessel, used for ventilation.

Cowling:
Removable covering on aircraft, as over a cockpit or around an engine.

Cow's tail:
Frayed end of a rope; also called a *Fag* or *Fag End.*

Coxcombing:
Fancy knot work consisting of coils of line worked around a tiller handle, stanchion, etc. See *Sennet, Square knotting, MacNamara Lace.*

Coxswain:
Man in charge of a small boat, pronounced COX-un.

Crab:
To move sidewise through the water. To catch a crab in rowing is to pull on the oar with the blade immersed insufficiently or twisted so that the rower fails to make a smooth stroke.

Crack:
Unnavigable break in sea ice caused by tide, temperature changes, current or wind.

Cradle:
A stowage rest for a ship's boat.

Crane:
Mechanical device for lifting weights.

Crash dolly:
Wheeled device for moving crashed aircraft on a carrier flight deck.

Creeping Attack:
Coordinated ASW attack using noiseless approach with all target information furnished by an assisting ship. The attacking ship does not echo range.

Crest of berm:
The seaward margin of the *Berm.*

Crew:
The men who operate a ship, boat, aircraft, turret, gun, missile, etc.

Crib:
>Rigid structure of timber, rock, concrete, and heavy wire used to close
>a harbor entrance, serve as a bridge support or temporary breakwater, etc.

Critical:
>Said of a reactor when the number of neutrons produced by fission is
>just enough to continue the reaction. Associated terms are Criticality
>and Critical Position of control rods.

Critical velocity:
>The speed at which a current can scour the bottom enough to maintain
>required channel depth.

Critique:
>Critical review of an operation or exercise held in the form of a conference.

Cromwell current:
>Sub-surface current of the Pacific which flows west to east under the
>north equatorial current.

Crossing the line:
>Crossing the equator.

Crossing the T:
>Classic tactic in surface engagement wherein one *Battle line* crosses
>and concentrates its fire upon the *Van* or leading units of the other.

Crosspointing:
>Line or strips of canvas or leather braided about a rail or stanchion as
>decoration and protection.

Cross signal:
>Illegal practice of answering ship's whistle signal of two blasts with one
>blast, or vice versa.

Crosstree:
>Superstructure member at top of a low mast or between two such masts;
>runs athwartships.

Crow:
>Slang: eagle on a petty officer's rating badge.

Crow's-nest:
>Lookout station aloft generally on the foremast.

Cruise:
>Tour of sea duty. A period of enlistment. Also, a voyage to several
>ports, such as a *Shakedown* cruise, or to a specific ocean area.
>See *Deployments.*

Cruiser:

A type of warship, smaller than a *Battleship,* more lightly armed and armored, cheaper to build and operate, suitable for any naval duty except combat against battleships. In the past, cruisers were faster than battle-ships, but no longer. Currently cruisers are employed as AAW escorts for *Aircraft carriers,* and nearly all have had some of their *Main battery* guns replaced with surface-to-air missiles. The type is however being replaced in the U.S. Navy by the more economical *Frigate.* Because of their re-maining main battery guns, U.S. cruisers were used for shore bombardment in Vietnam, but the only cruiser built by the U.S. Navy since WW II carries only surface-to-air missiles for her main battery. See *Destroyer, Frigate, Heavy cruiser.*

Cruising range:

The endurance of a ship in nautical miles at moderate or cruising speed.

CRUSADER:

Model designation: F-8; cognizant service: Navy.
Single-place, sweptback wing, carrier-based high-performance day fighter. Has variable incidence wing. 1-crew. Jet.

Cryptanalysis:

Solving encrypted messages without access to the decryption system.

Cryptoboard:

Group of personnel specifically designated for encrypting and decrypting messages.

Cryptocenter:

Compartment used by the cryptoboard.

Cryptochannel:

Crypto aids, indicators, and instructions that comprise a basic unit in cryptographic communications.

Cryptogram:

A communication in visible, secret writing.

Cryptographer:

One who encrypts or decrypts messages.

Cryptography:

The science of rendering plain text into unintelligible text and vice versa.

CUE-CAP:

An urgency designator of the JCS to show relative priority among programs; CUE-CAP is subordinate to *BRICK BAT.*

Cumshaw:

Something procured without official payment. Free; a gift. Comes from the beggars of Amoy, China who said "kam sia" meaning "grateful thanks." The historical reference is to graft for personal gain. In the U.S. Navy the term now relates to unauthorized work done for or equipment given to a ship or station, and usually no connotation of personal gain exists. A "cumshaw artist" is a man who is adept at getting cumshaw work done, frequently by liberal handouts of food and coffee to the shipyard workers.

Current direction:
> The compass heading toward which water moves.

Current, ocean:
> Continuous movement of water in the sea, sometimes caused by prevailing winds, as well as large constant forces, such as the rotation of the earth, or the apparent rotation of the sun and moon. Examples are the *Gulf Stream,* the *Cromwell Current,* and the Kurishiro (Japanese Current).

Current pattern secondary:
> Water movement which varies from the prevailing current pattern.

Current ship's maintenance project (CSMP):
> Card record of repairs, alterations, etc.

Current tables:
> Coast and geodetic survey publications giving data on currents for various localities throughout the world.

Current, tidal:
> Currents along the coast caused by the rise and fall of the tides. Water movement associated with the rising tide is the *Flood current;* that associated with the falling tide is the *Ebb current.* Between flood and ebb currents is a period of no current, *Slack water,* which corresponds to the *Stand* between flood and ebb tides.

Cusp:
> Sand deposited, by wave action, in the form of points or bars projecting seaward along a beach.

Custodian:
> Officer responsible to his CO for custody, handling, and safeguarding of classified publications.

Customs of the service:
> Unwritten naval practice having the force of usage and tradition. An example is the removal of caps or hats by officers entering a compartment where the crew is eating.

Cut:
> Landing Signal Officer's signal to a pilot to close the throttle, allowing the aircraft to settle aboard the carrier. Also, a bearing line or a set of bearing lines which result in a ship's position or visual fix.

Cut of the jib:
> General appearance of a vessel or of a person. Derivation dates back to sailing days when ships of different nationalities shaped their jib sails somewhat differently. Thus a ship would be identified by the "cut of her jib."

Cutter:
> A type of rig used on sailing yachts, having a single mast located further aft than that of a *Sloop.* The original revenue vessels used this rig and hence were called cutters. Today the term is applied to all Coast Guard ships above a certain size. Also a type of square-sterned pulling boat.

Cutwater:
> The *Stem* of a ship, the forward-most portion of the *Bow,* which cuts the water as she moves.

D

Daily Estimated Position Summary (DEPSUM):
Daily broadcast summary by the Operational Control Authority of the estimated positions of ocean shipping within a specific area. It includes courses, speeds and expected alterations whthin the next 24 hours.

Daily Movement Summary (MOVSUM):
Confidential tabulation of departures and arrivals of all merchant shipping (including neutrals) from ports during a 24-hour period.

Damage control:
Measures necessary to preserve and re-establish shipboard watertight integrity, stability, maneuverability and offensive power; to control list and trim; to make rapid repairs of materiel; to limit the spread of and provide adequate protection from fire; to limit the spread of, remove the contamination by, and provide adequate protection from toxic agents; and to provide for care of wounded personnel.

Damage control bills:
Written procedures for operating the various systems of a ship (such as ship's drainage system) to further efficient damage control.

Damage control book:
Contains material information in the form of texts, tables, and plates concerning facilities and characteristics of those ships that are highly subdivided with complicated piping and wiring systems.

Damage Control Center:
Compartment behind a ship's armor, if any—otherwise located in as protected a position as practicable—from which measures for control of damage and preservation of the ship's fighting capability are directed.

Damage controlman (DC):
Petty officer who assists in firefighting, damage control, and chemical warfare.

Damping:
The reduction of oscillation of a system by friction or other means.

Dan buoy:
Temporary marker buoy used during minesweeping operations to indicate boundaries of swept path, swept area, known hazards, etc.

Danger bearing (angle):
Limiting bearing (angle) of fixed object(s) on shore which may be used to insure safe passage clear of an outlying shoal or other danger.

Danger signal:
Five or more rapid short blasts of whistle to indicate possibility of collision or other emergency.

Dan layers:
Vessesl assigned duty of laying the *Dan buoys* during mine warfare operations.

Dark adaptation:
Becoming accustomed to darkness in order to achieve good night vision.

Darken ship:
 Blacking out all lights visible from outside the ship.

DARK FENCE:
 Alternate name for *Space Surveillance System* (SPASUR).

DASH:
 Model designation: QH-50C; cognizant service: Navy.
 Unmanned remote-controlled helicopter designed to carry an ASW torpedo
 to a combat radius of 30 miles and drop it on a submarine contact.

Data Communications:
 Electronic or electrical transfer of data from one place to another and
 the translation necessary to make it acceptable at its destination.

Date-time group (DTG):
 Six numerals and a letter indicating date (first two digits), time (four
 digits), and time zone description (letter) of origin of a message.

Datum and datum time:
 The last known position of a submarine is the datum, its time at that
 point is the datum time. If a ship is torpedoed and no additional
 information is available, the position and time of torpedoing are
 used as datum and datum time.

Datum plane:
 Same as *Chart Datum*.

Davit:
 Shipboard crane that can be swung out over the side; used for hoisting
 and lowering boats and weights. Often found in pairs. Pronounced "day-vit."

Davy Jones' Locker:
 The bottom of the sea.

Dawn alert:
 See *Alert*.

Dawn and Dusk Combat Air Patrol (DADCAP):
 Special application of night combat air patrol which fills the gap during
 dawn or dusk between the use of combat air patrol and night combat air
 patrol; an extension of the use of night fighters *(ZIPPERS)* over a target
 area.

Day and night distress signal:
 Hand-held smoke and flare projector.

Day beacon:
 Unlighted structure which serves as a daytime aid to navigation. See *Daymark*.

Daymark:
 The daytime identifying characteristics of any aid to navigation. Also
 the *Shape* or signals displayed by a vessel to indicate her special
 status, such as fishing, laying cable, etc.

Day's duty:
 A tour of duty or a watch lasting for 24 hours.

Day's work:
Twenty-four hours of navigation of a ship required periodically of junior officers.

D-Day:
Term used to designate unnamed day on which an operation commences. D+7 means 7 days after D-Day.

Dead ahead:
Directly ahead; bearing 000 degrees relative.

Dead astern:
Directly aft; bearing 180 degrees relative.

Deadhead:
Log floating on end and mostly submerged. Also called a sleeper.

Dead horse:
Slang: an advance in pay.

Dead in the water:
Said of a vessel that has stopped and has no way on.

Deadlight:
Ventilation cover, fitted with light-obstructing baffles, for a ship's *Air port,* to permit ventilation without the escape of light. Also, a heavy glass set flush with the deck for admitting light below.

Deadman:
Timber or similar object buried in ice or in the ground to secure guys, tackles, or a ship's lines. If in ice, can also be called *Ice anchor.* Also synonym for *Irish pennant.*

Dead reckoning (DR):
Method of navigation using direction and amount of progress from the last well-determined position to a new dead reckoning or DR, pronounced "dee-are," position.

Dead-Reckoning Tracer (DRT):
Plotting device that records track of ship by continuously integrating course and speed as input from compass and log.

Deadrise:
Vertical distance between a vessel's keel and the turn of the bilge.

Dead ship:
One without power. Also called a *Cold Ship.*

Dead space:
Area within maximum range of weapon, radar, radio, or observer which cannot be covered because of obstacles or inherent limitations.

Deadweight, Deadweight tonnage:
The difference between a ship's loaded and light displacement. Total deadweight refers to carrying capacity of a ship; cargo deadweight is the total deadweight less fuel, water, stores, dunnage and other items required on voyage—expressed in long tons.

Deadwood:
Part of a ship's hull between keel and keelson aft or between stem and keel forward. In wooden ships these were solid timbers because there was insufficient space for framing in the usual manner.

Debarkation net:
Rope net used as ladder on ship's side for troops embarking or disembarking.

Debarkation station:
Location on board a ship where men assemble to debark into boats.

DECCA:
Medium-frequency continuous-wave radio navigation system. For precise positioning within short range of transmitters. Currently used in heavily traveled coastal areas of Europe and the United States.

Decipher:
To convert an enciphered message into plain text by means of a system (not by cryptanalysis).

Deck:
A floor in a ship. The uppermost complete deck is the main deck. Complete decks below it are numbered from the top down: second deck, third deck, etc. Partial decks between complete decks are called half decks; those below the lowest complete deck are platform decks, or flats. Partial decks above the main deck, if they extend to the sides of the ship are called, according to location, the forecastle deck, middle deck, or poop deck. Those which do not extend to the side are superstructure decks. Weather deck(s) are those exposed to the weather. In *Aircraft carriers* however, the topmost deck is the flight deck, and the next one below is the hangar deck. The main deck is the one below the hangar deck, after which the numbering system proceeds normally, and partial decks above the hangar deck are called *Gallery decks*. Decks often get their names from construction, as armored flight deck, protective deck, splinter deck, all three of which are fitted with armor, or from employment, as boat deck, gun deck, berth deck. As an added use of the word deck, the OOD's watch is called "the deck," as in the expression, "---has the deck," meaning he has charge of all deck functions and, if underway, is supervising all maneuvers of the ship.

Deck gang:
All men attached to the ship's deck departments, as opposed to those attached to engineering, radio, or electronics departments. In old days the deck gang was distinguished by wearing rating insignia on the right arm, hence the term, "right-arm rate." All others wore their rates on the left arm and, of course, were known as "left-arm rates."

Deck hand:
A man who works topside, on deck, usually a seaman. Slang: swab jockey, deck ape.

Deckhouse:
Topside ship's structure.

Deck load:
Gear or cargo stowed topside on weather deck.

Deck log:
Official day-by-day record of a ship in commission and thus a legal document when signed. Distinct from *Engineering log.*

Deck pads:
Non-skid plates or mats secured to the deck where traffic is heavy.

Deck plane:
Standard fire control reference plane of a ship.

Deck seamanship:
Maintenance and operation of all gear topside including boats, anchors, rigging, etc.

Declassify:
Remove security classification from information. Notification of holders of the information is part of the process.

Declination:
Angular distance north or south of the celestial equator. Used as a coordinate with Greenwich Hour Angle to identify positions of celestial bodies.

Decode:
To translate code into plain text by means of code book. Loosely used as synonym for *Decipher.*

Decontaminate:
To free from the harmful residue of nuclear or chemical attack.

Decoration:
A medal or ribbon awarded for exceptional courage, skill, or performance.

Decrypt:
To convert a cryptogram into plain text by a reversal of the encryption process (not by cryptanalysis). See *Decode.*

Deep:
An ocean bottom depression of great depth, usually more than 6000 meters.

Deep air support:
Air action against enemy forces at such a distance from friendly forces that detailed integration of each air mission with fire and movement of friendly forces is not required. See *Close air support.*

Deep creep attack:
Surprise depth charge attack for use against a submarine deeply submerged and using slow speeds. Effective only when surprise can be achieved.

DEEP JEEP:
Deep diving vehicle designed to be mobile on ocean floor.

Deeps:
Deepest areas in the ocean. Also, fathoms of a hand leadline which are not marked.

Deep Scattering Layer (DSL):
Ocean layers which scatter sound or echo it vertically. Thought to be of biological origin, they range in depth from 150 to 200 fathoms during the day and migrate to or near the surface at night.

Deep-sea lead:
Heavy weight with line or wire and mechanism to lower and retrieve it for obtaining soundings in deep water. Now largely replaced by *Echo sounder.*

Deep-sea system:
Sub-division of *Benthic division.*

Deep six:
Slang: to throw an object away or overboard.

Deep-submergence rescue vehicle (DSRV):
Small submarine, able to be carried piggyback on a large submarine or air-transported to a disaster scene, then submerge, find the sunken submarine, and make a watertight joint with the submarine's *Escape trunk.* The development of the deep submergence rescue vehicle was made necessary by the far-ranging, deep-diving, high-speed nuclear submarine, for which the standard *Rescue chamber* was inadequate.

DEEPSTAR:
Self-propelled, deep-diving ocean research vehicle.

Deep tanks:
Compartments strengthened to carry water or liquid cargo.

Deepwater waves:
Surface wind waves having a wavelength less than one half the water depth.

Deflection:
Lateral angular correction applied to target bearing to obtain hits in naval gunnery.

Degaussing:
Reducing magnetic field of a ship by wrapping ship fore and aft permanently with energized wire, to protect against magnetic mines and torpedoes.

Delivery groups:
Four-letter pronounceable groups which assist in transmission and delivery of a message. Assigned to activities and commands.

Delta:
The alluvial deposit, usually roughly triangular, near the mouth of a river. Phonetic word for letter D. The triangular shape of supersonic aircraft wing.

DELTA DAGGER:
Model designation: F-102; cognizant service: Air Force.
A single-place, supersonic, all-weather, delta-wing interceptor aircraft. 1-crew. Jet.

DELTA DART:
Model designation: F-106; cognizant service: Air Force.
Similar to *DELTA DAGGER* except for engine, new tail, addition of fuselage fuel tank, and new electronic equipment. 2-crew. Jet.

Deltaic deposits:
Sediment laid down in a river delta.

DEMON:
The F3B and C, a transonic interceptor phased out of operation in 1965.

Demonstration group:
Component of a force organized to conduct deceptive operations involving a feint.

Demurrage:
: Charge made when a merchant ship is delayed while loading or discharging cargo.

Densitometer:
: Device for measuring sea water density.

Dentalman (DN):
: Enlisted man in paygrade E-3 who performs general duties in the dental corps.

Dental technician (DT):
: Petty officer who performs general dental corps duties.

Department of Defense (DOD):
: The Department of the Executive Branch of the Government including the Office of the Secretary of Defense and the Departments of the Army, Navy and Air Force.

Department of the Navy:
: The executive part of the Naval Establishment; the headquarters, United States Marine Corps; the entire operating forces of the United States Navy, including naval aviation, and of the United States Marine Corps, including the reserve components of such forces; all field activities, headquarters, forces, bases, installations, activities and functions under the control or supervision of the Secretary of the Navy; and the United States Coast Guard when operating as a part of the Navy pursuant to law. See *Navy Department*.

Departure:
: The technical point at which a ship leaves an anchorage or harbor. Thus a typical entry in the ship's log might read: "With Brenton Reef Lightship bearing 070° true, distance two miles, took departure for Portsmouth, England on course 135° true and per gyro compass (pgc), speed 15." See *Course*.

Departure report:
: Prepared by a repair activity upon the completion of a ship's overhaul, listing work undertaken, per cent completed, items deferred, with reasons therefor, and a summary of cost.

Deperming:
: Reduction of permanent magnetism of a ship by energizing coils temporarily placed vertically around the ship. The purpose is protection against magnetic mines and torpedoes.

Deploy:
: Specifically, to change from a cruising or approach formation to a formation of ships for battle or amphibious assault. Generally, to send ships or squadrons abroad for duty.

Deployment:
: A cruise in foreign waters.

Deployment bag:
: Part of a parachute gear that keeps canopy deflated until shroud lines are completely paid out.

Depth charge:
>   ASW explosive dropped from ships. Slang: *Ashcan.* Depth bombs are
>   dropped from aircraft, depth charges from ships. The difference is
>   that aircraft weapons must have a predictable trajectory and hence
>   require a standard bomb shape.

Derelict:
>   Abandoned vessel at sea, still afloat.

Derrick:
>   A device, consisting of a boom and tackle, used for hoisting heavy
>   objects. Named after Thomas Derrick, a well-known hangman of the time
>   of Queen Elizabeth, who devised a portable hangman's tree which he could
>   carry about to perform his duties wherever required.

Deserter:
>   Person absent from his command without authority whose apparent purpose
>   is to stay away. Absence over 30 days is presumptive, but not legal
>   proof, of desertion. See *Unauthorized absentee.*

Designator:
>   A 4-digit code number that describes an officer's qualifications and
>   specialties. See *File Number* and *Signal Number.* For example, an
>   1100 officer is an unrestricted line officer with no special qualifications.

Design class:
>   Ships of a type which, at the time of issue of specifications, are
>   intended to be identical. Change orders issued may eventually make
>   them dissimilar in some respects.

Despedida:
>   Farewell party for a person or group of people who are leaving a station
>   or command.

Dessican:
>   A can holding a dessicant *Moisture Absorbing Material* such as silica
>   gel.

Destroyer:
>   Small, high-speed, lightly armored warship, jack-of-all-trades. The type
>   comprises various configurations for special employment. *Destroyer
>   Escorts*—DE's are also considered destroyers. Very large destroyers,
>   which may go above 10,000 tons, are classed as Destroyer Leaders—DL,
>   *Frigates* in the U.S. Navy, although in foreign navies "frigates" are
>   smaller types. Modern surface navies consist of *Aircraft carriers* and
>   destroyers and a few Cruisers plus amphibious types and minecraft.
>   USS LONG BEACH, the only postwar cruiser built by the U.S. Navy,
>   is in reality a very big Destroyer Leader, nuclear-powered, and is so
>   employed. Slang: Can, *Tincan.*

DESTROYER:
>   Model designation: B-66; cognizant service: Air Force.
>   A light tactical bomber aircraft. Jet.

Destroyer Escort (DE):
>   An escort vessel, in reality a small destroyer, of about 4,000 tons,
>   with 5" guns and moderate speed (29 knots). DE is pronounced
>   "dee-ee."

Diagram   91

Destroyer Leader:
  See *Destroyer, Frigate.*

Destructor:
  An explosive or other device for intentionally destroying classified
  equipment, a missile or aircraft or their components because of safety
  considerations or to prevent compromise.

Detach:
  Term used when officers are ordered away from present duty; they are
  considered "attached" to ship or station. Enlisted men are "assigned
  to" and eventually "transferred." Occasionally a large transfer of
  men is termed an "issue," especially from training station or
  receiving ship.

Detachment:
  Temporary unit formed from other naval forces.

Detail:
  To assign men to a particular duty within their duty station; the men
  assigned to such duty.

Detail officer:
  An officer in the Bureau of Naval Personnel who assigns personnel.

Detailing, personnel:
  Assignment of personnel to fill exact requirements of billets.

Detent:
  Mine release gear on a minelayer.

Determination and Findings (D&F):
  Determinations and Findings required for a noncompetitive contract
  award.

Detonation, low order:
  Partial or slow explosion.

Detrius:
  Accumulation on the sea bottom of rocks or rock particles and of broken
  organic material.

Deviascope:
  Device for demonstrating the technique of compensating a magnetic
  compass.

Deviation:
  Magnetic compass error due to magnetic properties of ship. Expressed
  in degrees east or west.

Deviation table:
  List of compass errors due to deviation for representative headings through
  360 degrees, posted near each magnetic compass.

Devil's Claw:
  See *Compressor,* device used to hold anchor chain.

Diagram (beach, boat, landing, etc.):
  Graphic representation of beach limits, boat assignments, landing order,
  etc., in amphibious operations.

DIAL-X:
Internal communications system for *POLARIS* submarine.

Diaphone:
Fixed fog signal with a characteristic emission used as an aid to navigation.

Dicing:
High-speed, low-altitude, low-oblique aircraft photo operations.

Digital Geoballistic Computer (DGBC):
Computer for *POLARIS* Mark 84 fire-control system.

Dilbert:
Slang: a person who dopes off, acts stupidly, Dilbert was born during World War II as the hero of an effective series of instruction books and cartoons for naval aviators.

Dinette:
Slang: Mess hall in a submarine.

Dinghy:
Small (less than 20 ft.) handy pulling boat with a transom stern. May be rigged for oars or sail.

Dip:
To lower the national colors part way and then raise them as a salute to a passing warship. The merchantman dips first and holds his flag "at the dip." i.e., about one-third of the way down, until after the warship has dipped in answer and *Two-blocked.* Warships render *Passing honors* but do not dip to each other. A correction of observed sextant altitude because of the curvature of the earth. The sun or moon has dipped when its lower limb (bottom of observed curvature) touches the horizon.

Dip, magnetic:
The inclination to the horizontal of a magnetic compass needle caused by the earth's magnetic field.

Dipping sonar:
Sonar equipment used by helicopters or by hydrofoils.

Dip the eye:
To arrange the loops (eyes) of 2 mooring lines on the same bollard so that either line may be removed without moving the other. Accomplished by passing the eye of one line up through that of the other and then around the bollard.

Direct:
To give an *Order* in a specific manner. Positive action is expected.

Direct fire:
Gunfire delivered using the target itself as the point of aim for the guns or director. See *Indirect fire.*

Directive:
Military communication in which policy is established or a specific action is ordered; plan issued with a view to placing it in effect when so directed, or in the event that a stated contingency arises; any communication which initiates or governs action, conduct, or procedure.

Director (gun):
Mechanical and electronic device for control of gunfire.

Disbursing clerk (DK):
A petty officer who performs clerical duties in disbursing branch of supply department.

Disbursing officer:
Officer who keeps pay records and pays salary allowances and claims.

Discharge:
Process of separating enlisted men from the service. May be honorable, general, undesirable, bad conduct, or dishonorable.

Disciplinary barracks:
An activity to receive, confine, classify, segregate, and provide work, drill and training for courts-martial prisoners.

Dismantling shot:
Projectile fired from smoothbore cannon during the 17th, 18th, and early 19th centuries, intended to destroy rigging of enemy ship. Usually consisted of heavy iron bars chained together, or of two cannon balls chained together. See *Grape, Canister, Langridge, Double-shotted.*

Dispatch (Despatch):
Former term for message.

Dispatch money:
Bonus resulting from a ship loading or discharging before expiration of *Lay days.* Paid by shipowner to the charterer. Normally included in dry-cargo voyage charter parties.

Dispensary:
A medical and/or dental facility offering services less elaborate than those of a hospital.

Displacement:
The weight of water displaced by a vessel, expressed in long tons. See *Tonnage.*

Disposal, mine:
Clearance procedure which eliminates mine danger individually by any means requiring close approach of personnel to the mine; includes rendering safe, recovery, removal and destruction.

Disposition:
Prescribed arrangement of the stations to be occupied by the several formations and single ships of a fleet, or major subdivisions of a fleet, for any purpose, such as cruising, approach, maintaining contact, or battle; prescribed arrangement of all the tactical units composing a flight or group of aircraft.

Distance line:
A marked line used between ships replenishing underway to assist in maintaining correct distance apart.

Distance (tactical):
Distance between foremasts of adjacent ships or cockpits of adjacent air craft.

Distinctive mark:
Flag or pennant flown aloft in a ship to indicate that the ship is in commission and to indicate status of senior officer aboard. It may be commission pennant, broad or burgee command pennant, personal starred flag of a *Flag officer,* or the Red Cross flag.

District, naval:
Geographical area in which all naval activities except those of the operating forces come under the control of a *Flag officer,* the Commandant.

Ditching:
Controlled landing of a disabled aircraft on water.

Ditty bag (box):
Small canvas bag or a box used by sailors and marines to stow odds and ends of gear.

Diurnal inequality:
The difference in the height and/or time of the two high waters or the two low waters each day; also the difference in the velocity of either of the two flood, or ebb, currents each day.

Diurnal range:
Same as *Great diurnal range.*

Divided fire:
Directing the fire of one ship's batteries against two targets.

Dividers:
Instrument for stepping off distance on a chart.

Diving bell:
See *Submarine Rescue Chamber.*

Diving planes (bow and stern):
Control surfaces used to control motion of a submarine underwater in a vertical plane. In U.S. nuclear submarines, bow planes have been replaced by planes built into the "sail," and are called "sail planes."

Division:
The basic administrative unit into which Navy men are organized aboard ship, in aircraft squadrons, or at shore activities. Also, a tactical subdivision of a squadron of ships or aircraft.

Division book:
Division officer's record of men's names, watch quarter and station assignments and other pertinent data. Same data may also be kept in form of division personnel cards.

Division officer:
Junior officer assigned by the commanding officer to command a division of men.

Division Officer's Guide:
Standard handbook for junior officers.

Division parade:
Space on deck assigned for a division to fall in for muster or inspection. Also see *Foul Weather Parade.*

Division police petty officer:
Petty officer detailed by division officer to assist chief master-at-arms.

Dock:
Large basin either permanently filled with water *(Wet dock)* or capable of being filled and drained *(Drydock* or *Graving dock)*. The term is now used interchangeably with *Pier* or *Wharf*.

Docking plan:
Drawing showing details of a ship's bottom used for arranging supports in a dock in order to leave access for sonar domes, hull openings, etc., after docking.

Docking report:
One giving reason for docking, ship's condition, and work performed while docked.

Dock trials:
Test of ship's operating equipment including engines while alongside prior to sea trials after construction or overhaul. A part of *Builder's trials* for new construction.

DOD:
Department of Defense.

Dodger:
Canvas windshield on exposed bridge or conning station.

Dog:
Small metal fitting used to close ports and hatches. Also, to split a watch with a shipmate is to dog it.

Dog down:
Tighten dogs or clamps on a port, hatch, or door.

Dogface:
Slang: soldier.

Dog fight:
Aerial combat between fighter-type aircraft.

Dogtag:
Slang: identification disk.

Dog watch:
One of the two-hour watches, 1600-1800 (4-6 PM) or 1800-2000 (6-8 PM).

Doldrums:
Areas on both sides of the Equator where light breezes and calms persist. A person can be said to be "in the doldrums" if his personal affairs stagnate rather than progress.

Dolly:
A low platform with wheels used for transporting or shifting heavy objects. A large *Cable jack* mounted on wheels, used on aircraft carriers. See *Crash dolly*.

Dolphin:
A cluster or clump of piles used for mooring. A single pile or a *Bollard* on a pier is sometimes called a dolphin.

Dome:
A transducer sheathing device used to reduce the noise caused by passage of the transducer through the water.

Donkey engine:
Small auxiliary engine used for lifting, etc.

Door:
The closing device which closes an upright opening between compartments. A light-weight partition not intended to hold water might have a simple door; a watertight bulkhead would have a *Watertight door* of commensurate strength. For damage control, some watertight doors are electrically or hydraulically operated from a central control station (*Damage Control Center*). A *Hatch* is similar device in a deck.

Dope:
Slang: information or news, good or bad. Also called "the *Word.*"

Doppler:
Apparent change in pitch *(Frequency)* of sound or radio wave caused by change in effective length of travel between source and point of observation; caused by speed differential between source and observer.

Doppler effect:
In *ASW* this gives some indication of target motion and thus helps to confirm (or classify) a sonar blip as a submarine. See *Doppler.*

Dory:
Small, flat-bottomed pulling boat, used chiefly by fishermen. Easily nested in large numbers because of removable *Thwarts* and sloping sides, dories were the work boats of the famous Grand Banks fishing schooners.

Dosimeter:
An instrument used to measure personal cumulative exposure to radiation. Carried by all persons working on or around nuclear machinery. Is direct reading, hence can give the individual an immediate evaluation. Not as accurate nor as foolproof, however, as the *Film badge.*

Double-banked:
Boat with two men on a thwart or two men on an oar.

Double-bottoms:
Watertight subdivisions of ship, next to the keel and between outer and inner bottoms.

Double hooking:
Process of switching a boat or other load from one ship's crane to another.

Double luff:
A tackle in which the blocks have two sheaves each.

Double-shot:
The custom of loading two cannon balls into a single cannon with a single explosive charge, during 17th, 18th, and early 19th centuries. Reduced range and accuracy resulted of course, and the procedure was employed only at short range. See *Grape, Canister, Langridge, Dismantling shot.*

Double up:
To double mooring lines for added security. See *Single up.*

Doubling:
Sailing around a point of land, e.g., doubling Cape Horn.
See *Weathering.*

Doubtful Nonmilitary Vessel Category:
Condition between "Clean" and "Suspect" because of unexpected arrival, general characteristics, appearance of crew incompatible with declared nationality or with size and type of vessel, draft incompatible with declared cargo, reported length of voyage illogical, etc.

Down by the head (stern):
Lower in the water than normal at the forward (after) end of the ship.

Downgrade:
To lower a security classification previously assigned.

Downhaul:
Line or wire which pulls or leads downward.

Down time:
The time equipment that is out of commission because of failures of equipment, power, or other factors.

Dowse (douse):
To put out, to lower a sail quickly, or to wet down or immerse in water.

Draft:
Depth of a ship beneath the waterline, measured vertically to the keel.
A group of new men assigned to a command.

Drafting machine:
Mechanical parallel ruler used in navigational piloting and plotting.

Draft marks:
Numeral figures on either side of the stem and sternpost, used to indicate the amount of the ship's draft.

Draftsman (DM):
Petty officer who prepares technical drawings, plans, or sketches.

Drag:
Forces opposing direction of motion due to skin friction, profile, and other components. The amount that a ship is down by the stern. To pull the anchor along the bottom, as a ship drags due to high winds. Also slang at Naval Academy for girl or date.

DRAGON:
Model designation: XFGM-77A; cognizant service: Army.
Missile designed for use in medium antitank assault operations.

Dragon's Tail:
A towed thermister chain for measurement of sea temperatures.

Drag ring:
Plywood stabilizer for a torpedo launched from an airplane.

Drainage system:
Series of pipes which drain all spaces and compartments.

Drain, main:
Large suction line in the engineering spaces for pumping those compartments, connected to suction of main circulating pump.

Dredging:
Dragging an anchor along the bottom at short stay to steady a ship's head in narrow channels or when going alongside a pier. To deepen a harbor or channel.

Dress (right or left):
When in ranks, a command to form a straight line, guiding from the directed side.

Dressing lines:
Lines used in *Dressing ship.*

Dressing ship:
Displaying national colors at all mastheads and the flagstaff; full dressing requires a rainbow of flags from bow to stern over the mastheads.

Drift:
The lateral motion of a rotating projectile due largely to gyroscopic action. Displacement, due to wind, of aircraft's track from its true heading. Amount of anchor chain on deck for working purposes when mooring. Speed of current in knots.

Drift angle:
Horizontal angle between the fore-and-aft axis of an aircraft and its path relative to the ground.

Drift ice:
Any ice which has drifted from its point of origin.

Drift lead:
Lead weight dropped over the side with the line slack or leading aft. Indicates whether or not the ship is dragging her anchor.

Driftmeter (drift sight):
Device in aircraft used to observe *Drift.*

Drill:
Training exercise in which actual operation is simulated, such as a general quarters drill.

Driver (CD):
Petty officer who operates and maintains heavy automotive and construction equipment.

Drogue:
> Device used to slow rate of movement, e.g., a drogue on an aerial mine.
> See *Sea Anchor.*

Drone:
> Remotely controlled aircraft for target or data gathering purposes.

Drone Anti-Submarine Helicopter (DASH):
> Small, light weight, remotely controlled helicopter capable of operating
> from a destroyer and delivering an antisubmarine warfare weapon to an
> enemy submarine. It provided destroyers with a stand-off weapon.
> Discontinued because of high operational losses.

Drum:
> A capstan-head mounted with axis horizontal, usually as an adjunct to
> ordinary *Windlass* or *Capstan,* used for assistance in hauling
> lines.

Drum, steam:
> Large cylindrical shell at the top of a boiler in which the steam collects.

Drum, water:
> Cylindrical tank at the bottom of a boiler; also called *Mud drum.*

Drydock:
> See *Dock.*

Dry pipe:
> Perforated pipe at the highest point in a steam drum to collect the steam.

Dry run:
> Rehearsal of any kind, as in torpedo firing, when all motions are gone
> through except the release of the torpedo, shooting the gun, starting
> the engine, etc.

Ducts:
> Large sheet metal pipes that lead air from blowers to enclosed spaces.

Dud:
> An explosive, such as a bomb, that fails to detonate.

Dulcimer:
> Gong-like musical device used to announce dinner in the wardroom.

DUMBO:
> Seaplane formerly used for search and rescue.

Dummy message:
> Message sent for some purpose other than its content. Generally an
> entirely fabricated message.

Dump:
> Temporary stock of supplies or a storage place where military supplies
> are temporarily stocked.

Dump, floating:
> Supply of critical items held on landing craft for quick delivery ashore
> to assault troops during amphibious operations.

Dungaree(s):
Blue cotton work clothes.

Dunking (dunked) sonar:
Sonar gear towed submerged by an airship or helicopter. Also called *Dipping Sonar.*

Dunnage:
Material used in securing or protecting supplies aboard ship such as boards, mats, straps, etc. Also, a sailor's personal gear.

Duplex circuit:
One that permits radio communication traffic in both directions at same time.

Duplex pressure proportioner:
Shipboard foam firefighting device.

Dutch courage:
The courage obtained from drink. Comes from the custom initiated by the famous Dutch Admirals, Tromp and de Ruyter, of giving their crews a liberal libation before battle with the English. The practice was naturally belittled by the English, who nevertheless were forced to admit to the effectiveness of the Dutch Navy.

Dutchman:
A spacer piece in piping or duct aboard ship used to replace a piece of equipment such as the heating element in a ventilation duct.

Duty:
Adjective signifying status, i.e. duty engineer, duty section, etc. Meaning those who must remain on board ship in a work or "on watch" status instead of going ashore.

Dye marker:
Brightly colored chemical that spreads when released in water.

E

Eager:
Slang: overanxious for duty, employment, combat, and distinction, presumably to the detraction of his peers who are not so eager.

Eagle screams, the:
Slang: pay day.

Ear banger:
Slang: one who is overanxious to please.

Earliest complete freezing:
Earliest reported date on which ten-tenths ice coverage was observed at a specific location.

EARLY SPRING:
Same as *SKIPPER*.

Ease:
To do something slowly, as "ease away from the pier" or "ease the strain on a line." See *Handsomely*.

Ease her (the rudder):
Reduce the amount of rudder the ship is carrying.

Ease off:
To ease a line; slacken it when taut.

Easing-out line:
Line used to release something slowly, as an unshackled anchor chain or a fuel hose.

Easy:
Carefully, as in: "Lower away easy." See *Handsomely.*

E award:
Letter E, worn on enlisted men's uniforms, as mark of winning the *Battle Efficiency Award.* Also awarded to guns and mounts for efficiency in gunnery and to ships for excellence in communication, engineering, etc.

Ebb currents:
Currents caused by decrease in height of tide, generally set seaward.

Ebb tide:
See *Tide.*

Echelon:
A level of command. A subdivision, e.g., rear echelon of a headquarters.

Echo:
Phonetic word for the letter E.

Echo sounder:
> Oceanographic instrument for determining depth of water by measuring time for generated sound emission to reach bottom and return as an echo. See *Fathometer.*

Economizer:
> Heat transfer device on a boiler that uses the heat of the stack gases to preheat the feed water. See *Feed heater.*

Eddy:
> Circular motion caused by water passing obstructions or by action of adjacent currents flowing in opposite directions. Sometimes a synonym for *Countercurrent.*

Eductor:
> Pump used to empty flooded spaces.

Effective Program Projections (EPP):
> Normally includes the current fiscal year. Lists programs in the latest Five Year Defense Program with current budget and those for next four years.

Egg:
> Escape capsule for multiplace highspeed aircraft.

Eight-o'clock reports:
> Reports received by the executive officer shortly before 2000 (8 PM) from the heads of departments. He, in turn, reports eight o'clock to the commanding officer. Sometimes mistakenly called the twenty-hundred reports.

Ejection seat:
> Device which expels the pilot safely in an emergency from a high-speed airplane.

Electrician:
> Warrant officer advanced from *Electrician's mate* or *IC Electrician.*

Electrician's mate (EM):
> Petty officer who maintains and repairs power and lighting circuits.

Electromagnetic log:
> Speed log using an electromagnet to produce a voltage proportionate to the vessel's speed, using the water as a conductor.

Electronic Countermeasures (ECM):
> The use of electronics to reduce the effectiveness of enemy equipment, or to affect his resulting tactics. Active countermeasures are detectable by the enemy, passive are not.

Electronic Information Bulletin (EIB):
> Bi-weekly publication of *Ship Systems Command* containing general electronics information of interest to fleet and shore radio facilities.

Electronic Material Shipment Request (EMSR):
> Document authorizing shipment of designated Navy electronics equipment from one location to another. Originated in the Electronics Division, BuShips.

Electronic navigation:
(Navigation) using such devices as *Radar, Loran, Shoran.*

Electronic Repair Parts Allowance List (ERPAL):
Machine listing of parts and tubes for electronics equipment installed in a specific ship or activity.

Electronic Requirement Plan (ERP):
CNO listing by name and nomenclature of electronic requirement for ships, included as an appendix to the ship's Approved Characteristics. Originally Electronic Installation Plan.

Electronics nomenclature system:
See Appendix E.

Electronics Technician (ET):
Petty officer who maintains and repairs electronic gear.

Electronic Systems Command:
A functional command within the *Naval Material Command,* established May 1966.

Elevation, gun:
Vertical angle of the axis of the bore of a gun above the horizontal plane.

Elevator:
Movable section of the tail of a plane, usually hinged to the stabilizer and used to head the plane up or down in flight. A lift for passengers and freight. The largest elevators are those used to transfer aircraft between *Flight deck* and *Hangar deck* of an *Aircraft carrier.*

Elokomin rig:
Arrangement of tackle and hoses for fueling a ship underway from another ship alongside.

Embark:
To go aboard a ship or aircraft.

Embarkation officers (EMBO):
Landing force officers who advise naval unit commanders on combat loading and act in liaison with troop officers. Formerly called transport quartermasters (TQM).

Emergency drill:
Rehearsal of action taken by ship's crew in an emergency, such as fire.

Empennage:
Tail group or assembly of an aircraft.

Employment schedule:
Program of ship and aircraft activities promulgated by *Fleet* or *Type* commanders.

Encapsulted torpedo:
A homing mine under development.

Encipher:
To convert plain text into unintelligible language by a cipher system.

Encode:
> To convert plain text into unintelligible language by means of a code book.

Encrypt:
> To convert plain text into unintelligible form by means of a cryptosystem. "Encipher," "encode," and "encrypt" are often used synonymously.

End for end:
> To reverse something, as "end for end the boat falls," which means to shift ends to spread the wear evenly throughout the falls or line.

End item:
> The final combination of end products, sub-assemblies, components and materials ready for their intended use, i.e., ship, tank, aircraft, etc.

End on:
> Said of two vessels meeting, whose *Centerlines,* extended, lie upon a single straight line; or of another ship whose centerline projects through own ship. Generally refers to the bows-on or the head-to-head situations.

Endorsement:
> A form of letter, indicating approval, disapproval, comment, or other action, that is stamped or written on the basic letter or attached thereto.

Engagement stars:
> Small metal stars worn on campaign ribbons to denote the wearer's participation in specific battles or operations.

Engineering duty officer (EDO):
> Officer of the restricted line specializing in engineering afloat and ashore. The designation for *Aeronautical engineering duty officer* is AEDO, for *Ordnance engineering duty officer* is OEDO.

Engineer's bell book:
> See *Bell book.*

Engineman (EN):
> Petty officer who operates and maintains Diesel and gasoline engines.

Engine-order telegraph:
> Device on the ship's bridge to give orders to the engine room. Also called *Annunciator.*

Enlisted man:
> Male naval personnel below the grade of warrant officer. "Enlisted woman" is the WAVE counterpart.

Enlisted rating structure:
> See Appendix B.

Ensign:
> The most junior commissioned officer. The national flag flown by men-of-war from *Gaff* underway, *Flagstaff* in port.

ENTAC:
> Model designation: MGM-32; cognizant service: Army.
> Classified missile.

Entrance:
> That part of a ship's hull from amidships forward.

Entry Plan:
> Directive containing detailed instructions to a group of ships entering a port or roadstead.

Environmental test:
> Engineering test to evaluate natural climate or induced conditions of heat, cold, moisture, etc., on performance of a product.

Ephemeris:
> A publication giving the computed positions of celestial bodies for each day of the year, or for other regular intervals.

Equator:
> The great circle of the earth equidistant from the poles. Divides northern hemisphere from southern hemisphere.

Equatorial Tides:
> Tides occurring approximately every two weeks when the moon is over the equator.

Equinoctial:
> Celestial equator.

Equinox:
> A point marking the intersection of the ecliptic and the celestial equator, occupied by the sun when its declination is zero.

Equipage:
> General term used to designate material of a non-consumable nature which must be aboard for a ship to perform its mission properly.

Equivalent full-power hours (EFPH):
> A standard for indicating the amount of nuclear energy consumed. Naval reactors are rated in terms of the number of hours of full-power energy built into them, which is a direct measure of the amount of nuclear fuel. One-half hour at full power is the same as one hour at half power, although distances run and speeds attained vary as the cube law. Thus a 2,000-hour reactor which has logged 1,000 EFPH is half expended.

Equivalent service rounds (ESR):
> A standard for indicating gun erosion. All rounds fired, including reduced charges, are recorded in terms of service rounds.

Escape hatch:
> In general any hatch, usually small, installed to permit men to escape from a compartment when ordinary means of egress are blocked. Developed to a high degree in modern submarines, which have escape trunks fitted to receive a *Rescue chamber* or a *Deep Submergence Rescue Vehicle,* an additional hatch for unassisted escape, and numerous specialized operating mechanisms and devices.

Escape trunk:
> A specialized escape compartment in modern submarines, arranged to receive the *Rescue chamber* or *Deep Submergence Rescue Vehicle* or to permit individual escape from a disabled submarine.

Escort:
To convoy. Aircraft assigned to protect and accompany other aircraft. Combatant ships protecting a convoy or task force. A person who accompanies a body to a burial place.

Escort vessel:
Old name for *Destroyer Escort.* Now used to designate any warship escorting an aircraft carrier or a convoy.

Estimated position (EP):
The navigational position determined from estimates rather than from known data. Frequently an arbitrary datum from which to calculate the navigational *Fix.*

Estimate of the situation:
Logical process of reasoning by which a commander considers all circumstances and arrives at a decision.

Eulerian method:
Measurement of rate of flow past a given point by current meters.

Eulittoral zone:
Subdivision of the *Littoral system* of the *Benthic division* including waters from zero to 50 meters in depth.

Evacuation control ship:
In an amphibious operation, a ship designated as a control point for landing craft, amphibious vehicles, and helicopters evacuating casualties from the beaches.

Evaporator (Evaps):
Device aboard ship for making fresh water from salt by the process of evaporation.

Evasive steering:
Ship tactics to confuse submarines, including *Zigzagging, Sinuating,* and *Weaving.*

Even keel:
Floating evenly and level without *List* or uneven *Trim.*

Evolution:
The tactical maneuver or movement of ships or aircraft. Also a synonym for *Exercise.*

Execute:
To actuate, as "execute the signal!"

Executive officer:
The second in command of a ship, station, aircraft squadron, etc.

Exercise:
Naval maneuver, drill, or operation for training purposes.

Exercises, joint:
Exercises in which two or more of the Armed Services take part. *See Combined Operations.*

Expansion joint:
A joint which allows expansion, contraction, or flexing in a pipe, ship's decks or superstructure.

Explosimeter:
Device to test presence of explosive fumes.

Exposure suit:
Special clothing to assist downed aviators to resist exposure to cold water.

Extender:
Device for holding the detonator of a mine or depth charge in a safe position.

Extra duty:
Additional work assigned as punishment under *Uniform Code of Military Justice.*

Extremely high frequency radio (EHF):
Radio operating in the range of 30,000 to 300,000 MHz.

Eyebolt:
A metal bolt ending in an eye.

Eyebrow:
Elliptical metal ridge over an *Air port* designated to shed water.

Eyes of the ship:
The forward-most portion of the weather deck, as far forward as a man can stand, where *Fog lookouts* are customarily stationed. Most old ships had figureheads on their bows, and the term "eyes of the ship" is supposed to refer either to their eyes or to those of the fog lookouts. Interestingly, the Chinese, with an entirely different cultural history, for centuries have carved or painted eyes on the bows of their junks.

F

Facilities Engineering Command:
  A functional command within the *Naval Material Command*, established
  May 1966. Replaces Bureau of Yards and Docks (BuDocks).

Facsimile:
  The transmission of photographs or other material by wire or radio.

Fairlead:
  A fitting, such as a block, which provides a friction-free passage for
  a line or cable. Also, an unhampered route for a line or cable.

Fair tide:
  Tidal current running in same direction as the ship.

Fairway:
  The channel, the navigable part of a body of water.

Fair wind:
  A favoring wind.

Fake down:
  To lay out a line in long flat bights, the whole being much longer than
  wide, in such form that when needed it will pay out freely without
  bights or kinks. A coiled or flemished line cannot do this unless the
  coil of the line is able to turn, as on a reel, for otherwise a twist
  results in the line which will produce a kink and jam it. Also termed
  Flake down. See Coil and Flemish.

FALCON:
  Model designation: AIM-4; cognizant service: Air Force.
  Air-to-air guided, light-weight, and self-propelled missile.

Fall:
  The rope which, with blocks, makes up a tackle, e.g., a boat fall.

Fall in at quarters:
  Command to form ranks at *Quarters.* The command to disband or fall
  out is: "Leave your quarters."

Falling glass:
  Lowering atmospheric pressure as registered by the barometer;
  normally a sign of approaching bad weather.

Fall off:
  Said of a ship or the bow of a ship when it drifts away from a desired
  position or direction.

Fall out area:
  Area to windward of atomic explosion at sea where rain of contaminated
  matter is likely.

Fancy work:
  Decorative knots and pieces of canvas used particularly in *Gigs* and
  Barges. See *Square Knotting, MacNamara Lace.*

Fantail:
   The aftermost deck area topside on a ship.

Farm:
   Open storage area near pier entrance.

Fast:
   Snugly secured; said of a line when it is fastened securely.

Fast Automatic Shuttle Transfer System (FAST):
   Replenishment system designed to speed transfer of ordnance and
   supplies between ships at sea through specialized handling equipment
   aboard the supply ships.

Fast cruise:
   Trials of several days in length conducted while the ship is fast to
   a pier or at anchor, with only the ship's crew aboard. The purpose is
   to train personnel in all operations of the ship's equipment and to check
   out its proper operation in as many facets as practicable. Considerable
   ingenuity is commonly exercised to simulate actual conditions at sea.
   Originally devised to check out readiness of a nuclear ship and crew
   after completion of the construction period and prior to sea trials.
   Now extended to include postoverhaul trials, and nonnuclear ships as well.

Fast Deployment Logistic ship (FDL):
   Ship intended to permit fast transportation of necessary equipment to
   troubled areas, there to meet Army combat personnel transported by air.
   The program for development of these ships has struck many snags and has
   yet to be approved by Congress.

Fast ice:
   Sea ice which remains along coast or over shoals in the position of
   its growth. Same as *Landfast ice.*

Fast Reaction Integrated Submarine Control (FRISCO):
   A combat data processing and display system for submarines.

Fathom:
   Measure of length or depth, 6 feet.

Fathometer:
   Copyrighted trade name for *Echo sounder.*

Feather:
   To turn the blade of an oar horizontally at the finish of a stroke to
   reduce resistance of air or water. To change the pitch of a variable-
   pitch propeller or an airplane to vary the amount of bite into the air.
   Also, the bow *(Stem)* spray of a high-speed ship. Similarly, *Periscope
   feather,* the spray formed by the periscope of a submerged submarine
   moving through the water at moderate to high speed.

Feather merchant:
   Slang: uncomplimentary term of mild opprobrium, applied to men
   (especially reserves) new to the service.

Feedback:
   The audible return of a portion of the amplifier stage output to the input
   of that stage resulting in squealing when transmitting over a voice radio.

Feed heater:
Heat transfer device used to heat feed water before it goes to the boiler. See *Economizer.*

Feed water:
Fresh water made in *Evaporators* for use in boilers.

Feel the way:
To proceed cautiously, taking soundings with the lead. A ship will literally "feel its way" along an unfamiliar or uncharted channel.

Fender:
A device of canvas, wood, line, cork, rubber, wicker, or plastic slung over the side of a ship by means of a line, and placed in position to absorb the shock of contact between ships or between ship and pier.

Fend off:
To push away; pushing away from a pier or another ship when coming alongside, to prevent damage or chafing.

Fetch:
The distance a wind blows over the sea surface without significant change in direction, a factor in the build-up of waves.

Fiber rope:
General term for cordage made of vegetable fibers, such as hemp, Manila, flax, cotton, or sisal.

Fid:
Sharply pointed, round wooden tool used in separating the strands of a line for splicing. See *Marlinspike.*

Fiddle bridge:
Collapsible supports under the arresting cables on an aircraft carrier's deck.

Fiddle rack (boards):
Wooden device set on a table at sea in rough weather to hold table gear in place.

Fiddley, fidley:
Wide opening immediately above a fireroom, through which ventilators are led; iron framework around ladder of a deck hatch leading below decks.

Fidley deck:
Raised platform over the engine and boiler rooms, more particularly around the stack.

Fidley grating:
Steel gratings fitted over boiler-room hatches.

Field change:
Necessary parts and instructions to make an authorized post factory modification to machinery, ordnance, or electronic equipment.

Field-change order:
Written unilateral order by a field representative. Normally the technical and financial scope of such orders is less than that which can be authorized by the cognizant office or command.

Field day:
Cleaning day, traditionally Friday, the day before inspection.

Field ice:
Ice formed by freezing of the ocean surface. Also called sea ice.

Field music:
U.S. Marine term for bugle call or bugler.

Field scarf:
Marine term for khaki uniform necktie.

Field-strip:
To disassemble without further breakdown the major groups of a piece of ordnance for routine or operating cleaning and oiling; as opposed to *detailed stripping* which may be done only by authorized technicians.

Fife rail:
A wood or metal rail bored with holes to receive *Belaying pins;* seen on Navy ships at head of *Flag bags.*

Fighter direction:
Control of fighter aircraft. A fighter direction ship or aircraft is one specially equipped for that purpose. A fighter director is one who does the controlling.

Fighter sweep:
Offensive mission by fighter aircraft to destroy enemy aircraft or installations.

Figure-eight fake:
Method of coiling rope in which the turns form a series of overlapping figure-eights advancing about one or two diameters of the rope for each turn; usually done over the lifelines.

Filbert base:
A dummy air base intended to give the enemy false intelligence on positions and strength or to conceal removal or abandonment of a real base.

File:
Message files. Permanent: general, radio station, or visual station file. Temporary: tickler file, one that is designed to jog the memory. Also a line or rank of men standing in formation.

File closer:
Man who stands behind the file or rank, as the CPO or JO does during inspection.

File number:
Record identification number for naval officers, assigned upon commissioning and retained permanently. Corresponding term for Marine Corps officers is service number. Slang: serial number. File and service numbers will eventually be replaced by Social Security numbers.

Film badge:
A small piece of unexposed film, arranged in a badge worn pinned to clothing by personnel working in a nuclear environment. Changed periodically and read, i.e. developed and evaluated, in the nucleonics laboratory of the activity. Gives a more accurate measure of cumulative radiation exposure than the *Dosimeter.*

Final Acceptance Trials (FAT):
Final underway sea trials conducted by Navy operating personnel to show the ship meets all contractural requirements.

Final diameter:
Diameter of a circle made by a ship completing a turn with constant rudder angle.

Fire and rescue party:
Obsolete term for *Rescue and Assistance Party.*

FIREBEE:
Model designation: BQM-34; cognizant services: Air Force/Army/Navy. Turbojet target guided missile. For missile evaluation and training requirements. Also used as a high-performance target.

Firebox:
The section of a ship's boiler where fuel oil combustion takes place.

Fire, call:
Gunfire delivered on a target in response to a request from the supported unit.

Fire, continuous:
All guns firing independently when loaded; in contrast to *Salvo* fire.

Fire control:
Organized system by which the offensive power of the armament of a ship is directed.

Fire control, shipboard:
The entire system of directing and controlling the offensive and defensive weapons of a ship.

Fire control technician (FT):
A petty officer who performs major repair and overhaul of fire control equipment.

Fire-control tower:
May be either a separate structure or a part of the conning tower containing fire-control equipment; typical of major warships.

Fire, counter-battery:
Gunfire from a ship directed at enemy artillery ashore.

Fire, covering:
Gunfire delivered to protect or cover certain operations, such as minesweeping.

Fire, destruction:
Slow, deliberate, accurate gunfire to destroy a target ashore.

Fire, direct:
  Gunfire in which the weapon's sights bear directly on the target.

Fire, divided:
  One ship firing at two or more targets.

Fire, harassing:
  Sporadic shore bombardment gunfire to prevent enemy rest, regrouping,
  or movement.

Fire, illuminating:
  Starshell firing to silhouette the enemy and provide illumination for
  naval operations or troop operations ashore.

Fire, indirect:
  Gunfire at a target that cannot be seen from firing ship.

Fire, interdiction:
  Intermittent gunfire on roads, road junctions, railroads, airfields,
  etc., to prevent enemy use.

Firemain:
  The salt water line that provides firefighting and flushing water
  throughout the ship.

Fireman (FN):
  Enlisted man in paygrade E-3 who works in the engineering department
  spaces.

Fire mission:
  An assignment in shore bombardment to fire on a specific target.

Fire, neutralization:
  Gunfire designed to immobilize enemy activity in a specific area.

Fire party:
  Men aboard ship in the duty section organized to fight fire.

Fireroom:
  Compartment containing boilers and the station for firing or operating them.

Fire, salvo:
  Gunfire in which all guns of a battery fire together at regular intervals.
  In the British Navy, half the guns fire at a time, alternately. Thus,
  salvos are twice as fast for a given firing interval.

Fire, slow:
  Deliberate gunfire to permit careful adjustment.

Fire support:
  Gunfire to aid or assist a unit ashore. May be close support, deep
  support, or direct support fire.

Fire support area (sector):
  Specific terrain assigned ship for gunfire support during an amphibious
  operation.

Fire support ship, inshore (IFS):
  Shallow-draft rocket-firing ship for fire-support duty close to the beach
  during amphibious assault.

FIRETRAC:
System for measurement of performance of missiles fired at target drones.

Firing lock:
The mechanism in the breech of a gun which contains the firing pin.

Firing range:
Distance between firing ship and target at instant of firing torpedo.
See *Torpedo run.*

Firing stop mechanism:
Device that prevents a gun from firing into its own ship's structure.

First-aid kit:
Emergency medical equipment in a repair party locker or on a life raft.
At a gun, material is in a first-aid pouch or *Gun Bag.* In a boat, the
first-aid gear is in the *Boat Box.*

First call:
A bugle call sounded 5 minutes before quarters, colors, or tattoo.

First dog watch:
The watch from 1600 (4 PM) to 1800 (6 PM).

First lieutenant:
Officer responsible for the upkeep and cleanliness of the ship, boats,
ground tackle, and deck seamanship in general.

First light:
The beginning of morning nautical twilight, i.e., when the center of the
morning sun is 12 degrees below the horizon.

First watch:
The 2000-2400 watch (8 PM to midnight).

Fish:
Streamlined weight on the end of an aircraft's trailing, suspended
antenna. Also, slang for torpedo. A tapered batten of hard strong
wood bound to a spar to strengthen it. To fish a spar is to strengthen
it in this way.

Fist:
A radio operator's key or sending hand. A slow or rusty operator is said
to have a "glass fist."

Fita Fita guard (band):
American Samoans enlisted in the Navy for duty in Samoa. Disestab-
lished in 1951.

Fitness report:
Periodic evaluation of an officer's performance of duty and worth to
the service, by his commanding officer.

Fitting:
Generic term for any part or piece of machinery or installed equipment.

Fitting out:
Preparing a ship for commissioning and active service by placing on
board the material authorized by the *Allowance List.*

Fix:
>   A navigational position determined from terrestrial, electronic, or
>   astronomical data.

Flag bag:
>   Container on the bridge holding the signal flags.

Flag bridge:
>   In a ship designed for service as *Flagship,* a separate bridge for use
>   of a *Flag officer* and his staff. Usually on a different level from the
>   ship's *Navigating bridge* and distinctly separate from it.
>   See *Signal bridge*

Flaghoist:
>   Method of communicating between ships by using flags run up on
>   signal *Halyards.*

Flag lieutenant:
>   Personal aide to a *Flag Officer* afloat. Acts as flag visual signal
>   officer underway.

Flag officer:
>   Officer above the grade of captain authorized to fly a personal flag.
>   Equivalent to General Officer. See *Admiral.*

Flag plot:
>   An enclosed tactical and navigational center used by the flag officer
>   and his staff in exercising tactical command of ships and aircraft.

Flag secretary:
>   Personal aide to a flag officer who directs the paper work of a staff.

Flagship:
>   The ship from which an admiral or other unit commander exercises
>   command.

Flags, signal:
>   Colored flags, including international alphabet flags, used for
>   visual communications.

Flagstaff:
>   Vertical spar at stern of ship where the Ensign is displayed when anchored
>   or moored.

Flagstaff insignia:
>   Distinguishing devices such as eagles, halberds, stars, etc., fitted at
>   top of flagstaffs used in boats of officers or of important civil officials.

Flake:
>   Same as Fake in *Fake Down.*

Flake out:
>   Slang: to lie down, take a nap or "take an equal strain on all parts".

Flame-out:
>   Jet aircraft casualty—the fire goes out.

Flame safety lamp:
>   Special lamp designed to test oxygen content of air in a compartment.

Flank speed:
   Maximum *Speed.*

Flap:
   Slang: excitement or confusion.

Flapper valve:
   A valve, usually large, closed by swinging a hinged plate on to its seat,
   seated firmly by pressure above the plate or disc. Lends itself to quick
   closing, remote operation, and automatic action if water instead of air
   comes down the pipe. Disaster to USS SQUALUS in 1939 established
   requirement for such valves in hull air-induction system of submarines.

Flare:
   Pyrotechnic used to attract attention.

Flareback:
   Backfire of flame and hot gases into a ship's fireroom from the firebox.
   Also, an ejection of flame and hot gas from the breech of a gun.

Flare (of a ship's hull):
   The outward curve, away from the centerline, of the sides of a boat
   or ship, above the waterline; reverse of *Tumble Home.* Flare causes
   the sides of a ship's bows to be concave. Thus they force water away
   as she plunges, and simultaneously greatly increase displacement of the
   bow, reducing depth to which the bow plunges.

Flash burn:
   The burn from the flash of a bomb or projectile, countered on board ship
   by flashproof clothing *(battle dress).*

Flashing:
   Reducing the amount of permanent magnetism in a ship by placing
   temporary energizing coils horizontally around the ship.

Flashing light:
   Communication using code transmitted by blinker or signal searchlight.
   A navigational aid whose period of light is less than the period of
   darkness. See *Occulting Light.*

Flashless charges:
   Powder that reduces flash of detonation for concealment of firing ship
   at night.

Flash message:
   A category of precedence reserved for initial enemy contact messages or
   operational combat messages of extreme urgency.

Flash plate:
   Metal plate on forecastle on which anchor chain rests. So called because
   of the sparks when the anchor is let go.

Flashproof:
   Clothing worn to prevent flash burn.

Flat:
   A partial deck below the lowest complete deck. See *Deck.*

Flat hat:
   Blue cap formerly worn by enlisted men.

Flathatting:
>Slang: low flying and stunting.

Flattop:
>Slang: aircraft carrier.

Flaw:
>Sudden gust of wind. A very light puff during a calm is called a
>*Cat's-Paw.*

Fleet:
>An organization of ships, aircraft, marine forces and shore-based fleet
>activities, all under a commander or commander in chief who may exercise
>operational as well as administrative control. Also, all naval operating
>forces.

Fleet aircraft service squadron (FASRON):
>A unit which maintains and repairs fleet aircraft.

Fleet air detachment (FAD):
>Fleet aircraft, personnel and units based on shore. CFAD is Commander FAD.

Fleet air wing:
>A group of patrol squadrons, land- and tender-based, with tenders and
>supporting FASRONS.

Fleet Ballistic Missile (FBM):
>Shipborne ballistic missile, normally used in connection with
>*POLARIS* and *POSEIDON.*

Fleet Ballistic Missile Submarine (SSBN):
>Nuclear-powered submarine designed to deliver ballistic missile
>attacks against assigned targets from either a submerged or surfaced
>condition.

Fleet Guides:
>Naval publications describing each major U.S. port from which the fleet
>operates.

Fleet Improvement Program (FIP):
>Quarterly listing of all ships scheduled for overhauls or other
>availabilities and including all material or operational improvement
>plans planned for these periods.

Fleet in being:
>A naval force which acts as a factor of strength because of its existence.
>A classic example is the German High Seas Fleet during World War I.

Fleet Introduction Program (FIP):
>An accelerated flight program to indoctrinate fleet personnel in operation
>and maintenance of new weapons systems and provide additional checks
>on the system's fleet readiness.

Fleet logistics air wing (FLOG-WING or FLAW):
>Fleet aircraft which maintain essential air transport for fleet operations.

Fleet Marine Force (FMF):
>A balanced force of combined arms comprising land, air, and service
>elements of the U.S. Marine Corps. A Fleet Marine Force is an integral
>part of a U.S. Fleet and has the status of a type command.

Fleet Rehabilitation and Modernization (FRAM):
A program to extend useful life of certain ships and aircraft through a general overhaul and modernization program.

Fleet up:
To advance in position or importance, as the gunnery officer may "fleet up to executive officer."

Flemish (down):
To coil down a line on deck in a flat, circular concentric arrangement. See *Fake* and *Coil.*

FLEXBEE:
Lightweight, flexible wing reconnaissance drone used by the Marine Corps.

Flight:
In naval and Marine Corps usage, a specified group of aircraft usually engaged in a common mission.

Flight clearance:
Permission to make a flight.

Flight deck:
Top deck of an aircraft carrier.

Flight gear:
Clothing and equipment worn by an aviator.

Flight leader:
Pilot in tactical command of a mission, flight, sweep, or patrol station.

Flight line:
Prescribed path of airplane taking photographs or making other observations; also, relating to an airfield, a line of the field on which planes are lined up prior to takeoff.

Flight log:
Naval aviator's record of his flight time.

Flight pay:
Extra pay earned by aviation personnel. Slang: *Flight Skins.*

Flight plan:
Specified information filed either orally or in writing with Air Traffic Control relative to intended flight of an aircraft.

Flight quarters:
Manning of all stations for flight operations aboard ship.

Flight skins:
Slang for *Flight Pay.*

Flight surgeon:
Medical officer specially qualified for duty with an aviation unit.

Flinders bar:
Iron bar inserted in the binnacle of a magnetic compass to help compensate for deviation.

Floater net:
  Net made up of floats connected by line. Used to supplement life rafts
  and life boats.

Floating drydock:
  Movable dock floating in water; ships are floated into it when the dock
  is "down" (i.e., partially submerged). Then the dock is raised by pumping the tanks, lifting the ship for repairs to the *Underwater body.*

Floating dump (offshore dump):
  Reserve of critical supplies held afloat for quick delivery to the assault
  troops ashore in an amphibious assault.

Float, life:
  Emergency equipment used by ships and aircraft in case of disaster
  at sea.

Floating reserve:
  Amphibious troops kept aboard ship until needed.

Floe:
  Fragments of ice, other than icebergs, of no specific size.

Flood currents:
  Currents due to increase in height of tide.

Flood tide:
  Incoming tide.

Floor:
  Wide web beams inside ship's bottom. Also, the inside of the ship's
  bottom plating. See *Bilges.*

Floor plates:
  Removable deck plating of any machinery space.

Florida Current:
  Water moving into the Atlantic Ocean through the Straits of Florida,
  part of Gulf Stream system.

Flotation gear:
  Devices designed to insure floating, as in a landplane that flies over
  water.

Flotilla:
  Administrative or tactical organization consisting of two or more squadrons
  of ships together with a flagship and/or tender.

Flotsam:
  Floating wreckage or trash. See *Jetsam.*

Flow chart:
  Graphic display, using symbols, showing the step-by-step sequence
  of operations or processes.

Flow diagram:
  Graphic display of major steps of work in process emphasizing where
  the work is done and who is responsible.

Flukes:
Broad arms or palms of an anchor.

Flushdecker or Flush-deck destroyer:
Ship whose weather deck extends unbroken the length of the ship. A
World War I destroyer.

Fly:
The long dimension or length of a flag. Also, the outboard end of a
flag, away from the *Halyard.*

Fly 1, 2, 3:
Subdivisions of a carrier flight deck. Fly 1 is under the direction of
the flight deck officer and catapult officer; Fly 2, the taxi signal
officer, and Fly 3 the landing signal officer.

Flyable dud:
An aircraft that can be flown but is not in shape for combat.

Flycatcher operations:
Those against enemy small craft in an amphibious objective area.

Fly control:
The station on a carrier that gives landing and takeoff instructions
to flight deck personnel.

Flying boat:
Type of seaplane which can float on its hull in the water.

FLYING BOXCAR:
Model designation: C-119; cognizant service: Air Force.
A twin-boom, high-wing aircraft designed for carrying cargo with easy-
loading facilities through a rear door. 5-crew. 42 troops. Propeller-
driven.

Flying bridge:
Topmost bridge of a ship, usually above the navigating bridge or conning
tower.

FLYING CLASSROOM:
Model designation: T-29; cognizant services: Navy/Air Force.
Nonpressurized version of the popular Convair airliner, equipped for
navigation and bombardier training. 4-crew. 10-students. Propeller-driven.

Flying moor:
See *Moor.*

Flying officer:
Officer designated as a naval aviator; includes aviation observers and
Flight Surgeons.

Foam:
Chemical which produces large quantities of smothering suds for
fire fighting.

FOCUS I:
  Model designation: AGM-87; cognizant service: Navy.
  Classified Missile.

Fog buoy:
  Towing spar.

Fog lookouts:
  Special lookouts because of fog. Generally sent to the *Eyes of the ship*
  since in the thick fog they might well be the first to see another ship with
  which danger of collision might exist. The *Rules of the Road* specify that
  in fog a ship must proceed sufficiently slowly that she can come to a
  complete stop in half the distance of visibility. Lookouts may also be sent
  aloft when the fog is dense but close to the surface of the water.

Fog nozzle (applicator):
  Firehose fitting which forces water into very fine spray or fog.

Fog signal, major:
  Shore signal with normal range of one and one half miles or more.

Fogy:
  Slang: increase in pay because of length of service. Pronounced "foh-gy."

Following sea:
  Waves moving in the same general direction as the ship.

Foofoo:
  Slang: face lotion or hair tonic.

Footline:
  The bottom *Lifeline.*

Footrope:
  The rope attached to the underside of a yard upon which sailors stood while
  loosing or furling sail, now obsolete except for the few sailing ships
  used for training.

Force:
  A body of troops, ships, or aircraft, or combination thereof; major
  subdivision of a fleet. Measure of wind intensity as "Force 4." Part
  of a (Task Force).

Forced draft:
  Air under pressure supplied to the burners in a ship's boilers, characteristic of all naval ships.

Force tabs:
  With reference to war plans, the statement of time-phased deployments
  of major combat units by major commands and geographical areas.

Fore-and-aft:
  Lengthwise of a ship, from stem to stern.

Fore-and-aft sail:
>A sail designed to have a leading edge *(Luff)* and a trailing edge *(Leech,)* cut in a triangular or a quadrilateral shape, but neither square nor rectangular. Designed to be fitted to *Booms* instead of to *Yards*—except that the *Lateen* sail, as a special and obsolete case, had a yard slung at an angle from the horizontal. Most small craft have fore-and-aft sails because of their far greater versatility than the *Square sails,* but large *Sailers* found the huge fore-and-aft sails which they would have had to carry to be impracticable—in fact, some very large multimasted *Schooners* were equipped, late in the days of sail, with steam *Winches* to help handle their acres of canvas.

Forebody:
>Ship's hull forward of amidships.

Forecastle:
>Forward section of weather deck. Pronounced "FOK-sul." Vicinity of the ground tackle.

Forecastle deck:
>Partial deck over the main deck at the bow.

Forefoot:
>Part of the keel that curves up to meet the stem or where the stem joins the keel of a ship.

Fore leech:
>The *Luff* of a *Fore-and-aft* sail. See *Leech.*

Forel scale:
>Basic scale for measuring color of sea water.

Foremast:
>The forward-most mast of a ship with two or more masts, unless the second mast is so much smaller than the first that the first is called the *Mainmast* and the second the *Mizzenmast,* or *Jigger,* as in a *Yawl* or *Ketch.*

Forenoon watch:
>The 0800-1200 watch.

Foresheets:
>Space in an open boat, at the bow, not occupied by Thwarts. See *Sternsheets.*

Foreshore:
>Portion of the shore or beach lying between low water and the upper limits of normal wave action.

Forestay:
>A *stay* supporting a mast from forward.

Foretop:
>Heavy structure supported by a foremast; houses fire-control equipment. See *Top.*

Formation:
>Any ordered arrangement of two or more ships or aircraft proceeding together.

Forward:
Towards the bow.

Forward bow (quarter) spring:
Mooring line at the bow (quarter) that leads forward from the ship to the
pier or wharf. Both forward and after spring lines are necessary to prevent
fore-and-aft movement of the ship.

Foul:
To entangle, confuse, or obstruct. Jammed or entangled; not clear for
running. Covered with barnacles, as foul bottom. For one ship to foul
or run afoul, of another is to collide broadside or with insufficient
force to do serious structural damage.

Foul anchor:
Anchor entangled in its chain.

Foul deck:
Aircraft carrier deck that is obstructed and cannot be landed upon.

Foul ground:
Shallow sea area marked by rocks, reefs, shoals, wrecks, etc.

Foul hawse:
Condition marked by the twisting of the chains when moored with
two anchors down. See *Clear hawse.*

Fouling:
The attachment of various marine organisms to underwater bodies, a problem
in ships because it reduces speed.

Foul up:
Slang: to get into trouble. Also, trouble, disturbance, or confusion.

Foul weather:
Rainy or stormy weather. "Foul weather parade" is an assembly below
decks or under shelter.

Founder:
To sink.

Four O:
Perfect; one hundred per cent.

Foxer gear (FXR):
Noise-making device towed astern to foil acoustical torpedoes.

Foxtail:
Short-handled brush for sweeping small areas. Also, short line
attached to a *Jackstay.*

Foxtrot:
Phonetic word for letter F.

Frames:
Athwartships strength members of a ship's hull, numbered from bow aft
and used as reference points to locate fittings, division parades, etc.

Frap; frapping gear:
To frap is to wrap with line. Frapping gear is the line used.

Frapping lines:
>   Lines passed around forward and after boat falls to steady the boat in a
>   seaway as it is being hoisted or lowered.

Free:
>   To clear or untangle.

Freeboard:
>   Distance from weather deck to waterline.

FREEDOM FIGHTER:
>   Model designation: F-5; cognizant service: Air Force.
>   A single-place, mid-wing, fighter version of the *Talon*. 1-crew. Jet.

Freeing port:
>   A deck-level opening in the ship or in *Bulwark* to permit water to escape.

Free surface:
>   Liquid in a partially filled ship's compartment or tank that is free to
>   move from side to side as the ship rolls. Because the liquid always goes
>   to the low side, a large free surface is always dangerous to stability.

Frequency:
>   The rate at which a cycle is repeated, originally given in terms of cycles
>   per second (or kilocycles, megacycles, etc.) The term kHz (kilohertz) is
>   replacing kc, and mHz is replacing mc.

FRESCANAR:
>   Three dimensional radar used with *TALOS, TARTAR* and *TERRIER.*

FRESH I:
>   A catamaran design foil research supercavitation hydrofoil formerly
>   designated HTC (Hydrofoil Test Craft).

Freshen the nip:
>   To shift a rope to equalize the wear. Not a drinking term.

Freshwater king:
>   Enlisted man in charge of the ship's evaporators.

Freshwater system:
>   Series of freshwater piping to supply galley, washrooms, scuttlebutts,
>   and boilers.

Frigate (DL, DLG, DLGN):
>   In days of sail, a *Full-rigged ship* mounting guns on two decks. Fast
>   and maneuverable, comparable to the *Cruiser* of a later day. Currently
>   in the U.S. Navy, a frigate is a large *Destroyer,* designed principally
>   to be the primary escort ship for the *Attack aircraft carrier.* In
>   foreign navies, however, the World War II system is followed, in that a
>   frigate is a convoy escort smaller and slower than a full-fledged destroyer.

Frogmen:
>   Slang: underwater demolition personnel.

Front:
>   Boundary between two dissimilar air masses marked by turbulence, squalls,
>   rain, and change in temperature.

Fuel depot:
> An activity that provides petroleum to other activities and to ships.

Full and bye:
> Said of a *Square-rigged* sailing ship sailing with the wind abeam with all sails set and drawing. She is sailing by the wind, with all sails full.

Full and down:
> Said of a ship when all spaces are full of cargo and ship is down to specified draft and drag.

Full bag:
> Complete outfit of uniforms and related gear, required of all enlisted men.

Full-rigged ship:
> A *Ship* with bowsprit and three masts, entirely *Square-rigged* except for the lowest sail on the *Mizzenmast.*

Full speed:
> A prescribed speed that is greater than *Standard speed* but less than *Flank speed.* See *Speed.*

Funnel:
> Ship's smokestack; stack.

Furl:
> To make up in a bundle, as "furl the sail."

FURY:
> AF-1E jet-powered fighter bomber.

Fuselage:
> Body of an airplane.

Fuze:
> Mechanical, electrical, electronic, or magnetic device for detonating an explosive charge in a weapon.

Fuze (projectile):
> A fuze of the following types: auxiliary detonating, base detonating, mechanical time, point detonating, or *Proximity fuze* (VT). See *Projectile.*

Fuze, proximity (VT):
> A fuze activated by external influence in close vicinity of target. Also called VT fuze.

G

Gaff:
Small spar on the aftermost mast from which the ensign is displayed while underway.

Galactic Radiation Experiment Background (GREB):
A series of solar radiation research satellites developed by the Navel Research Laboratory (NRL).

GALAXY:
Model designation: C-5A; cognizant service: Air Force.
A very large high-speed subsonic transport designed for logistic support mission. Has visor front door and rear cargo openings for straight-through loading and unloading. Has become highly controversial because of high-cost overruns on the initial construction contract. 6-crew. Jet.

Gale:
Strong wind, usually described as: a moderate gale (28-33 knots); a fresh gale (34-40 knots); a strong gale (41-47 knots); or a whole gale (48-55 knots).

Gallery deck:
Partial deck below a flight deck of an aircraft carrier.

Galley:
Kitchen.

Gangplank:
Temporary bridge from the ship to a pier or to another ship alongside. See *Brow*.

Gangway:
Opening in the rail or bulwarks giving access to the ship; an order to stand aside or to stand clear. Not a synonym for *Accommodation Ladder.*

Gantline:
Line passing through a single block aloft.

Garble:
Error which renders a message incorrect or unintelligible.

Garboard strake:
The strake next to the keel.

Gasket:
Strip of sealing material, usually rubber, set along edge of watertight door, port, or hatch. The gasket opposes a knife-edge. Also in pipelines, cylinder blocks, etc.

Gate vessel:
Ship used to open and close gate or opening in anti-submarine nets protecting a harbor or narrow passage.

Gather way:
To gain headway.

Gauge glass:
: Device for indicating water level in a tank or boiler.

Gazetteer:
: Alphabetic lists of names of geographic features of various locations, published by the Oceanographic Office.

Gear:
: General term for equipment, material, supplies, or baggage.

Geedunk:
: Slang: ice cream, soda, etc. Items from soda fountain.

General alarm:
: The signal for manning battle stations. Nowadays given by musical notes over a ship's general-announcing system, but in days past various other means, such as bugle calls, the fife and drum, the drum alone, a loud rattle, or the *Boatswain's pipe,* were used.

General announcing system:
: System of loud-speakers throughout a ship or station over which the *Word* may be passed to all hands. PA system.

General Classification Test (GCT):
: A test for scoring basic capabilities of enlisted men.

General mess:
: Arrangement for feeding all hands except those whose rations are commuted to a flag, cabin, wardroom or CPO mess.

General message:
: One having a wide standard distribution, originated by the Navy Department or by a fleet commander. Usually serially numbered, as an *AlNav.*

General muster:
: Massed formation of all hands at a designated place.

General Operational Requirement (GOR):
: Document prepared by CNO stating broad capabilities required in the fleet to meet long-range needs.

General orders:
: Numbered directives of a general nature and wide application issued by the Navy Department and signed by the Secretary of the Navy.

General prudential rule (Rules of the Road):
: "In obeying and construing these rules due regard shall be had for all dangers of navigation and collision and to any special circumstance which may render a departure from these rules necessary to avoid immediate danger." The general caveat which permits a privileged vessel to maneuver to avoid collision or other hazard when in extremis (but only then).

General quarters:
: Stations for battle. To "sound general quarters" is to give the signal, the *General alarm,* which will bring all hands of the crew to their battle stations as quickly as they can get there.

General service rating:
: Those enlisted *Ratings* normally authorized in peace time.

General stores material (GSM):
Material listed in the catalogue of Navy material.

GENIE:
Model designation: AIR-2; cognizant service: Air Force.
A missile.

GEOREF:
A geographic reference system used to facilitate reporting and plotting of ships and aircraft.

Gibson girl:
Portable radio for sending distress signals, carried on life rafts.

GI can:
Trash can.

Gig:
Ship's boat designated for the use of the commanding officer.

Gilhoist:
Wheeled vehicle used to transport landing craft overland.

Gilligan hitch:
Any unseamanlike, unorthodox knot, hitch, or bend.

Gimbals:
A pair of rings, one within the other, with their axes at right angles. Usually they support a compass or gyro repeater, in which case their purpose is to keep it horizontal despite motion of the ship. Any gyroscope requires a set of gimbals, however, to give it the requisite three degrees of freedom, i.e., freedom to move its axis in any direction. Almost always used in pairs, hence referred to in the plural.

Gipsy, gipsy head:
An auxiliary drum on a windlass or capstan used for handling lines.
See *Warping head, Capstan.*

Give way:
An order to begin pulling oars together.

Glacier:
Field or stream of ice moving down a slope and spreading because of its own weight.

Glacon:
A fragment of sea ice ranging in size from brash to medium floe.

Gland:
A seal designed to prevent leakage of water, steam, or oil along a movable shaft, such as propeller shafts, submarine periscopes, or turbine rotors.

Gland Steam:
Steam introduced into shaft gland packing to prevent air leakage into and steam leakage out of a turbine.

Glass:
Barometer. A hand-carried telescope is a *Long Glass*. Binoculars are referred to as "glasses."

Glide bomb:
A winged missile, unpowered.

GLOBEMASTER:
Model designation: C-124; cognizant service: Air Force.
A low-wing monoplane having clamshell cargo doors in front fuselage and
loading elevator in center fuselage capable of transporting heavy ground
force and ordnance equipment in main cabin. 5-crew, 200-troops, or
127-litters plus 25 ambulatory patients. Propeller-driven.

Go adrift:
To break loose.

Gob:
Slang: enlisted man; not good usage.

Go by the board:
To go over the side; to be swept away; forgotten.

Godown:
Warehouse or storehouse along the waterfront, especially in the Orient.

Goldbrick:
Slang: a loafer or to loaf.

Golf:
Phonetic word for letter G.

Gook:
Slang: a Latin or Asiatic; a derogatory expression to be avoided.

Go-to-hell hat:
Slang: overseas, or garrison cap.

Gouge:
Slang: to cheat. Also, a prepared solution to a problem or examination.

Grab rope:
A safety line secured along a boat boom or gangplank.

Grade:
Graduations in authority and pay among petty officers and officers. "Grade" can only be
used as a noun, but *rank* can be both noun and verb. Generally, "rank" represents relative
position within a specific grade, but this is not rigorously true. Thus one could say, "Lieutenant Jones ranks Lieutenant Smith," meaning that Jones is senior to Smith; "grade"
could not be used in this context. "Rank" can, however, also be used to denote a grade, as,
"His rank is Captain." It would be equally correct to say, "His grade is Captain." The term
"seniority" is sometimes used with the meaning of "rank" within a grade.

Granny Knot:
A false, unsymmetrical square knot, to be avoided because it slips.

Grape:
Small iron ball, an inch or so in diameter, bound together in clusters
and fired from smoothbore cannon. A common form of ammunition 150 years
ago. See *Canister, Langridge*

Grapnel or Grappling iron:
>   Small, 4-armed anchor used nowadays mainly to recover objects in the water.
>   Also used, especially in days of sail, to secure alongside another ship
>   or to dock by force, and occasionally still so used today, as in Vietnam.

Grass:
>   Visual representation of static on a radar or loran scope.

Grating:
>   Metal or wooden lattice work used to cover hatches while still providing
>   ventilation below or to provide a platform for the steersman.

Graving dock:
>   Basin with a gate or caisson sealing the entrance, in which ships
>   can be built or dry-docked.

Gravity waves:
>   Waves controlled by gravity and inertial forces whose wave-length is
>   greater than 1.73 centimeters.

Great circle:
>   The intersection of the earth's surface and a plane through the earth's
>   center.

Great diurnal range:
>   The difference in height between mean higher high water and mean lower
>   low water. Also called diurnal range.

Great tropic range:
>   Difference in height between tropic higher high water and tropic lower
>   low water. Also called tropic range.

Greenwich Hour Angle (GHA):
>   Angular distance west of the Greenwich *Celestial meridian.* Used to
>   identify positions of celestial bodies for navigation.

Greenwich meridian:
>   The meridian through Greenwich, England, near London; the reference meridian
>   for measuring longitude and time. The prime meridian.

GREYHOUND:
>   Model designation: C-2; cognizant service: Navy.
>   Carrier-based landplane used for logistic support for Fleet and Marine
>   operations. 3-crew. Prop-jet.

Grid, JAN:
>   Joint Army-Navy grid system covering entire earth adopted to afford secure
>   means of referring to geographical positions.

Grid navigation:
>   Navigation by the use of grid directions. Generally used in polar navigation,
>   with grid coordinates on the chart replacing latitude and longitude.

Grinder:
>   Paved area at a shore activity, for drill and parades.

Gripe(s):
>   Device for securing a boat at its davits or in its cradle. "Gripe in"
>   means to secure by use of gripes.

Grog:
Slang: any alcoholic drink, particularly rum.

Grommet:
Reinforced hole in a sail or awning. The round metal or fiber stiffener in a flat hat or officer's cap.

Groove:
Flight path of an aircraft making a perfect approach for a carrier landing.

Ground:
To run a ship ashore; to strike the bottom through ignorance, violence, or accident.

Ground Controlled Approach (GCA):
Aircraft approach to landing ashore during which the pilot is guided in altitude, speed and heading by advice from a controller at the airfield.

Ground Controlled Interception (GCI):
Technique by which a pilot is guided to intercept his target by provision of speeds, headings and altitudes from a controller ashore.

Ground Effects Machine (GEM):
A vehicle designed to move across the earth's surface supported by a downward blast of air. Also known as an air cushion vehicle or hovercraft.

Ground speed:
Speed made good over earth's surface along *Course* or *Track.*

Ground swell:
The sea swell encountered as a result of distant or past storms. Same as *swell.*

Ground tackle:
General term for all anchoring equipment aboard ship. Tackle is pronounced "take-ul."

Ground waves:
Signals of a radio transmission that travel along the ground. *Sky Waves* travel upwards and the ionosphere reflects them back to earth.

Group:
Several ships or aircraft, normally a subdivision of a force, assigned for a specific purpose. The squadrons assigned to an ASW carrier comprise an air group. The words or collections of letters in a cipher or code message are known as "groups."

Group flashing light:
Navigational aid showing groups of two or more flashes at regular intervals.

Group grope:
Slang: full deck launch of a carrier air group for a specific mission.

Group occulting light:
Navigational aid showing two or more eclipses at regular intervals, the eclipses being shorter than the flashes.

Group-rate marks:
Short diagonal stripes worn on upper part of left sleeve by non-rated men: white for seamen, red for firemen, green for airmen, light blue for construction men.

Grouse:
Slang: to complain; to find fault.

Growler:
Small piece of floating ice with two to six feet showing above surface. See *Bergy-bit.*

G-suit:
Antiblackout suit.

Guard:
To maintain a continuous radio receiver watch with transmitter ready for immediate use. See *Copy, Cover, Listen.*

Guard flag:
One flown by a ship to denote having the guard e.g., specific responsibility for having a doctor aboard.

Guard mail:
Mail delivered by guard mail petty officers between naval activities.

Guard of the day:
That part of the ship's Marine guard on duty for the day, kept in readiness for a call to the quarterdeck.

Guardship:
A ship ordered to maintain a readiness to get underway immediately. Also, a ship maintaining a prescribed communication watch on certain radio frequencies, or generally to perform common duties for a group of several ships in port together.

Guestwarp, guess-warp, geswarp:
Rope rove through a *Thimble* on a *Boat boom* for the convenience of boats making fast alongside. Usually terminated in an eye-splice for simplicity in securing. Also may refer to a rope run along a ship's side as a grab line, guy rope, or additional towline to steady a boat towed astern, or to a hauling-line run by a boat to a *Buoy, Wharf, Dolphin, Bollard,* etc. for *Warping* purposes. "Guestwarp" is the preferred spelling.

Gudgeon:
Metal loops or rings on the hull of a boat into which the *Pintles* of the rudder fit.

Guidance:
The process of intelligence and flight control involved in directing a missile to the target. Types of guidance are: base-line, beam-rider, command, homing, self-control.

Guide:
Vessel designated in a formation or disposition as the one for others to keep station on.

Guided missile:
> Self-propelled airborne weapon capable of seeking a target or of following a radar beam to the target.

Guided missile cruiser:
> With exception of the CGN, these ships are converted heavy cruisers. Some guns are replaced by *TALOS, TARTAR,* or *TERRIER* missile launchers. The CGN is a nuclear powered long-range ship equipped with TALOS TERRIER missile and ASROC launchers. Designated as CG and CGN. For designed mission, see *Cruiser, Heavy Cruiser.*

Guided missile designation system:
> See Appendix D.

Guided missile destroyer:
> Equipped with *TERRIER TARTAR* guided missile launchers, improved naval gun battery, long-range sonar and antisubmarine warfare weapons.

Guided missile frigate:
> A large destroyer-type vessel designed for CVA escort in *Task force* formation. Essentially an anti-air warfare ship. Latest contruction exceeds 10,000 tons displacement. Equipped with *TERRIER* or *TARTAR* missile launchers and, in some cases, 5''/54-gun battery; also ASROC. Designated as DLG and DLGN; the DLGN is nuclear-powered. For designed mission, see *Frigate*. See *Destroyer.*

Guidon:
> Company identification pennant for naval units ashore.

Gulf Stream:
> Current originating in the Atlantic end of the Florida Straits, running northward past the Grand Banks, and then dispersing as it passes across the Atlantic Ocean, passing Iceland and bathing England and Ireland. Generally considered to be responsible for the mild climate of Northern Europe despite its latitude, which is the equivalent of Labrador.

GULFSTREAM I:
> Model designation: C-4; cognizant service: Coast Guard. Low-wing monoplane designed for medium range. Staff personnel transport. 3-crew. Prop-jet.

GULFSTREAM II:
> Model designation: VC-11; cognizant service: Coast Guard. Small long-range personnel transport. 4-crew, 12-passengers. Jet.

Gulf Stream System:
> System of three currents in the Atlantic, including the Florida Current, the Gulf Stream and the North Atlantic Current.

GULL:
> A floating radar target used to simulate surface targets for deception purposes.

Gunar:
> Electronic fire control system for ships.

Gun bag:
> First-aid material kept at a gun station.

Gunboat:
>   Small, moderate-speed, relatively heavily armed vessel for general patrol
>   and escort duty.

Gun captain:
>   Petty officer in charge of gun's crew.

Gundeck:
>   Slang: to fake or to falsify something, such as a report. To pretend
>   to be drunk. See *Smokestack.*

Gun house:
>   Visible part of a turret extending above the *Barbette.*

Gun mount:
>   A gun structure with 1 to 4 guns which can rotate and
>   carry them to various points of aim. It may be either open or enclosed
>   in a steel shield. While they resemble *Turrets* and are frequently
>   so-called, enclosed mounts are not so heavily armored as turrets and
>   carry no guns larger than 5-inch. Some World War II cruisers had 8-inch
>   guns which were carried in "gun mounts" instead of turrets, according
>   to technical purists of the day, because the mounts did not have all the
>   appurtenances of regular turrets as installed in battleships. The enclosure,
>   whether of a turret or mount, which actually housed the guns, was some-
>   times called a *Gun house.*

Gunner:
>   Warrant officer who has normally advanced from *Aviation Ordnanceman,*
>   *Fire Control Technician,* or *Gunner's Mate.*

Gunner's mate (GM):
>   Petty officer who performs unkeep and repair of ordnance.

Gunnery:
>   The science of using *Ordnance.*

Gunnery officer:
>   Officer ordered to head the Gunnery Department and who is responsible for
>   the ship's or squadron's armament. Now known as Weapons Officer.

Gunport:
>   Aperture in the front armor plate of a turret through which a gun projects.

Gun salute:
>   Blank shots fired to honor a dignitary or in celebration. The national salute
>   is 21 guns.

Gun tackle:
>   One using two single-sheave blocks. Tackle is pronounced "take-ul."

Guntub:
>   The cylindrical splinter protection around a deck gun aboard ship.

Gunwale:
>   Upper edge of a boat's side. Pronounced GUN-el.

GUPPY:
>   "Greater Underwater Propulsive Power." A World War II fleet submarine
>   which has been streamlined, given a more powerful battery, and fitted
>   with a snorkel.

Guy:
  Line used to steady or support a spar or boom. Also called a *Vang*.

Guyot:
  A flat-topped submarine mountain. See *Tablemount*.

Gypsey:
  See *Gipsy*.

Gyrene:
  Slang: Marine.

Gyro angle:
  In torpedo firing, angle between axis of own ship and final torpedo track, measured clockwise from own bow.

Gyro Erected Optical Navigation (GEON):
  A system permitting use of gyro reference plane instead of horizon in celestial navigation.

Gyro compass:
  A compass having one or more gyroscopes properly torqued to indicate true north. PGC Means "per gyro compass," and is always nearly the same as a true direction.

Gyropilot:
  Automatic steering device connected to the repeater of a gyrocompass; designed to hold a ship on its course without a helmsman. Also called automatic steerer, iron mike, and iron quartermaster.

Gyro repeater:
  An instrument containing a compass card driven by a remotely located gyro compass. Used for steering, taking bearings, azimuths, etc.

H

Hack chronometer:
Spare or comparison chronometer.

Hack, under:
Colloquial for punishment for officers, involving restriction to their quarters. Formal term is "suspension from duty, confined to quarters."

Hail:
To address or call to a near-by ship or boat. Also a ship or man is said to hail from such-and-such a home port. See *Ahoy!* and *Boat hails.*

Half-breadth plan:
Engineering drawing of a ship showing the outlines of horizontal sections of the hull from main deck to keel. Ship is shown from above, i.e., plan view, and only half the full is shown since the outlines of the other side are identical.

Half deck:
A partial deck between complete decks. See *Deck.*

Half hitch:
Usually seen as two half hitches; a knot used for much the same purposes as a clove hitch.

Half-mast (half staff):
To fly a flag halfway up the mast, as a sign of mourning.

Half speed:
See *Speed.*

Half-tide level:
Plane midway between mean high water and mean low water.

Halocline:
Area of rapidly changing water salinity.

Halyard (Halliard):
The line used to hoist a flag, pennant, or sail.

Hammerbox:
Noise-making device for sweeping acoustic mines.

Hammock:
A traditional sailor's bed, made of heavy canvas and swung from a pair of hooks on the underside of the deck above, i.e., "swung from the overhead."

Hammock ladder:
Non-existent item, like a "bucket of steam," often requested of new men aboard ship. Theoretically, a ladder to help men to climb into their hammocks.

Hand:
Member of the ship's crew. "All hands" means every person on board.

Handie-talkie:
Ship-to-shore, portable, battery-powered radio.

Hand lead:
Weight and line used in taking soundings.

Handrail:
Metal or wood rail on brow, ladder, etc.

Hand rope:
See *Grabrope.*

Hand salute:
Gesture of respect exchanged between military men. See *Salute, Hand.*

Handsomely:
Carefully; deliberately. See *Ease, easy.*

Handy billy:
Small portable water pump.

Hangar:
Building in which aircraft and airships are stored and serviced. Large compartment in a ship for similar purpose.

Hangar deck:
Deck, below the flight deck of a carrier, where aircraft are parked and serviced.

Hangfire:
Delayed detonation of an explosive charge in a gun. See *Misfire.*

Hank:
Loose group of bights of line, secured together with twine. Lifelines on a balsa float are made up in hanks.

Happy hour:
Period of entertainment aboard ship, including refreshments. Same as *Smoker.* Also period at bar of club ashore when prices are reduced.

Harbor defense:
Technique or organization for protecting a harbor against enemy ships, submarines, and aircraft.

Harbor Entrance Control Post (HECP):
The control and tactical command post from which the harbor defense commander controls and coordinates the harbor defense system.

Harbor master:
Officer in charge, under Port Director, of piloting, berthing, and traffic in harbor; responsible for navigational aids and hydrographic information.

Hard:
Section of a beach especially prepared with a hard surface for amphibious operations. Also, an adjective meaning full or extreme, as in the command: "Hard right rudder."

HARPOON:
Model designation: XAGM-84A; cognizant service: Navy.
Missile specifically designed to destroy land and sea targets.

Harrison cargo gear:
Cargo handling system using traveling overhead cranes instead of usual booms and winches.

Hash mark:
Slang: *Service stripe.*

Hatch:
Access opening in deck of a ship, fitted with a *Hatch cover* for water-tight closure.

Hatch beam:
Steel support for a cargo hatch cover.

Hatch coaming:
Raised framework around a hatch on which the hatch cover rests.

Hatch cover:
Wooden or steel cover for a hatch.

Hatch hood:
Canvas cover rigged over an open hatch to keep out rain, spray, and wind.

Hatch list:
List and location of all cargo loaded through a particular hatch.

Hatchway:
Same as hatch, but with emphasis on the opening.

Haul:
To pull or to drag. The wind "hauls" when it changes in direction with the sun, i.e., clockwise. When a ship changes course so that her head lies nearer to the wind she is said to "haul up." "Bear up" means the same. "Haul off," "fall off," or "bear off" mean the reverse. *Veers* means the same as "hauls." *Backs* means the wind direction changes counterclockwise.

Haul down:
Term used as a directive to execute a flag hoist by lowering it.

Hauling part:
The part of a tackle to which power is applied, in contrast to *Standing part.*

Haul out:
To make fast at the boat boom. To move out of a line of ships.

Haven, submarine:
Sea area in which no attacks on submarines are permitted, allowing a safe passage for own submarines in wartime.

HAWK:
Model designation: MIM-23; cognizant services: Army and Marine Corps. A low-altitude air defense weapon.

Hawk, anchor:
> A multipronged device used at end of anchor chain, usually by salvage vessels, to recover a lost anchor.

HAWKEYE:
> Model designation: E-2; cognizant service: Navy.
> Aircraft designed to maintain station from a Task Force at some distance for Early Warning mission. Can vector friendly aircraft to attack position on approaching enemy aircraft. 5-crew. Prop-jet.

Hawse:
> Area at bow of ship where hawsepipes are located; also, that space between the bow of a ship and the anchors.

Hawse buckler:
> Metal cover for hawseholes to prevent entrance of water.

Hawsepipes:
> Heavy castings through which the anchor chain runs. Hawseholes are the openings.

Hawser:
> Heavy line of fibre or wire. A towing hawser. Any line over 5 inches in diameter.

Head:
> Toilet and washroom. Also the upper corner of a triangular sail.

Header box:
> An extension of the salt water compensating line that is open to the sea and that equalizes fuel tank pressure and sea pressure in a submerged submarine.

Headers:
> Reservoir into which or from which the tubes of a boiler or heat exchanger terminate.

Heading:
> That part of a message or an order preceding the text. The direction in which a ship or aircraft is pointed.

Head line:
> Mooring line which is made fast forward of the ship's *Pivot point.*

Headroom:
> Clearance between the decks.

Headway:
> Forward movement of a vessel through the water.

Heart:
> Center strand of a fiber or wire rope.

Heave:
> To throw, as in heaving the lead. Also means to pull, as "heave in." See *Heaving.*

Heave around or heave 'round:
> To activate a windlass to which a line or chain is attached. To turn to and work hard.

Heave away:
   An order to start heaving on a capstan or windlass so as to pull
   on a line.

Heave in:
   To haul in.

Heave out (roll out):
   "Rise and shine:" get up out of bed.

Heave short:
   To heave around on the anchor chain until the anchor is at *Short stay*,
   just short of breaking ground. Done in preparation for getting underway.

Heave to:
   To stop--in an affirmative sense; to bring the ship to a halt, dead in
   the water. In case of heavy weather, a ship may heave to in order to
   take the most comfortable and safest heading. She is in this case considered to be "hove to" even though making considerable way through the
   water from the action of wind and sea.

Heaving or *Heave:*
   The vertical displacement, or up-and-down movement of a ship in a seaway, as distinguished from pitching, which is essentially a rotation
   about an athwartship's axis. Heave generally refers to an upward movement, bodily, of the entire ship, but is sometimes applied only to bow
   or stern in a less specific sense, as "her heaving bows." Also, to
   come into sight, e.g. "as soon as she heaves into sight" or "when
   she heaves over the horizon."

Heaving line:
   Light, weighted line thrown across to a ship or pier when coming along-
   side to act as a messenger for a mooring line. The weight is called a
   Monkey Fist.

Heavy Cruiser:
   Term has lost original meaning and is useful only to distinguish cruisers carrying 8-inch
   guns (heavy) from those with 6-inch (light). Size and displacment not a factor. Conversion
   to missiles with removal of all or part of main battery produced proliferation of types
   based on the original heavies; CA, CAG, and CG; also, from light cruisers, CL, and CLG.
   The Nuclear Guided Missile Cruiser, CGN, was built from keel up. See *Cruiser, Destroyer,*
   and Appendix A.

Heavy weather:
   Stormy weather with large seas.

Hedgehog:
   An ASW ahead-thrown weapon; a mortar-type projector mount that fires a
   contact-fuzed projectile.

Heel:
   To list over; the amount of inclination or list.

Heel and toe:
   Period of duty (watch) alternating with a period of rest. Also called
   Watch and Watch.

Helicopter:
> An aircraft supported in flight by rotating airfoils instead of fixed
> wings. Used for spotting, rescue, evacuation, transport, and general
> utility. Also called pinwheel, egg beater, whirly-bird, windmill,
> copter, or chopper.

Helm:
> The helm proper is the tiller, and thus the order to put the helm to
> port, for example, is the same as an order to put the rudder right.
> The term has now developed to mean the rudder and the gear for turn-
> ing it, and the *Helmsman* is of course the man who steers. Because
> of possible confusion as to intended direction, however, orders are
> today given with respect to the rudder, and never with respect to the
> helm.

Helmsman:
> *Steersman,* a man who steers a ship or boat.

HERALD equipment:
> Sonar and listening devices used in harbor defense.

HERCULES:
> Model designation: C-130; cognizant services: Navy and Air Force.
> Medium-range land-based transport aircraft. 4-crew, 92-troop. Prop-jet.

Hermaphrodite brig:
> Two-masted sailing vessel with the foremast *Square-rigged* and the
> mainmast *Fore-and-aft* rigged. See *Brigantine.*

Hertz:
> A unit of frequency equivalent to one cycle per second. Hz. See *Frequency*

H-Hour:
> Term used to designate the time, usually on D-day, for an operation
> to commence.

Higher High Water (HHW):
> The higher of the two high waters during any tidal day.

Higher Low Water (HLW):
> The higher of the two low waters of any tidal day.

HIGH LANDER:
> LCVP/H experimental landing craft program.

Highline:
> A simple line rigged between two ships underway transferring stores.
> The simplest transfer rig. Stores and personnel are transferred on a
> wheeled trolley riding on the highline and hauled back and forth
> between the ships.

Highlining:
> Simple exchange of material or personnel at sea using the highline
> with associated trolleys and skids, both ships underway.

Highly Unusual Geophysical Operation (HUGO):
> A meteorological research vehicle.

High Performance External Gun (HIPEG):
> A 20 mm gun pod for aircraft with very high firing rate.

HIGH POINT:
PCH-1 experimental hydrofoil ASW patrol craft program.

High water:
The maximum height of a tide due to tidal and weather conditions.

High water line:
The intersection of the plane of mean high water with the shore.

HI-HOE:
Space probe program for launching CALEB rockets from F-4H aircraft.

Hitch:
Method of securing a line to a hook, ring, or spar, e.g., clove hitch.
Slang: term of enlistment.

Hit the deck:
Get up; same as "rise and shine."

Hit the sack:
Slang: turn in, go to bed. See *Rack* and *Sack*.

Hit the silk:
Make a parachute jump.

Hobby shop:
Recreational workshop.

Hogging:
Distortion of a ship's hull which results in bow and stern being
lower than amidships section; opposite of *Sagging*.

Hogging line:
Line passed under the keel and secured on opposite sides of the ship.

Hoist:
Display of signal flags at a yardarm. The wide dimension of a flag. Also, to lift.

Hoist, boom:
A whip, or single part of a line, running over a block at the head
of a boom and thence to the deck where it may be used to handle weights.

Hoist in:
Hook on, hoist and stow, or secure a boat aboard ship.

Hoisting eye (ring) (rod):
Fittings in a boat to which the boat falls are attached for hoisting.

Hoisting pad:
Metal plates supporting a pad eye or ring by which a boat is hoisted.

Hoist out:
To lower a boat from a ship to the water.

Hold:
Compartment of a cargo ship. A command to a line handler which means
to take sufficient turns around his *Cleat* to prevent any more line
from running out. See *Check*.

Holdback:
Catapult fitting for holding down the airplane prior to firing.

Hold captain:
In amphibious operations, an enlisted man who supervises the
loading and unloading in a ship's hold.

Holding ground:
The bottom in an anchorage. Usually described as good or bad,
depending on ability to hold an anchor.

Holiday:
Unscrubbed or unpainted section of a deck or bulkhead.
Any space left blank or unfinished through inadvertence
or carelessness.

Holiday routine:
Schedule aboard ship involving no work or drills; normal for
Saturday (sometimes Wednesday) afternoons and Sunday.

Holy Joe:
Slang: Chaplain.

Holystone:
Small stone used with sand and water to scrub wooden decks.

Home:
To be guided by a signal emanating from the target, is to home on it.

Home of record:
Address which an officer may desire to use for personal reasons.

Home port:
Port or air station on which a ship or aircraft unit normally bases.

Homeward bound pennant:
Pennant flown by ships returning to U.S. after absence of year or more.

Home yard:
Now designated as *Planning and Overhaul Yard* of a ship.

HONEST JOHN:
Model designation: MGR-1; cognizant services: Army and Marine Corps.
Tactical nuclear weapon for battlefield use.

Honey barge:
Garbage scow.

Honors and Ceremonies:
Collective term: official guards, bands, salutes, and other
activities that honor the colors, celebrate a holiday, or greet
a distinguished guest or officer.

Hood:
Canvas cover, e.g., hatch hood, periscope hood. Also, a metal
or plastic cover for a *Binnacle.*

Hooker control:
A station that assists the *Landing signal officer* for night
carrier landings.

Hook on:
> To attach the *Boat falls* to the padeyes at bow and stern of a boat, then hoisting it clear of the water. *Hoist in* is a more complete evolution which includes the entire operaton of taking a boat out of the water and securing it for sea.

Hookmen:
> Men who disengage arrester hook from cable on carrier flight deck. They wear green jerseys and helmets.

Horned scully:
> Underwater beach obstacle designed to tear holes in boats.

Horns:
> Horizontal arms of a cleat or chock; projecting timbers of a stage to which rigging lines are secured.

Horse Latitudes:
> Sea areas on outer margins of trade winds, around $30°$ north and south where prevailing winds are light and variable.

Hospital corpsman (HM):
> Petty officer who performs general hospital corps duties.

Hospitalman (HN):
> Enlisted man in paygrade three who performs general semi-skilled hospital corps duties.

Hospital ship (AH):
> An unarmed ship, marked in accordance with the Geneva Convention, staffed and equipped to provide complete medical and surgical facilities.

Hostile Nonmilitary Vessel category:
> Vessel which refuses to be brought to, commits an unquestionably hostile act, offers resistance to the examining party, or flagrantly disobeys orders.

Hot caseman:
> Man who disposes of the ejected cases from a gun using case ammunition. Also called hot shellman.

Hot suitman (hot poppa):
> Man wearing asbestos suit trained to rescue crews of burning aircraft.

Hotel:
> Phonetic word for letter H.

HOUND DOG:
> Model designation: AGM-28; cognizant service: Air Force. A supersonic, jet-propelled, air-to-surface, inertial guided, standoff strategic missile.

House:
> To stow or secure in a safe place, as to house the anchor. Has a special meaning in connection with ship's awnings: in case of rain, to loose alternate stops from *Ridge rope,* to haul down and secure to *Rail, Lifeline* or, most properly, to the *Housing line,* thus creating gutters or valleys to carry off the water.

Housing anchor:
> An anchor having no stock: houses itself in hawsepipe when hove in.
> See also *Stockless anchor, Patent anchor.* Compare *Old-fashioned anchor.*

Housing chain stopper:
> Slip stopper fitted with a screw turnbuckle; used for securing anchor
> in hawsepipe.

Housing line:
> The middle one of the three lifelines around the perimeter of a
> ship. From top, they are lifeline, housing line, and foot line.
> When an awning is housed, gutters to carry off rain are formed by
> bringing alternate lashings down to the housing line.

Hove:
> Nautical past participle of "heave." The leadsman hove the lead—not
> "heaved."

Hovering:
> In submarines, the maintaining of depth with no way on by use of ship's
> pumps controlling on-board ballast. See *Balancing.* In helicopters,
> to maintain altitude over a fixed point.

Hove taut:
> Pulled tight.

HUEYCOBRA:
> Model designation: AH-1G; cognizant service: Army.
> Attack helicopter incorporating reduced cabin frontal area, tandem
> seating for pilot and copilot/gunner, integral chin-mounted gun
> turret, and provisions for external armament on stub wing. 2-crew.

Hug:
> To keep close. A vessel might "hug" the shore.

Hulk:
> A worn-out vessel, stripped of all useful gear.

Hull:
> The body or shell of a ship or seaplane.

Hull board:
> Group of officers who inspect and report on the condition of the ship's hull.

Hull down:
> Said of a ship visible over the horizon by her upper works alone.

Hull Report:
> Result of weekly inspection made of his spaces by a *Division Officer.*

Hummock:
> An irregular ridge or hillock on sea ice.

Hunter-Killer Force (HUK):
> A naval force consisting of an anti-submarine warfare carrier,
> associated aircraft and escorts.

Hunter-killer operations:
> Coordinated search-and-destroy ASW activities by surface and/or air units.

Hunting:
Mechanical self-perpetuating oscillation between two limits, as in a follow-up or servo system. See also *Mine Countermeasures*.

Hunting, mine:
Branch of mine countermeasures which determines the positions of individual mines and concentrates countermeasures on these positions; includes locating, clearance and watching.

Hurricane:
Destructive cyclonic storm with winds above 65 knots. In the eastern hemisphere it is called a *Typhoon.*

HUSKIE:
Model designation: H-43; cognizant services: Navy and Air Force. General purpose helicopter. 2-crew, 6-passengers.

HUSTLER:
Model designation: B-58; cognizant service: Air Force. Long-range, high-altitude bomber aircraft with a distinctive delta wing. Jet.

HYDAC:
Single-stage sounding rocket. Also Hybrid Digital-Analog Computer.

HYDRA:
Program investigating techniques for sea launch of large rockets.

Hydro-flap:
Planing surface swung down beneath the fuselage of land aircraft to assist in emergency water landings.

Hydrofoil:
A surface craft designed to "fly" in water. By use of submerged foils, the hull is lifted from the water much as an aircraft is lifted from the ground. Reduction of hull drag permits greater speed.

Hydrographic Office:
The office of the Navy Department that produced charts and navigational publications. Now called the Naval Oceanographic Office.

Hydrography:
The science of determining the condition of navigable waters.

Hydrophone:
An underwater microphone.

HYDRO SKIMMER:
An air cushion vehicle experimental program.

Hydrospace:
See *Inner space.*

Hydrostatic Pressure:
Pressure at a given water depth due to water mass above, normally measured in pounds per square inch.

I

Ice anchor:
Timber, or *Deadman,* buried in ice, to which ship's lines are secured.

Iceberg (Berg):
Large ice mass of glacial origin, floating in the sea.

Ice blink:
White glare on sky produced by reflection from ice.

Ice breaker (AGB):
A specially designed vessel with a spoon-shaped bow, protected propellers, and powerful engines for operations in heavy ice.

Ice concentration:
The percentage of ice cover, usually expressed in tenths, in a given area of water.

Ice fields:
Mass of drifting ice, offshore. A form of *Pack Ice.*

Ice-free port:
Port in which winter ice does not interfere with navigation of harbors or terminals.

Ice lane:
An area of the ocean where ice frequently may be found.

I.C. Electrician (IC):
Petty officer who maintains shipboard interior communications systems.

Ice period:
Period between first appearance and final clearance of ice during any given year.

Identification card:
Personal, official, identification card. Commonly called "ID Card."

Idler:
Enlisted man who normally has a full schedule of daytime duties, but is excused from night watches.

IFF:
Identification, Friend or Foe. An electronic system of exchanging identification. With radar and radar-controlled missiles this is a necessity.

Immediate message:
A category of precedence reserved for messages relating to situations which gravely affect the security of national or allied forces or populace, and which require immediate delivery.

Impact, center of:
Center of the dispersion pattern in the fall of projectiles or bombs.

Impact, mean point of:
> Geometrical center of all the points of impact of the shots of a
> salvo or of the bombs in pattern bombing, excluding wild shots.

Impulse charge:
> Propellant designed to start a self-propelled missile, such as a
> torpedo, on its way.

In:
> A Navy man serves "in" a ship, not "on" her.

Inactivate:
> To place a ship in the Reserve Fleet. "Put into mothballs" is the
> slang term.

Inactivation:
> Process of preparing a ship for Reserve Fleet status.

Inboard:
> Towards the center of a ship or a group of ships.

In bows:
> An order to bow oarsmen to boat their oars and to prepare to come
> alongside a vessel or dock.

Incentive pay:
> Extra pay for hazardous duty such as that involving flying or for
> specialists such as doctors.

Inclination diagram:
> Polar coordinate graph used to record roller data in making a gun
> battery alignment aboard ship.

Incline:
> To list a ship and compute its stability. See *Inclining experiment.*

Inclining experiment:
> Computation of the *Metacentric height* of a ship by use of weights
> to cause a list. The result is a measure of the stability of the vessel.

Inclinometer:
> Instrument for measuring the roll of a ship. Same as *Clinometer.*

Indefinite Delivery Contract:
> Used where the exact time of delivery is not known. May be one of
> three types: definite quantity—provides for specific quantities and
> materials to be delivered on order; requirement—for supplies or
> services during specified period; indefinite quantity—specifies
> maximum and minimum limits, provides for a period of delivery.

Indefinite Quantity Contract:
> A form of *Indefinite Delivery Contract.*

Index correction:
> Correction to sextant altitude in celestial navigation to allow for
> index error of the sextant caused by the index and horizon mirrors
> not being parallel.

India:
> Phonetic word for letter I.

Indicator:
>In cryptography, an element within the text which provides a guide
to prompt decryption.

Indirect fire:
>Aiming guns by *Laying* them a target which is not intended to be
hit and by bringing them on to the intended target by artificial
range and deflection corrections. Employed when the target cannot be seen.

Industrial security:
>The portion of internal security concerned with protection of
classified information in the hands of industry.

Inertial guidance:
>System designed to guide a missile, aircraft, or ship by devices
independent of outside information, using the inertial properties
of gyroscopes. The system measures and converts minute accelerations
experienced by the ship, aircraft, or missile to distance in the
direction of the acceleration.

Inertia reel:
>Device for automatically restraining a pilot's shoulder harness when
a force of 2 or 3 G's is applied.

Infrastructure:
>Term used in NATO, generally applicable to all fixed and permanent
installations, fabrications, or facilities for the support and control
of military forces.

Inhaul:
>Any line used to haul in on something.

Initial provisioning:
>Process of determining range and quantity of spare repair parts,
special tools, test equipment and support equipment required by an
end item during initial service period.

Initial velocity (i.v.):
>Velocity of projectile at start of trajectory.

Injector:
>Device using jet of steam to force water into boiler.

INJUN:
>Series of radiation research satellites.

Inland Rules:
>Rules of the nautical road that are applicable in most inland U.S. waters.

Inner bottom:
>Top of the double bottom of a ship; consists of watertight plating.

Inner space:
>Popular term used to describe the area below the ocean's surface.

In ordinary:
>A ship not in commission, maintained by a skeleton crew.

In-port watch:
>See *Port watch.*

Inshore:
Toward land. If already ashore, "Inshore" means away from the sea.

Inshore currents:
The motion of water inside the surf zone, includes longshore and rip currents.

Inshore Fire Support Ship (IFS):
An amphibious warfare vessel of shallow draft capable of providing heavy fire cover for military landings.

Inshore water:
Water adjoining land whose physical properties are influenced by land conditions.

Inspection:
Careful and critical examination, of personnel, material, and records, or a ceremonial Captain's or Admiral's Inspection of personnel and of ship or station.

Instruction:
Serially numbered directive issued by commanders ashore and afloat. May contain policies, procedures, orders, doctrine, and information of a continuing or permanent nature. See *Notice.*

Instrument landing system:
ILS Radio enabling aircraft to land in low visibility.

Instrumentman (IM):
Petty officer who tests and repairs watches, gauges, meters, clocks, and other precision instruments.

Insular shelf:
Sea bottom surrounding islands from their point of permanent immersion to about 200 meters, where slope increases measurably toward greater depths.

Insular slope:
The sea bottom from the seaward limit of the insular shelf to the sea floor.

Interagency Committee on Oceanography (ICO):
The top national planning council for oceanographic matters.

Intercardinal points:
The four points midway between the cardinal points of the compass: northeast, southeast, southwest, and northwest.

Intercom:
Ship's voice intercommunication system. Also called *Squawk-Box.*

Interdict:
To prevent or hinder enemy use of a certain area.

Interdiction:
Destruction of roads, bridges, railroads, tunnels, supply dumps, etc., to prevent the support of enemy front lines.

Interface:
Term used to describe areas of common interest between items of hardware or philosophies.

Interim Clearance:
Clearance issued temporarily and based on investigation insufficient
to meet final security-clearance requirements.

Interim Parts List (IPL):
An interim stock number identification table used for equipment new
to naval service.

Interior communications:
All telephones, call bells, alarms, and other forms of communications
within the ship.

Interlock:
Safety switch which cuts off high voltage when access covers, doors,
or panels on an electrical device are opened.

Intermediate Waves:
Waves with a relative depth (water depth/wave length) of between
0.5 and 0.05.

Internal security:
The prevention of actions against the United States and protection
of life and property by employment of all measures other than military
defense.

Internal waves:
Waves which occur along the interface separating two water masses;
usually at the thermocline. Wave heights, periods, and lengths are
usually large compared to surface waves.

International Ice Patrol:
A patrol operated by the Coast Guard in accordance with an international
agreement for the prevention of disasters caused by collisions of
vessels with ice.

International Low Water (ILW):
Reference plane below mean sea level calculated by multiplying half the range
between mean lower low water and mean higher high water by 1.5.

International Rules:
Rules of the nautical road made effective by agreement of the
major maritime powers for use on high seas and most inland waters
of the world, except of the U.S.

Interrogatory:
In any naval message, means: "question;" "I do not understand;"
"meaning not clear;" etc.

Interrupted quick-flashing light:
A navigation light showing quick flashes for several seconds followed
by a period of darkness.

Intertidal zone:
Generally, the zone between mean high water and mean low water.

Interval (tactical):
Distance between foremasts of adjacent *Guides* of ships in formation.

Intervalometer:
Device for measuring depth charge interval, used to lay a barrage or pattern.

INTRUDER:
Model designation: A-6; cognizant service: Navy.
All-weather, low-altitude, carrier-based, two-place attack aircraft.
Primary mission is to conduct interdiction close-air-support missions
and attacks on land bases and ships under any weather conditions.
2-crew. Jet.

INVADER:
Model designation: A-26; cognizant service: Air Force.
A light bombardment aircraft. 3-crew. Propeller-driven.

Inventory Control Point (ICP):
Organizational unit within a military service assigned primary
responsibility for management of a group of items either for inter-
or intra-service use.

Ionosphere:
Layer of ionized air above the earth which reflects some radio transmissions.

IRA:
Improved guidance head for the *SIDEWINDER* missile.

Irish pennant:
Loose, untidy end of line left adrift. Also *Deadman* and *Cow's tail.*

IROQUOIS:
Model designation: UH-1; cognizant service: Army.
A single-rotor, two-bladed helicopter with a gas turbine engine.
1-crew, 5-passengers.

Island:
Structure above the flight deck of an *Aircraft carrier.*

Isobar:
A line on a chart connecting points of equal atmospheric pressure.

Isobath:
A contour line connecting points of equal depth on a bathymetric
chart.

Isohaline:
Having no change in salt content on the reference plane or line
connecting points of common salinity.

Isopiestic:
Condition of constant pressure on the sea surface.

Isopleths:
Lines of equal wave heights on a wave chart used for optimum
track ship routing.

Isotach:
Line connecting points of equal current velocity.

Isotherm:
Line connecting points of equal temperature.

Isothermal:
Having no change in temperature.

Isothermal layer:
 A layer of water throughout which a constant temperature exists.

Isotherm follower:
 Device used to study the movement of subsurface layers of sea water.

Isovelocity:
 A phenomenon in which sound velocity is the same throughout a given water layer.

Iswas:
 Slang; any crude or improvised measuring or calculating device.

J

Jack:
Short for *Union Jack*, a blue, white-starred flag flown at the bow *(Jackstaff)* of a vessel at anchor. To jack over the engines is to turn them over. Short for *Cablejack.*

Jackass:
Cover over *Hawsepipe* to keep water out. See *Buckler.* Also, similar cover over entrance to pipe leading to chain locker, after anchor chain comes off *Wildcat.*

Jackbox:
Receptacle into which telephone plugs or jacks are fitted.

Jack-of-the-dust:
Man in charge of the provision issue room.

Jackstaff:
Flagpole at the bow of a ship from which the *Union jack* is flown when the ship is not underway.

Jackstay:
Wire or line rigged for a special purpose, such as hanging *Seabags.*

Jacob's ladder:
Portable ladder, with rope or wire sides and wooden rungs, slung over the side for temporary use. See *Sea Ladder.*

Jamming:
Deliberate radio or radar interference.

Jeep:
Small truck-like auto, built for military service in WW II.

Jeep carrier:
Small aircraft carrier built in great numbers during World War II.

Jeheemy:
Salvage rig to rescue swamped or stranded boats during an amphibious landing.

Jet-assisted take-off (JATO):
An auxiliary rocket device providing short, intense thrust during take off of an aircraft.

Jetsam:
Material which sinks when thrown overboard. See *Flotsam.* The term "flotsam and jetsam" is however loosely used to denote floating debris.

JET STAR:
Model designation: C-140; cognizant services: Navy and Air Force. A small transport aircraft. 2-crew, 8-passengers. Jet.

Jettison:
Throw over the side, as when emergency reduction of topside weight is required.

Jetty:
Pier or breakwater extending into the water to protect channels or shoreline from erosion, or to form a boat or ship harbor.

Jewelry:
Gear used to fasten together sections of a *Pontoon* causeway.

Jew's-harp:
Ring at upper end of shank of an anchor to which anchor chain is secured.

JEZEBEL:
AN/SSQ-38 sonobuoy, passive, used for localization of targets.

Jigger, or jiggermast:
The fourth mast in a four-masted ship, sometimes also called the "pusher." In case of a ship with a very tall first mast and a relatively tiny second, they may be known as the "mainmast" and the "jigger," but at this point the nomenclature becomes largely a matter of choice and preference. *Yawls* and *Ketches* are generally fitted with jiggers instead of a mizzenmast, and most frequently the other mast is called the main. Also, light tackle for general use.

Jimmy legs:
Slang: Guard; *Master-at-arms.*

JINDIVIK:
Jet target drone.

Job analysis:
Detailed description of all tasks that make up a job. Results in a job description or a *Billet specification.*

Job classification:
A group of similar jobs which can be described by the same job definition and can be identified by the same job title and job code.

Job order:
Order issued by a repair activity to its own people to perform a repair job in response to a *Work Request* from the unit to be repaired.

Joe pot:
Slang: coffee pot.

Joiner Door:
Conventional non-watertight door aboard ship

Joint:
Involving elements of more than one of the Armed Services. See *Combined Operation.*

Joint Command:
Similar to *Specified Command* except composed of all Services.

Joint Long-Range Strategic Study (JLRSS):
  Broad appraisal to assist in development of guidance based on
  military strategies and concepts for the period from eight to twelve
  years hence. Provides general guidance for military research and
  engineering objectives. JLRSS is pronounced "jellers". Updated
  annually.

Joint Strategic Capabilities Plan (JSCP):
  Annual translation of national objectives into terms of military
  objectives which becomes directives for conduct of military operations
  during life of the plan. JSCP is pronounced "jay-scap." Updated
  annually.

Joint Strategic Objectives Plan (JSOP):
  Annual mid-range plan for operations anticipated five years hence
  and extending for the following three years. JSOP is pronounced
  "jay-sop". Updated annually.

JOLLY GREEN GIANT:
  Model designation: HH-3E; cognizant service: Air Force.
  Similar to SEA KING with modifications which provide armor
  protection, equipment, and subsystems applicable to aircrew recovery
  operations in combat areas. Helicopter.

Jolly roger:
  Skull-and-crossbones flag flown during crossing-the-line ceremonies.

Journal:
  That part of a shaft, pin, or rotating piece fitted into and working
  in a bearing.

Journalist (JO):
  Petty officer who does news reporting, editing, and related work.

Jubilee pipe patch:
  Damage control patch for piping resembling an elongated hose clamp
  under which a sheet of packing is laid.

Judge Advocate General (JAG):
  The senior legal officer in the Navy.

JULIE:
  The AN/SSQ-23A sonobuoy which releases charges to explode at
  predetermined depths to provide echo-ranging information.

Juliett:
  Phonetic work for letter J.

Jumbo boom:
  Heavy-lift boom aboard ship capable of handling wieghts up to 50 tons.

Jumper:
  Connecting pipe, hose, or wire for emergency use aboard ship.
  Enlisted man's blue or white uniform shirt.

Jump ship:
  Slang for leaving ship without authority or permission.
  See Over the Hill.

Junior officer:
Technically, lieutenant commanders and below. In practice, usually
ensigns and lieutenants are considered junior officers and addressed
as "mister." Lieutenant commanders are often addressed as "commander,"
following traditional army practice of addressing lieutenant colonels
as "colonel."

Jury rig:
Any temporary or makeshift device, rig, or piece of equipment, such
as a jury rudder, jury mast, etc. Can be a term of mild derision,
but need not be.

K

Kamikazi:
Japanese suicide aircraft, World War II, which crashed into ships.
Also, the pilots of such craft. Term is now used to refer to any
deliberate suicidal tactic in war.

Kapok:
Natural, light, waterproof fiber used in stuffing life jackets.

Karry krane:
Mobile, crash-handling crane for small aircraft carriers.

Kedge:
To carry out an anchor in a small boat, then haul the ship or craft
up to the anchor, then repeat. See *Anchor*.

Kedge anchor:
Usually an old-fashioned *Anchor* for pulling off when aground or
for *Warping*. Now rare. See *Stern anchor* for amphibious adaptation.

Keel:
Central, longitudinal beam or timber of a ship from which the frames
and hull plating rise.

Keel depth:
For surface ship, the distance of the keel below the waterline; for
a submarine, the depth at which operating. Some foreign navies use
the depth of water over the deck as the measure of depth of submergence.

Keelhaul:
Slang: To reprimand severely, derived from ancient barbaric punishment:
the hauling of a man from one side of the ship to the other under
the bottom by means of ropes passed under the keel.

Keelson:
Timber or steel fabrications bolted on top of a keel to
strengthen it.

Keeping ship:
Observing the routine of a ship when not engaged in exercises or
operations.

Kekle:
To 'dress up' mooring lines, wrapping them where they come together
with *Small Stuff*.

Kelp:
The largest known seaweed which grow on rock or stone bottom; may
be as long as 600 feet with fronds four feet wide.

Kentner shackle:
Patented anchor chain link which disassembles upon the removal of a pin.

Ketch:
> A small sailing ship, usually but not always *Fore-and-aft* rigged, fitted with a tall *Mainmast* and a much shorter *Mizzenmast* or *Jiggermast,* stepped in front of the rudder post. In appearance the ketch is similar to a *Yawl,* but the yawl has its aftermost mast stepped behind the rudder. Bomb ketches were extensively employed by the British Navy, for blockade or siege operations from sea.

Keying Interval:
> The elapsed time between successive pings on echo-ranging sonar.

K-gun:
> Depth charge projector. See *Y-gun.*

Kick (of the rudder):
> Swirl in the wake of a ship caused by rudder action when making a turn. Same as *Knuckle.*

Kick plate:
> Bright metal plate, to absorb scuff marks on the vertical parts (steps) of a ladder. Also the dark stripe near the deck on a light-painted bulkhead.

Killer submarine (SSK):
> One designed to detect and destroy submarines.

Kilo:
> Phonetic word for letter K.

KINGFISHER:
> Model designation: AQM-60A; cognizant service: Army. A supersonic, high-altitude, ramjet target vehicle.

King posts:
> Posts that support the cargo booms on cargo ships. Usually erected in pairs.

King spoke:
> The spoke of a ship's wheel that is up when the rudder is amidships.

Kingston (valve):
> Large valve in the hull of an old submarine. Obsolete.

KIOWA:
> Model designation: OH-58; cognizant service: Army. Single-rotor, light observation, helicopter. Has provisions for installing armament systems and a passive defense system consisting of both fixed and removable compounds. Two-crew plus two-passengers or 400 pounds of cargo.

Kit (kid):
> Small container, such as a mess kit or *Spit Kit.*

KITE:
> Airborne radar reflector used to simulate a target for deceptive purposes. May be dropped from aircraft or streamed from a ship.

KITTY:
Model designation: PWN-6; cognizant service: Air Force.
A rocket-borne radiosonde system used to carry a sounding instrument
to approximately 220,000 feet. Atmospheric data, transmitted by the
instrument to a ground receiver station, and precision radar give
wind information.

Kiyi:
Small brush used to scrub clothing or canvas.

Knee:
An angular piece connecting a ship's frames to the beams.

Knife edge:
The rim of a door frame, hatch, or port that meets the *Gasket* for
a watertight fit. Has the appearance of a very dull knife blade.

Knock off:
To stop; cease.

Knot:
Unit of speed equivalent to one nautical mile (6080 feet) per hour;
a collective term for hitches and bends; a knob in a rope. See
Nautical mile.

Knuckle:
See *Kick.* Also a sudden change in curvature of a ship's hull.

Kytoon:
Helium filled balloon supporting a temporary radio antenna.

L

Labeled cargo:
Cargo such as explosives and chemicals, which require special handling.

Labor:
A ship is said to labor when she works heavily in a rough sea.

Labrador Current:
A cold-water current flowing south along the coast of Labrador, which is the principal carrier of icebergs that menace the sea lanes of the North Atlantic.

Lace, gold:
Officer's gold braid, now often synthetic.

Lacing:
Line that secures canvas by passing through the eyelets or grommets in the canvas.

Ladder:
Stairs. Also, a succession of salvos with established differences in range, fired to establish hitting gun range.

Ladder screen:
Canvas or metal sheet secured on the underside of a ladder.

Lagging:
The insulation around pipes aboard ship.

Lagrangian method:
Current measurement by use of drifting objects, such as bottles.

LANCE:
Model designation: XMGM-52B; cognizant service: Army. Classified missile.

Land breeze:
Breeze coming off the land (as the land cools faster than the sea after sunset).

Landfall:
The arrival or first sighting of land at the end of a voyage.

Landfast ice:
Ice of any type which is attached to the shore, beached or stranded in shallow water.

Land ice:
Any ice floating on the sea that originated from a glacier.

Landing craft:
Craft employed in amphibious operations, specifically designed for carrying troops and equipment and for beaching, unloading and retracting. Also used for logistic cargo resupply operations. See Appendix A.

Landing craft, Assault (LCA):
Personnel and cargo carrier, 30 ton.

Landing Craft, Medium (LCM):
An amphibious assault boat capable of beaching and discharging personnel and tanks.

Landing Craft, Rubber (LCR):
Rubber landing craft. for 10 people (L) or 7 people (S).

Landing Craft, Vehicle and Personnel (LCVP):
A small amphibious assault boat capable of beaching.

Landing force:
The troops organized for an amphibious assault. Also, a portion of a ship's crew detailed to go ashore in an organized unit for any military operation, a term obsolete since World War II.

Landing party:
An organized force of infantry from the ship's company detailed for emergency or parade duty ashore. Formerly called *Landing force.*

Landing ship:
An assault ship which is designed for long sea voyages and for rapid unloading over and onto a beach. See Appendix A.

Landing signal officer (LSO):
Officer who directs pilots in landing on an aircraft carrier.

Landing team:
See *Battalion landing team.*

Landing Vehicle, Tracked, Engineer (LVTE):
Lightly armored amphibious vehicle designed for minefield and obstacle clearance in amphibious assaults and operations inland.

Landlubber:
Seaman's term of derision for one who has never been to sea, hence a *Lubber* or *Lubberly.*

Lands:
The raised part of the rifling of a gun between grooves.

Lanyard:
Small line made fast to an object to secure it, as a pistol lanyard.

Lapping head:
Abrasive device for removing copper fouling from the bore of a gun.

Laser:
Light amplification by stimulated emission of radiation.

Lash:
To secure with line or wire by wrapping and tying with seamanlike knots in the case of line, or with an approved hitch in the case of wire. Lashing or wire-lashing are the materials used. LASH (Lighter aboard ship) is a new method of shipping in which loaded lighters or barges are transported in a specially designed merchant ship.

Latitude:
> The measure of angular distance in degrees, minutes, and seconds of arc from
> $0°$ to $90°$ north or south of the equator.

Launch:
> To float a ship upon completion of building, traditionally by sliding
> down the *Building ways* although many ships, especially big ones,
> are now launched by floating them out of the drydock in which they
> were built. Also, an open powerboat.

Launcher:
> Device for holding and firing a rocket, guided missile, or any
> projectile, such as a depth charge, which does not qualify as being
> a bullet or projectile shot from a gun.

Law officer:
> Officer member of a court-martial who is a qualified lawyer.

Lay:
> To go, as in "lay aft on the fantail." The direction of the twist
> of strands of a rope.

Lay before the mast:
> To assemble or fall in, usually to make reports.

Layer depth:
> The thickness of the mixed layer nearest to surface of the sea; the
> depth to the top of the *Thermocline.* A term much used in
> antisubmarine warfare.

Lazarette:
> Storage compartment in the stern of a ship or boat.

Lazy line:
> General term for a line used for various purposes in securing boats,
> specifically the line made fast to stern of boats at a *boat boom.*

Lead:
> Weight used in taking soundings.(Pronounced "led").

Lead Bureau Concept:
> An approach to system development by which one bureau, laboratory,
> or command is assigned overall responsibility for a development even
> thought the entire effort will not be conducted within that bureau,
> laboratory, or command. Lead (Pronounced "leed").

Lead (in ice):
> Long narrow passage or lane in pack ice through which a ship can
> navigate. (Pronounced "leed").

Leadline:
> Lead with attached line, used for taking soundings. Also called a
> *Hand lead.* (Pronounced "led").

Leadsman:
> Man who uses the leadline. Pronounced "led".

Lead time:
>   The length of time before end item delivery in which an operation
>   must be performed to meet delivery schedules. Pronounced "leed".

Lead yard:
>   Shipyard which builds the first ship of a design class. It furnishes
>   specified services to yards which build other ships of the class.
>   Pronounced "leed".

Leak stoppers:
>   Wooden plugs and metal fittings designed to stop leaks in the hull of a
>   ship or boat.

Leatherneck:
>   Slang: Marine.

Leave:
>   Authorized vacation or absence from duty other and longer than
>   *Liberty.* Term *Shore leave* is no longer used. Leave carries with
>   it permission to travel beyond the allowed radius of liberty.

Leave rations:
>   Cash payment in lieu of rations in kind while on leave, for enlisted
>   personnel.

Leaver (Convoy):
>   A section of a convoy which breaks off from the main convoy to proceed
>   separately to its own prearranged terminal port. When detached the
>   leaver section becomes a leaver convoy. If it is a single ship, it
>   is referred to simply as a "leaver."

Lee:
>   The direction away from the wind, i.e., away from which the wind is
>   coming. Opposite to *Weather.* If the wind is blowing from the
>   west, westerly directions are "weatherly," while easterly directions
>   are to *Leeward.*

Leech:
>   The after edge of a *Fore-and-aft* sail.

Lee helm:
>   To carry a lee helm means that the sailing ship tends to come up to
>   the wind and it is necessary to compensate by a little rudder toward the
>   lee side to keep her on course. Compare with *Lee helmsman.*

Lee helmsman:
>   Assistant steersman. Compare with *Lee helm.*

Leeward:
>   Away from the wind. Pronounced "LOO-urd," but only for this specific
>   word. In all other cases, the word or syllable "lee" is pronounced
>   as spelled.

Leeway:
>   Drift of an object with the wind, on surface of the sea.

Left-handed rope:
>   Twisted from right to left. Strands and cables are usually left-handed.
>   Also called left-laid rope.

Let fall:
An order to let oars fall into the rowlocks; from the position of toss also, when lowering a boat, to let the falls go by the run just before the boat is waterborne.

Let go by the run:
Allowing a line to run free.

Letters of censure:
Non-judicial punishment inflicted upon an officer by his commanding officer or reporting senior and entered in officer's record. Most severe is letter of reprimand; of lesser severity—letter of admonition; least severe—letter of caution.

Level(s) of supply:
A general term for quantities of material held for issue.

Liberty:
Authorized absence of an individual from place of duty, normally not more than 48 hours. Sometimes incorrectly called "shore leave". Liberty sometimes carries geographical limits to provide possibility of quick recall.

Lie off:
To remain stopped a short distance away.

Lie-to (lay-to):
To stop a ship but not anchor or moor it.

Lieutenant (LT):
Junior officer ranking above a lieutenant junior grade and below a lieutenant commander.

Lieutenant commander (LCDR):
Officer who ranks just below commander and above a lieutenant.

Lieutenant junior grade (JG):
Officer who ranks just above ensign and just below a full lieutenant.

Lifeboat:
In merchant ships, a boat required by international law, which can be quickly launched for safety of passengers and crew. The number required is determined by the number of persons permitted to voyage in that ship (as a result of the *Titanic* disaster, when there were not enough). In a warship the lifeboat is a ready boat which may quickly be launched with a crew trained and equipped for rescue day or night. The motor whaleboat is traditionally the most seaworthy of all ship's boats and is much the preferred type for this use.

Life buoy (ring):
Buoyant device, usually fitted with a light and smoke maker, for throwing to a man in the water.

Lifeguard:
Aircraft and ships detailed to recover aircraft personnel at sea.

Lifeguard submarine:
One stationed to rescue downed airmen in an area where surface vessels cannot operate.

Life jacket, preserver:
>Device to keep individual afloat. May be jacket, ring, knapsack,
belt, yoke, or vest type.

Lifeline:
>Line secured along the deck to lay hold of in heavy weather; line
thrown on board a wreck by a lifesaving crew; knotted line secured
to the span of lifeboat davits for the use of the crew when hoisting
and lowering. The lines between *Stanchions* along the outboard
edges of a ship's weather decks are all loosely referred to as
lifelines, but specifically the top line is the lifeline, middle is
the *Housing line,* and bottom is the *Footline.*

Life raft:
>Float either constructed with a metallic tube covered with cork and naval
canvas, or made of balsa wood or other suitable material. Modern life rafts
are usually of rubber which automatically release and inflate if submerged.

Lift:
>Specified quantity of cargo requiring transportation. To transport
cargo or personnel.

Lift, amphibious (or assault):
>Total capacity of assault shipping utilized in an amphibious operation.

LIFTMASTER:
>Model designation: C-118; cognizant service: Navy/Air Force.
Long-range, low-wing, monoplane equipped with fully retractable
landing gear and pressurized cabin. Used as cargo, personnel, ambulance,
or staff transport. 5-crew, 79-troops, or 61-litters.
Propeller-driven.

Lightening hole:
>Hole cut in steel plate in order to lighten it without sacrificing
much strength.

Lighter:
>Barge-like vessel used to load or unload ships.

Lighter-than-air (LTA):
>Blimps, dirigibles, and other lighter-than-air devices.

Lighthouse:
>A building in which an aid to navigation light is located.

Light lists:
>Publications describing aids to navigation maintained by U.S. Coast
Guard.

Light lock:
>Double door permitting passage without showing light to the outside.

Light off:
>Start, literally "to start a fire in," as in "light off a boiler."
Slang: to "light off" an engine, controversy, investigation, etc.

Light period:
>The length in time in seconds required to complete one cycle of the
characteristics of an aid to navigation.

Light ship:
> Command or word passed which permits lights to be shown as the ship is secured from being darkened. See *Lightship.*

Lightship:
> An anchored, manned, floating navigational light, in the form of a ship. It has the desirable feature of being able to go to harbor for upkeep.

Light ship condition (Condition A):
> Ship which is complete, ready for service and has all permanent ballast and spare parts aboard but without variable load.

Lignum vitae:
> Very dense wood used in propeller shaft bearings.

Lima:
> Phonetic word for letter L.

Limb (of the sun or moon), upper or lower:
> The upper or lower edge as sighted against the horizon in taking sun or moon sights.

Limited Duty Officer (LDO):
> An ex-enlisted man who has won a commission because of his high quality. Because of the branch and experience through which he has risen, he is limited to duties of his specialty.

Limpet mines:
> Small explosives attached to the hull of a ship by enemy swimmers. See *Mine.*

Line:
> General term for rope; the equator; a formation in which ships or personnel are formed in any direction from the guide. See *Rope.*

Lineal number:
> Precedence number for naval officers. Replaces old *Signal number.* Changes with each promotion, becoming smaller as officer becomes more senior. See *Number in grade.*

Line chief:
> Aircraft maintenance man, the "straw boss" of the hangar deck.

Line item:
> A descriptive entry in any document which describes the item, unit of issue, stock or part number, and quantity of the item involved.

Line of departure:
> In amphibious assault, the line from which the scheduled boat waves leave, on signal, for the beach.

Line officer:
> One who is concerned with the operation of the forces afloat in contrast to *Staff Officers.* Engineering Duty, Special Duty and Limited Duty Officers are line officers restricted to duty in their own specialty.

Line of Fire (LOF):
  A straight line joining gun and point of impact (or burst) of the
  projectile.

Line-of-sight:
  Straight line, used to describe radio frequency transmission that does
  not follow the curvature of the earth.

Lines drawing:
  The representation of the ship's form in three separate planes. The
  longitudinal is known as the *Sheer plan.* The transverse section
  as the *Body plan,* and the horizontal as the *Half-breadth plan.*

Line service:
  Fueling, arming, engine warm-up, and minor adjustments of aircraft.

Line squall:
  A violent windstorm characteristic of a weather front.

Line-throwing gun:
  A 45-cal. gun for throwing a line. The projectile carries a light
  line which is used to pull a *Messenger* across.

List:
  Inclination of a ship about a fore and aft axis i.e. she lists to
  port or starboard.

Listen:
  To maintain a continuous radio receiver watch.

Listening sweep:
  Sonar search conducted without sound emanation; passive use of sonar.

Lithographer (LI):
  Petty officer who does printing of all kinds.

LITTLE JOHN:
  Model designation: MGR-3A; cognizant service: Army.
  A missile.

Littoral:
  The coastal region.

Littoral currents:
  Same as *Longshore currents.*

Littoral system:
  Subdivision of *Benthic division.*

Lizard, traveling:
  A short section of line with a thimble at one end, through which
  passes a small wire cable stretched taut between two fixed structures
  on board ship. The lizard can move freely along the wire, while firmly
  gripped by a man needing to make the passage safely from one structure
  to the other in bad weather.

Load:
  Single round of ammunition. Command to put ammunition into the gun.
  Also, to stow supplies into a boat, vehicle, ship, or aircraft.

Loading, combat:
Loading assault troops and equipment for rapid debarkation in predetermined priority.

Loading, commerical:
Loading of troops and/or equipment for maximum utilization of space.

Loading machine:
Dummy gun used to train gun crews in loading.

Loading, rail:
Loading of boats during amphibious assault at the rail of the ship
instead of after they are waterborne.

Load List:
Items carried in a ship of the mobile support force which supports
the fleet underway.

Loafer's loops:
Slang for *Aiguillettes.*

Local Apparent Noon (LAN):
The instant that the center of the sun is exactly over the upper
branch of the meridian of the observer, i.e., the highest altitude
to which the sun will climb on that day. Time of LAN, pronounced
Ell-Ay-Enn, varies with the time the ship is keeping; thus the instant
that the sun "dips," i.e., when its altitude begins to decrease,
can be converted directly to the difference in longitude between
the actual position of the ship and that of the meridian whose time
the ship happens to be keeping. This is why the search for an accurate
timepiece was so important for navigation. At this same moment,
calculation of latitude from altitude of the sun and its declination
is easy. Thus LAN has long been a favorite of navigators,
and a sun unobscured by clouds at noon is always desired.

Lock:
Compartment in a canal for lowering or lifting vessels to different
levels.

Locker:
Metal cabinet, fitted with a lock, in which men keep their gear. Any
small compartment or cabinet.

Lodgement area:
The area, resulting from a consolidation of several beachheads, which
is the base for subsequent operations inland.

Log:
Device for measuring a ship's speed and distance traveled through
the water. See *Taffrail log, Pitometer log,* and *Electromagnetic
log.* To record something is to log it. Short for *Logbook.*

Logbook:
Any chronological record of events, as an engineering watch log.

Log, deck:
Official record of a ship in commission submitted to the Chief of Naval
Personnel in accordance with Navy Regulations and the BuPers Manual.

Log, engineering:
>   Daily record of important events and certain data concerning the
>   machinery of a ship.

Loggerhead:
>   A piece of iron on a long handle used for melting pitch in seams to
>   make the seams more water-tight. The loggerhead was thus a deadly
>   weapon readily available to fractious members of a ship's crew.

Logistics:
>   The science of planning and carrying out the movement and
>   maintenance of forces.

Logroom:
>   Engineer's record room on board ship.

Longevity pay:
>   The increase over base pay that is computed on years of service.

Long glass:
>   Medium-powered (up to 16) monocular telescope used on ships, specially
>   for spotting signals. Short term is *Glass.* The long glass is the
>   traditional symbol of authority on board ship, and some ships still
>   provide the OOD in port with a ceremonial one to carry about while
>   standing his watch.

Longitude:
>   Measure of angular distance in degrees, minutes, and seconds east
>   or west of the prime meridian at Greenwich.

Longitudinal frames:
>   Frames of a ship running fore and aft.

Longitudinal wave:
>   A wave in which particles of the transmitting medium are displaced
>   perpendicularly to the wave itself, i.e. sound waves in air or water.

Long-Range Active Detection System (LORAD):
>   A shipboard active long-range sonar system.

Long-Range Objectives (LRO):
>   Basic guidance for the achievement of ship, aircraft, and weapons
>   goals for period ten to fifteen years hence using self-imposed fiscal
>   assumptions. It is used internally within the Navy only and is based
>   on *Long-Range Requirements.*

Long-Range Requirements (LRR):
>   Estimate of the ship, aircraft and weapons capabilities required
>   during the period to fifteen years hence.

Longshore currents:
>   Currents within the surf zone which parallel the shoreline and are
>   caused by waves breaking at an angle to the shoreline. Derived from
>   "alongshore current."

Longshoreman:
>   Laborer who loads and unloads marine cargo.

Long Wave:
  Waves occurring when phase velocity is dependent on water depth alone
  and whose relative depth (water depth/wave length) is 0.05 or less.

Loofa sponge:
  Formerly sponge used in the hot well of a feed water heater aboard
  ship.

Look alive:
  Meaning "be alert," "move quickly."

Lookout:
  Man stationed as a visual watch; air, horizon, surface, fog, etc.
  See *Reports, Lookout.*

Loom:
  The shine of a light that is below the horizon. Also, the rounded
  part of an oar from blade to handle.

Loran:
  A system of electronic navigation in which the time difference in
  the reception of pulse signals originated simultaneously at a master
  and slave station is utilized to locate the ship as being upon a
  charted hyperbolic curve that is the locus of all possible positions
  which would observe the identical time difference. The intersections
  of two such lines gives a fix. (LOng-RAnge electronic Navigation).

Lower High Water (LHW):
  The lower of the two high waters on any tidal day.

Lower Low Water (LLW):
  The lower of the two low waters during any tidal day.

Lower Water Datum:
  The approximation of mean low water adopted as a standard for a
  limited area.

Lowest Low Water:
  Plane of reference lower than mean sea level by an amount equal to
  the difference between mean sea level and the lowest low water of
  any normal tide.

Lowest Normal Tides:
  Reference plane lower than mean sea level by half the maximum tide
  range without consideration of wind or barometric pressure influences.

Low-order burst (detonation):
  The incomplete, less destructive detonation of an explosive.

Low Water (LW):
  The minimum height reached by a tide, can be due solely to tidal
  action or may include weather factors as well.

Low Water Datum:
  The approximation of mean low water used as a standard for limited areas.

Lubberly:
  Unseamanlike; clumsy. A lubber is an unseamanlike person.
  See *Landlubber.*

Lubber's line:
Reference mark on a compass or radar scope corresponding to ship's head.

Lucky bag:
Container or stowage for articles found adrift. Aboard ship unclaimed articles are periodically sold at auction.

Luff:
To head into the wind so that the upwind edge of the sail ripples with wind passing on the back side. The leading edge of a Fore-and-aft sail. See *Leech.*

Luff tackle:
A tackle having one single- and one double-sheave block. See *tackle.* Pronounced "Tay-cul".

LULU:
Air-delivered atomic depth charge.

Lunar Day:
Time for one rotation of the earth with respect to the moon, approximately 24.84 hours.

Lyle gun:
Gun used in lifesaving to throw a lifeline to a ship in distress.

M

MACE-A:
Model designation: MGM-13; cognizant service: Air Force.
Tactical surface-to-surface guided missile.

MACE-B:
Model designation: CGM-13; cognizant service: Air Force.
Long-range, tactical surface-to-surface guided missile employing a
self-contained jam-proof inertial guidance system.

Machine accountant (MA):
Petty officer who operates and maintains punched card accounting
machines.

Machinery index:
Comprehensive listing of all machinery and related equipment, other
than electronic, installed on board.

Machinery repairman (MR):
Petty officer who works as a shop machinist, using precision tools.

Machinery spaces (engineering spaces):
That part of a ship containing propulsion and auxiliary machinery and
under the cognizance of the Engineer Officer.

Machinery trials:
Tests of main propulsion plant of a ship.

Machinist:
A warrant officer advanced from Machinist's Mate.

Machinist's mate (MM):
A petty officer who maintains and operates machinery.

Mach number:
Ratio of speed of an object to speed of sound in air through which
object is moving. Pronounced "mock."

MacNamara lace:
Fancy curtains and trimmings for barges and gigs worked from unlaid
canvas threads. Nautical corruption of macrame lace. See *Sennet,
Square Knotting, Coxcombing, Fancy Work.*

Mae West:
Pneumatic life jacket.

Magazine:
Compartment aboard ship or ashore fitted for the stowage of ammunition.

Magazine flooding (sprinkling) system:
Network of water pipes for wetting down quickly the contents of a
magazine.

Magnetic Airborne Detector: (MAD):
A device that detects a submerged submarine from low-flying aircraft
making use of the magnetic field of its submerged mass.

Magnetic compass:
A compass using the earth's magnetic field to align the compass card.
See *Compass.*

Magnetic storm:
Worldwide magnetic disturbance which usually starts suddenly and
lasts a minimum of several hours.

Magnetometer:
Device for measuring magnetic force on the sea bottom.

Mailbuoy:
An ancient sailor's joke: the mid-ocean buoy in which mail is kept
for delivery to passing ships.

MAILBUOY:
Communications satellite for UHF relay.

Mailgram:
Dispatch transmitted by mail.

Main battery:
The largest caliber guns carried by a warship.

Main body:
The major part of the important ships of a formation or disposition.

Main deck:
Uppermost complete deck of a ship.

Main drain:
Suction line for pumping out engineering spaces.

Mainmast:
The second mast of a ship with two or more masts, except when the first
mast is much the larger of the two. See *Foremast.*

Main radio:
Main radio room *Radio Central* aboard ship.

Maintop:
A Top in the *Mainmast*, not necessarily at the highest point. See
Top, Foretop, Masthead.

Make:
A ship makes headway, makes good a course steered. A line is made
up ready for use, and is made fast to an object. To the report
from the OOD, "Twelve o'clock, sir" the CO replies: "Make it so."
A lookout makes out a light before reporting it. A leaking boat makes
water. A man being promoted makes a rate.

Make it so:
Response by captain to 12 o'clock report at sea. See *Make.*

Make-up feed:
　　Water of required purity with boiler compound added ready for use in
　　ship's boilers. It is the water needed to replace that lost in the
　　cycle between the boiler and the condenser.

Mameluke sword:
　　Cross-hilted type worn by Marine officers.

Man:
　　To assume station, as in: "Man your planes."

Maneuver:
　　The skillful operation or movement of a ship or aircraft.

Maneuvering board:
　　A compass rose containing polar coordinates used in solving problems
　　of relative motion.

Maneuvering rudder:
　　See *Pilot Rudder.*

Manhelper:
　　A paint brush lashed to a long wooden handle.

Manhole:
　　Round or oval hole cut in deck, bulkhead, or tank top to provide
　　access.

Manifest:
　　A list of all cargo with details as to shippers, consignee, etc.

Manifold:
　　A piping complex with many valves and pipes permitting suction or
　　discharge into various pipelines. Sometimes designed in the shape of
　　a large waterproof or pressureproof chest with valves built in.

Manned and ready:
　　Report made by a gun or station when all hands are present and ready
　　for action. See *Ready.*

Manning level:
　　Mathematical percentage of personnel actually on board vs *Allowance.*
　　Not presently figured against *Complement,* though this might be
　　done in wartime. Thus has only a second-order relation to combat
　　effectiveness of unit. See *Complement, Allowance.*

Manning the rail:
　　All hands evolution in which the men line up along the ship's rail
　　to honor some personage or occasion.

Man-of-war:
　　Fighting ship; armed naval ship. A warship. Most commissioned vessels
　　of the navy are men-of-war, but not all, e.g., a hospital ship.

Manrope:
　　Side rope to a ladder, used as a handrail; a rope used as a safety
　　line anywhere on deck; a rope hanging down on the side of a ship
　　to assist in ascending the ship's side.

Mare's-nest:
Slang: any mess or disarray.

Marine:
A member of the U.S. Marine Corps. If the word is not capitalized,
it refers to anything relating to the sea.

Marine Corps:
An elite, sea-going soldier corps of the Navy, first of the armed
services to be founded. Mission is to be available on short notice
for tough combat and police duty, worldwide. Slang: Leathernecks.

Marine Corps Air Station:
Provides operating, testing, overhaul, and personnel facilities for
Marine aviation.

Marine Corps Institute:
An official training activity charged with the educational development
of Marine Corps personnel.

Marine Division/Wing Team:
Marine Corps air-ground team consisting of one division and one
aircraft wing.

Marine Expeditionary Corps:
Marine air-ground task force built around two Marine divisions and
two Marine aircraft wings.

Marine railway:
A device on tracks leading into the water on which a ship can be hauled
out.

Marine regatta:
A boat race.

Mark:
An exclamation used in taking a reading of an amount, quantity, dial,
etc., when it is necessary that the reading be marked by time. "Mark!
Bearing is 279" or, as in celestial observations, "Stand by—Mark!
Altitude is 46° 27.6'." Also the marked fathoms on a hand
lead: "By the mark seven."

MARK:
Term used to identify specific type of weapon or equipment always
followed by a number to indicate the specific equipment and frequently
followed by a MOD number to indicate variety of equipment, e.g.
Torpedo, MARK 46, MOD 1.

Marker ship:
In an amphibious operation, a ship which takes accurate station on
a designated control point. It may fly identifying flags by day and
show lights to seaward by night. (NATO term is marker vessel.)

Marline:
Tarred cord; small stuff.

Marlinspike:
Tapered steel tool for separating strands of rope or wire in splicing.
See *Fid.*

Marlinspike seamanship:
Skill with rope, line and related gear topside.

Marry:
To join, as an LST is married to a pontoon causeway, or two lengths of line are married.

Martinet:
A very strict officer who goes by the rule book and never permits any deviation. Not necessarily always harsh, "He's a martinet, but he's fair." Similar to a *Sundowner* but in lesser degree.

Mary Anne:
Floating crane used to salvage aircraft in the water.

Maser:
Microwave amplification by stimulated emission of radiation.

Maskee or moskee:
Slang: expression of Asiatic origin, meaning, "O.K." or "all right."

Mast, captain's:
Actually a sort of court held in a designated place at which the commanding officer awards punishment, listens to requests *(Request mast),* or commends men for special services *(Meritorious or commendatory mast).* Derived from the old practice of actually holding this court publicly at the mizzenmast, which, in a three-masted ship, separated officers quarters from those of the crew. Such terms as "before the mast" also relate to the significance of the mizzenmast.

Master-at-arms (MAA):
Ship's police, headed by a chief MAA. There may be special MAA such as the one in charge of the mess decks. In the old Navy the chief MAA had custody of the ship's hand weapons and trained the crew in their use.

Masthead:
Highest point of a mast that a person can reach. Does not include staffs, poles, etc., which might project above that point. Traditionally, a midshipman might be "mastheaded" for training or discipline. See *Top.*

Masthead light:
White 20-point light required by *Rules of the Road* to be carried on the foremast of a ship.

MATADOR:
Model designation: MGM-1; cognizant service: Air Force. Surface-to-surface missile.

Material condition:
State of damage control security within a ship. Designated X, Y, Z. depending on number and type of closures made.

Material history:
Loose-leaf card system for keeping a record of ship's machinery and hull.

Material Improvement Plan (MIP):
Annual compilation establishing priority order for budgeting and accomplishment of class improvement items in ships.

Material Inspection (MI):
Conducted by the Board of Inspection and Survey, in order to identify funding responsibility for deficiencies on ships which do not receive final acceptance prior to expiration of shipbuilding contract. Also conducted to determine material readiness of ship at other times.

MAVERICK:
Model designation: ZAGM-65A; cognizant serivce: Air Force.
An electro-optical homing, tactical air-to-surface missile.
Design details classified.

Mayday:
International distress signal, voice radio.

Meaconing:
System of receiving enemy beacon signals and rebroadcasting them to confuse enemy navigation.

Meal break or pennant:
Echo flag hoisted from port yardarm of a naval vessel at anchor when the crew is at mess. Significance is that only routine honors may be expected at such times. Also called *Bean rag or Chow rag.*

Mean depth of the sea:
Depth above and below which half of the earth's submerged surface lies, usually considered to be 3800 meters.

Mean Higher High Water (MHHW):
Average height of higher high waters.

Mean high springs:
The average height of the high waters at *syzygy.*

Mean High Water (MHW):
The average height of high waters.

Mean High Water Neaps (MHWN):
The average height of high water calculated at the first and last quarters of the moon.

Mean Lower Low Water (MLLW):
The average height of lower low water.

Mean low water (MLW):
The average height of all low waters at a given place. The tidal datum used for most charts.

Mean Low Water Neaps (MLWN):
The average height of low water at the first and last quarters of the moon.

Mean range:
The average difference between mean high and mean low water.

Mean river level:
The average height of the surface of a river at a given point for all tide stages. Calculation is usually based on hourly readings with unusual variations excluded.

Mean Sea Level (MSL):
Surface level determined by averaging all stages of the tide.

Mean sounding velocity:
Average velocity of sound through a vertical column of water based
on velocities in different sections of the column.

Mean sphere depth:
The uniform depth to which water would cover the earth if the solid
surface were leveled, generally thought to be 2440 meters.

Mean Tide Level:
The average of the high waters and the low waters.

Mean Water Level (MWL):
The mean surface level determined by averaging the height of water
at equal time intervals over a long period.

Measure black, blue, green, white:
Lighting conditions used for night landings on carriers.

Measured mile:
An exact nautical mile delineated by beacons or markers ashore used
in calibrating pit logs and propeller shaft revolutions per mile.

Meatball:
Battle Efficiency Pennant.

Meathead:
Slang: an uncouth and stupid person.

Mechanic (CM):
Petty officer who overhauls and repairs heavy construction machinery.

MECHANICAL MULE:
A 1/2-ton carrier, designated the M-274, for light infantry weapons
and cargo.

Mechano decking:
Portable aluminum decking for a tanker.

Meet her:
An order to the steersman to apply opposite rudder in order to check
or stop ship from swinging.

Mend clothes:
An ancient order in the British Navy signifying that there were to
be no drills or exercises and that the crew was free to carry out
any desired or personally needed activity. Admiral David Beatty's
famous signal to the Grand Fleet at Scapa Flow at the end of World
War I ended with this order.

MENTOR:
Model designation: T-34; cognizant service: Navy/Air Force.
Primary basic-training aircraft. Two-crew. Propeller-driven.

Merchant ship broadcast system (MerCast):
System providing communication with merchant ship under Government
lease or charter.

Mercator chart:
Most commonly used chart for marine navigation. Mathematically compiled but often illustrated as a projection from the center of the earth onto a cylinder tangent to the earth.

Merchant Ship Report (MEREP):
Daily report indicating total number of merchant ships arriving or departing a specified port.

MEREP:
Merchant ship arrival and departure summary.

Meridians:
Great circles of the earth that pass through the poles. Used for measuring longitude.

MESCALERO:
Model designation: T-41; cognizant service: Army/Air Force. A conventional high-wing aircraft with dual controls, dual brakes, a rear window to improve visibility, and patented spring steel landing gear. Two-crew. Propeller-driven.

Mess:
To eat. A group of people eating together. Crew's mess is called the general mess.

Message:
Any thought briefly expressed in plain or secret language in a form suitable for rapid transmission.

Messboy:
Old term for stewardsman and never used today.

Messcook:
Old term for *Messman.*

Messenger:
Light line used to carry across a larger line or hawser. Man who carries messages for officer of the deck (watch).

Messenger Buoy:
See *Buoy.*

Messenger mail:
See *Guard Mail.*

Mess gear:
Knives, forks, spoons, etc. Also, the word passed before meals to clear the messing spaces.

Messman:
An enlisted person detailed to serve food to the crew. Slang: bean jockey.

Mess treasurer:
Person who administers finances of any mess.

Metacenter:
 The mathematically computed instantaneous center of the arc generated by the center of buoyancy as it changes when the ship rolls is called the transverse metacenter. That generated when the ship pitches is called the longitudinal metacenter. Location of the appropriate metacenter with regard to the ship's center of gravity is a measure of her stability against roll or pitch. For surface ships, the transverse metacenter is the only one of concern, unless there has been serious damage adversely affecting the longitudinal metacenter. For a submerged submarine the entire calculation is different because the center of buoyancy cannot shift, no matter what the ship's attitude. See *Metacentric height.*

Metacentric height:
 Distance between the metacenter and the center of gravity of a ship: a measure of stability. See *Metacenter.*

Metalsmith (ME):
 Petty officer who works in metal including welding, soldering, and metal shaping.

Microseismograph:
 Instrument for detecting distant storms by minute movements in earth's crust.

Mid-channel buoy:
 A buoy placed in the middle of a channel, to be passed on either side. In the U.S. waters it has black and white stripes.

Mid-ocean ridge:
 A great median arch or sea-bottom swell extending the length of an ocean basin and roughly paralleling the continental margins. The Atlantic mid-ocean ridge is a most prominent example.

Midshipman:
 A student officer, enrolled at the U.S. Naval Academy or at a civilian university under the NROTC program who is commissioned as a Naval or Marine officer upon graduation. Unlike a cadet, he wears gold braid and has a legal status between CPO and Warrant Officer. Acceptable slang: "Mid"; "Middie" is term of derision.

Midwatch:
 The watch from midnight to 4 AM (0000 to 0400).

MIGHTY MOUSE:
 A 2.75" air-to-ground rocket.

Mike:
 Phonetic word for the letter M.

Mil:
 Unit of angular measurement defined by the Navy as the angle whose tangent is 1/1000 of the radius and equivalent to 3.44 minutes of arc. The Army defines the mil as 1/6400 part of the circumference of a circle. The Navy mil is 0.065 minutes greater than the Army mil.

Mile, nautical:
 A minute of arc of earths' circumference measured at equator. U.S. nautical mile is 6,080 feet. See *Nautical mile.*

Milestones:
Recognizable points in time at which specific tasks or activities start or end.

Military:
Marine Corps slang for anything tough or uncomfortable.

Military Inspection:
Appraisal of a command or activity in terms of ability to carry out mission.

Military Occupational Specialty (MOS):
Numerical system used by the Marine Corps and Army to identify special skills of an individual.

Military Sealift Command:
Ocean freight and passenger service, operated by the Navy for the Department of Defense. Includes specially equipped ships for support of ocean, missile, and space research. Formerly known as Military Sea Transportation Service, MSTS.

Military Sea Transportation Service (MSTS):
See *Military Sealift Command*.

Military Specifications:
Used primarily in procurement to provide clear, accurate descriptions of technical requirements.

Military Standard:
Document setting engineering and technical limitations to assure uniformity in materials and products.

Mind your rudder:
Admonition to the steersman to steer a proper course.

Mine:
An explosive charge, submerged and designed to explode against a ship. Automatic mines are self-actuating; controlled mines are fired from afar. Mines may be ground, moored, or drifting. Firing may be acoustic, contact, influence, or pressure. Sometimes called sea mines to distinguish from land mines, which are usually antipersonnel mines.

Mine Countermeasures:
The branch of naval warfare which embraces all methods, procedures and techniques for preventing or reducing damage to ships from mines. It includes: *Channel Conditioning, Clearance, Disposal, Hunting, Locating, Sweeping,* and *Watching.*

Minefields:
Minefields are classed according to their location. Defensive minefields are planted in one's own or in friendly waters. Offensive fields are classed as: Attrition, Countered, Nuisance, Strategic, Sustained Attrition, and Transitory Attrition.

Mineman (MN):
Petty officer who performs upkeep and repair of mines and ASW ordnance.

Mine sterilizer:
Device to make a mine harmless after a pre-set number of days.

Minesweeping:
  Procedure of removing or destroying mines to permit safe passage
  of friendly ships.

Minesweeping boat (MSB):
  Specially constructed boat used for sweeping mines.

Mine tracks:
  Tracks fitted on the deck of a minelayer to permit mines to be dropped
  over the stern.

Mine vessels:
  Those designed to plant or sweep mines. Principal types are:
  Minelayer; Destroyer Minelayer; Minesweeper; and Destroyer
  Minesweeper.

Mine winch:
  Winch aft on a minelayer for actuating the *Bogie wire.*

MINIBUOY:
  AN/SQQ-46 air drop sonobuoy.

Minimize:
  A condition wherein normal high speed communications are drastically
  reduced so that actual or simulated emergency messages will not be
  delayed.

Mining effect:
  Destructive effect of an explosion under water.

Minute-guns:
  Saluting guns fired at intervals of a minute as a sign of mourning
  in military funerals for officers and officials entitled to gun
  salutes.

MINUTEMAN:
  Model designation: LGM-30; cognizant service: Air Force.
  Silo-launched solid-propellant inertial-guided intercontinental
  ballistic missile (ICBM).

Misfire:
  Propellant charge that fails to fire when the trigger has been pulled.

Missile designation system:
  See Appendix D.

Missile technician:
  A petty officer who tests, fires, and maintains guided missiles.

Mission:
  The objective or purpose usually stated in general terms.

Mission, call:
  Type of air support operation in which a specific request is made
  for an attack against a target.

Mizzenmast:
  The third mast of a ship with three or more masts, except when the
  vessel has only two masts and the first is much taller than the
  second, as in *Yawls* and *Ketches.* See *Foremast.*

Mizzentop:
Top in the mizzenmast. See *Top, Maintop, Foretop, Masthead.*

MO:
Radio signal--a series of dashes sent from a scene of action or
emergency for aircraft or ships to home on.

Mobile Noise Barge (MONOB):
A ship especially instrumented for recording noise emanations.

Mock-up:
Model or replica, sometimes life-sized, of a machine or device, used
for planning, design, instruction, or training purposes.

Model basin:
Large tank or basin for testing new ships in the form of models.

Moderate speed:
Speed required by the *Rules of the Road* to be made in a fog, at
which a vessel can stop in half the distance of visibility.

Modification number (MOD):
Part of equipment identification, always follows *Mark Number.*

MOHAWK:
Model designation: OV-1; cognizant service: Army.
Surveillance aircraft with visual and photographic observation
capabilities. Two-crew. Prop-jet.

MOJAVE:
Model designation: CH-37; cognizant service: Navy/Air Force.
All-metal helicopter having a single rotor with five blades. Engines
are mounted in nacelles at ends of high stub wings. Three-crew, 23-passengers.

Molder (ML):
Petty officer who constructs molds for metal castings.

Mole:
A large solid-fill nearshore structure of earth, masonry or large
stone, used as a breakwater or a pier.

Monkey drill:
Slang: physical drill, usually setting-up exercises.

Monkey fist:
Weighted knot in the end of a *Heaving line.*

Moor:
To secure a ship alongside a pier. To secure to a *Mooring buoy.*
To anchor with two anchors and a *Mooring swivel.* To make a
regular moor, the ship drops the upstream anchor first, then backs
down and drops the second. Then the second anchor chain is paid out
while the first is *hove* in--until the ship is centered between
the two, for insertion of the mooring swivel. In a *Flying moor*
the ship drops the downstream anchor first as she approaches her
anchorage, pays out the chain as she steers for the spot to drop
the upstream anchor, then veers the upstream chain and heaves in
on the first one dropped until centered. The most spectacular
maneuver of all is a flying moor upon entering harbor on a strong
flood tide. See *Mooring swivel.*

Mooring:
>Securing a ship to a pier or wharf or to a mooring buoy. Anchoring
>with two anchors connected to a single chain by means of a mooring swivel.

Mooring buoy:
>A heavy round buoy anchored with several extremely heavy and strong anchors, usually
>concrete blocks known as sinkers, and fitted with a swivel and link in the center of the
>buoy's top surface. Mooring buoys are numbered and marked on harbor charts, and of
>course are always in the center of their *Berths*. To moor to a buoy, the ship first
>unshackles the anchor, then leads the chain, with shackle, to the mooring link on the
>buoy. The process of mooring is complete when the chain is properly shackled to the
>buoy, and the stoppers put on it on deck in the usual manner. When mooring to a buoy,
>of course, much less chain is used, and the ship's swing around the buoy is much
>smaller in radius than it would be to a single anchor.

Mooring line:
>Line used to secure a ship to a pier.

Mooring swivel:
>A huge swivel fitted into the *Ground tackle* to restrict the ship's
>swing in her berth by using two anchors some distance apart, generally
>one upstream and one downstream so that as the current shifts from
>ebb to flood the ship will alternately ride to each. Anchor chains
>are usually fitted with regular swivels, inserted in the chain near
>the anchor to prevent kinks in the chain as the ship swings to the
>current. The mooring swivel differs from these in that it has two
>links to which an anchor chain can be attached instead of only one.
>After the two anchors are down, their chains are broken and both
>shackled to the swivel; then a single chain is led from the other
>end of the swivel through one of the hawse pipes and stoppered on
>deck in the usual manner. See *Moor* and *Flying moor.*

Morning call book:
>See *Call book.*

Morning-order book:
>Book in which executive officer writes his instructions for the next
>morning's ship work. See *Plan of the Day.*

Morning orders:
>Published schedule of activities for the day aboard ship. A part of
>*Plan of the Day.*

Morning watch:
>The watch from 0400 (4 AM) to 0800 (8AM).

Morse code:
>Code of dots and dashes used in radio and visual signaling.

Mosaic:
>An assembly of overlapping aerial photographs used as intelligence.
>A controlled mosaic is rectified to fit known reference points.

Mothball fleet:
>Slang: ships out of commission, but maintained in good condition.
>Same as *Reserve Fleet.*

Motor launch:
   Large, sturdily built powerboat used for liberty parties and
   heavy workloads.

Motor torpedo boat:
   A small (100'), high-speed (60 knots) boat armed with torpedoes
   and machine guns.

Motor tube:
   The part of a rocket that contains the propellant charge.

Motor whaleboat:
   A small, double-ended, diesel-powered ship's boat, sometimes called
   the *Life boat* if held ready for quick lowering.

Mount:
   To assemble, organize, and prepare for embarkation a unit of Army
   or Marine Corps troops.

Mount (gun):
   System of gun-supporting parts, elevating and training mechanisms,
   and recoil and counter-recoil equipment.

Mounting:
   All preparations made to load personnel and material for an amphibious
   operation.

Mounting area:
   A general locality where forces of an amphibious expedition are assembled,
   trained, and loaded.

Mourning badge:
   Three-inch band of black crepe worn on left arm by officers when
   prescribed as a mark of mourning.

Mousetrap:
   Ahead-thrown ASW weapon used on small ships.

Mousing:
   Small line strung across a hook to prevent a sling from slipping off.

Movement Report Center or Office (MRC, MRO):
   Both are part of the movement report system which accounts for all
   ship and command movements.

Movement Report System:
   System established to collect and make available to certain commands
   information on the status, location, and movement of flag commands,
   commissioned fleet units, and ships under operational control of the
   Navy.

Movement, ship-to-shore:
   Act of debarking troops and their equipment from assault shipping
   via assault craft and vehicles to the assigned landing area.

Moving Havens:
   Restricted areas established to provide a measure of security to
   submarines and surface ships in transit through areas in which the
   existing attack restrictions would be inadequate to prevent attack
   by friendly forces.

Moving Submarine Haven:
   A moving submarine haven is established by Submarine Notices, extending
   50 miles ahead, 100 miles behind, and 15 miles on each side of the
   estimated position of the submarine along the stated track, while in
   transit.

Moving Surface Ship Haven:
   Established by Surface Ship Notices: normally a circle with a specified
   radius centered on the estimated position of the ship or the guide of a group
   of ships.

Moving Target Indicator (MTI):
   A device that enables a moving target to be distinguised on a radar
   scope.

Mud drum:
   See *Drum,* water.

Mushroom anchor:
   A large anchor having the general shape of a mushroom, used on light-
   ships and modern submarines.

Musician (MU):
   Petty officer who plays musical instruments, conducts, or arranges
   music.

Mustang:
   Slang: Officer who was formerly an enlisted man.

Muster:
   Roll call.

Muster on stations:
   Roll call taken aboard ship while the men are at work or drill.

Muster out:
   Discharge or release from active duty.

Mutiny:
   Rebellion against constituted authority aboard ship, a crime that,
   when committed at sea in a civilian ship, comes under the jurisdiction
   of the Coast Guard.

Muzzle bag:
   Canvas cover fitted over the muzzle of a gun to shield the bore from
   water.

N

Nadir:
   That point on the celestial sphere vertically below the observer,
   or 180 degrees from the zenith.

Nancy:
   A system of visual communications using a special light visible only
   by means of special equipment.

Nansen bottle:
   Oceanographic water-sampling bottle.

Napalm:
   A powder used to thicken gasoline for use in flame throwers and
   incendiary bombs.

NASTY:
   Class name given to group of Norwegian-produced high-speed patrol
   boats used in the Vietnam War. Derived from the building firm
   name: Naste.

National Agency Check (NAC):
   Cursory review of individual's background usually restricted to
   search of police and security records for derogatory material.

Nautical mile:
   Length of one minute of arc of a great circle of the earth; 6080
   feet compared to 5280 feet of a statute mile. The USA and UK standard
   is 6080 feet, most other maritime countries use 6076 feet.

Naval activity:
   Unit of the *Naval Establishment* established under an officer in
   command or in charge.

Naval Air Base:
   Collective term comprising all Naval and some Marine aviation shore
   facilities in each *Naval District.*

Naval Air Facility (NAF):
   Provides operating aid in some cases and maintenance facilities to
   meet special requirements.

Naval Air Station (NAS):
   Provides operating, testing, overhaul training, and personnel facilities
   for naval aviation.

Naval alteration (NAVALT):
   Specific alteration affecting the military characteristics of a ship.

Naval attache:
   A naval officer on duty at an embassy abroad, whose major tasks are
   advising and representing his ambassador on naval matters and coll-
   ecting intelligence. Abbreviated *ALUSNA.*

Naval Auxiliary Air Station:
> Provides facilities similar to an air station but less extensive.
> Requires logistic support from its parent *NAS.*

Naval Barracks:
> An activity to house, clothe, pay and administer nontransient en-
> listed personnel.

Naval Base:
> A shore command in a given locality which includes and integrates all
> naval shore activities in the assigned area.

Naval Beach Group:
> Permanently organized naval command, within an amphibious force,
> comprised of a commander, his staff, a beachmaster unit, an amphibious
> construction battalion, and boat unit.

Naval campaign:
> An operation conducted essentially by naval forces for the purpose
> of gaining control of the sea.

Naval Communications System (INCS):
> The world-wide network of transmitting and receiving stations providing
> service to the Navy ashore and afloat.

Naval Control of Shipping Officer:
> When assigned, officer who controls and coordinates the routing and
> movements of merchant convoys and independently-sailed merchant
> ships subject to the directives of the operational control authority.

Naval Control of Shipping Organization:
> Organization within the Navy which carries out specific responsibilities
> to provide for the control and protection of movements of merchant
> ships in time of war.

Naval Establishment:
> Unofficial term for the entire Navy, consisting of Operating Forces,
> the *Navy Department,* and the *Shore Establishment.* See *Navy Department.*

Naval gunfire team:
> Men organized to control and direct naval gunfire from the shore.

Naval landing party:
> Part of ship's complement organized for military operations
> ashore. Formerly called the landing force.

Naval Material Command:
> Activated May 1966, successor to the Naval Material Support
> Establishment. Command includes six functional commands:
> Air Systems, Ship Systems, Electronic Systems, Ordnance Systems,
> Supply Systems and Facilities Engineering. Commander, Naval Material
> Command reports directly to CNO.

Naval mission:
> Group of officers and men who assist a friendly foreign power in the
> administration of its navy.

Naval Oceanographic Office (NavOceanO):
> The office of the Navy that produces navigational charts and publications.

Naval Ordnance Laboratory (NOL):
   Test and research facility for naval weapons, located at White Oak, Maryland.

Naval Ordnance Plant (NOP):
   Navy owned and operated industrial plant for production of weapons.

Naval Port Control Office:
   An authority that coordinates logistic support and harbor services
   for any services for any ships under naval control.

Naval Research Advisory Committee (NRAC):
   Advisory committee of private civilians reporting to the Secretary
   of the Navy to provide advice on all research matters to SecNav.

Naval Research Requirement (NRR):
   Prepared by the Chief of Naval research to start basic and applied
   research in support of future needs.

Naval Reserve:
   A force of qualified officers and men available, in an emergency,
   to meet the needs of an expanding Navy while an adequate flow of
   new personnel is being established. Component parts are Fleet, Organized Volunteer, and Merchant Marine Reserves.

Naval Ship Maintenance Facility:
   See *Reserve fleet.*

Naval Ship Research and Development Center (NSRDC):
   Activity formed in 1967 from integration of David Taylor Model Basin,
   Carderock, Maryland and Marine Engineering Laboratory, Annapolis,
   Maryland into single command.

Naval shipyard:
   An industrial activity charged with building, repairs, alterations,
   overhauling, docking, converting, or outfitting of ships, together
   with necessary replenishment.

Naval station:
   Naval shore *Activity,* having fixed boundaries and a commanding officer.

Naval stores:
   Oil, paint, turpentine, pitch, and other such items traditionally
   used mainly for ships.

Navigable waters:
   Waters that can actually be used for passage of ships.

Navigation:
   The art and science of conducting a ship or aircraft from one position
   to another.

Navigational light:
   A light with rigidly described characteristics, marked on charts
   so that passing navigators can use it to fix their positions. May be
   in a *Lightship* but most frequently mounted in a lighthouse. Among
   the given characteristics are height above sea level, arc of visibility,
   color, period of repetition, etc. Known as Alternating--showing
   color variations; Fixed—a steady light; Flashing—off more than it
   is on; Occulting—on more than it is off; Group flashing—flashing in
   groups of two or more flashes followed by a period of darkness.

Navigation Head:
>A transshipment point on a waterway where loads are transferred between
>water carriers and land carriers. A navigation head is similar in
>function to a railhead or truckhead.

Navigation, pressure pattern:
>The selection and control of a flight path or track for aircraft by
>considering the atmospheric pressure pattern in order to take advantage
>of the most favorable wind conditions.

Navigator:
>Officer who is head of the Navigation Department, responsible for
>the safe navigation of the ship.

NAVIGATOR:
>Model designation: RC-45J, UC-45J; cognizant service: Navy.
>A two-engine Beechcraft. Used as a small utility transport and for
>maintenance of flight proficiency. Two-crew, four-passengers.

NAVION:
>Model designation: U-18; cognizant service: Air Force.
>Four-place, low-wing monoplane with tricycle landing gear. Aircraft
>returned to Air Force inventory and used by AF Aero clubs. Propeller-driven.

Navol:
>Solution of hydrogen peroxide in water, used as a fuel in MK. 16 torpedo.

Navy Capabilities Plan (NCP):
>This plan with its annex, the Navy Logistic Capabilities Plan, supports
>the Joint Strategis Capabilities Plan and covers the short-range period.

Navy contract symbol (NO):
>Followed by lower case letter indicating bureau or office concerned—
>NOy, BuDocks.

Navy Department:
>The executive part of the Navy located in Washington, D.C. Differs
>from *Department of the Navy* in that by long usage it refers only
>to the administrative offices at the seat of government. See *Naval
>Establishment.*

Navy Enlisted Scientific Education Program (NESEP):
>A four-year scholarship for enlisted men designed to educate and retain
>certain selected men, particularly technical specialists, for a full
>career as officers in the Navy.

Navy Exchange:
>Stores for naval personnel that sell at small profit for welfare and
>recreation fund.

Navy Industrial Fund (NIF):
>Working capital fund for industrial activities which is replenished
>by billings to activities for which work is performed.

Navy League of U.S.:
>A national organization that believes in and works for a strong Navy;
>headquarters, Washington, D.C. Completely independent of the Navy;
>active duty officers may not belong to it.

Navy Long-Range Strategic Study (NLRSS):
> An appraisal of the strategic environment for from eight through twenty years hence with consideration given to scientific and technological factors likely to affect naval warfare.

Navy Mid-Range Objectives (NMRO):
> Provides mid-range force structure goals (10 to 11 years) based on the NMS, NLRRS, etc. Considers alternate force goals in relation to threats and assesses risks involved in each case to serve as a base for PO and JSOP submissions based on a balanced force goal.

Navy Mid-Range Study (NMS):
> Provides internal planning guidance for the portion of the mid-range period between five and ten years hence.

Navy navigation satellite system (NAVSAT):
> Navigational system using the Doppler shift from signals transmitted by the satellite to establish position.

Navy Objectives Plan (NOP):
> Covers strategic concepts and objectives during the next ten years.

Navy Oceanographic and Meteorological Automatic Device (NOMAD):
> A 20- by 10-foot platform moored at sea to monitor and report weather and oceanographic data automatically.

Navy Procurement Directives:
> Navy implementation of Armed Services Procurement Regulations establishing uniform procurement policies within the Department.

Navy Program Objectives (PO):
> Contains annual increments of the Navy and Marine Corps force levels required for orderly progress towards objectives in the Navy Mid-Range Objectives.

Navy Relief Society:
> The quasi-official relief agency operated for the benefit of Naval personnel and their dependents.

Navy Standard Requisitioning and Issue Procedure (NAVSTRIP):
> Mandatory procedures for requisitioning supplies from Army, Navy, Air Force, DSA or GSA. Applies to Marine Corps when ordering from the Navy Supply System. Known as MILSTRIP when inter-service requisitioning is involved.

Navy Tactical Data System (NTDS):
> Computerized system for assembly and evaluation of all available tactical information, including friendly and enemy ships and aircraft, which offers this information for study by tactical commander and also offers possible solutions to the situation.

Navy Technical Data Office (NTDO):
> An element of the Office of the Chief of Naval Material responsible for implementing, reviewing and monitoring policies for handling technical data and keeping the ADL.

Navy Unit Commendation (NUC):
> An honor accorded a naval unit for distinguishing itself in combat or other operations, of lesser degree than *Presidential Unit Citation.*

Neap Range:
    Average diurnal range of tide occurring during the first and fourth quarter points of the moon.

Neap Tides:
    Tides of decreased range occurring at the first and fourth quarter points of the moon.

Nearshore Currents:
    Currents adjacent to coastal areas.

Nearshore Water:
    Same as *Inshore water.*

Need-to-Know:
    Requirement, in addition to security clearance, that disclosure of classification to an individual or contractor is necessary for the proper performance of his work.

Negative:
    In any naval message means: no; not granted; do not concur; not approved; etc.

Negotiated Contract:
    Contract obtained by direct negotiation without formal advertising but after the solicitation of price quotations from qualified sources.

Nekton:
    Oceanic life forms capable of spontaneous swimming.

Neptune:
    Mythical god of the sea.

NEPTUNE:
    Model designation: P-2; cognizant service: Navy.
    Old reliable workhorse of Navy Antisubmarine patrol squadrons. Famous for dependability, versatility, and extraordinary range. Underwent many successive modifications, adding bigger engines and jet pods for high-speed attack. The "Truculent Turtle" of this class held the distance nonstop record for years, from Australia to the United States. Nine-crew, propeller-driven, jet pods.

Nest:
    Two or more ships moored together, side by side. Also, a boat stowage on board ship in which one boat is placed inside, or partially inside, another.

Net:
    A group of connected radio stations. A steel mesh to protect ships and harbors from torpedoes, submarines, and surface craft.

Net-laying ship:
    Ship designed for laying and tending submarine or anti-torpedo nets.

Nets and booms:
    Combination of underwater steel mesh nets and surface floating booms for harbor defense against submarines, torpedoes, and small surface craft.

Netting:
    Same as *Snaking.*

Niggerhead:
An obsolete term for a *Gipsy* or *Warping head*. See *Capstan*.

NIGHTINGALE:
Model designation: C-9; cognizant service: Air Force.
A medium-size transport aircraft for domestic and intratheater
aeromedical evacuation. Commercial model is DC-9. Jet.

Night order book:
Official ship's record in which the commanding officer writes his
orders to the officers of the deck for the night's activities. The
engineer of a ship uses a similar book to leave directives for the
engineer officers of the watch.

Night stick:
A short wooden club carried by men on shore patrol duty.

Night vision:
Faculty of seeing well at night. See *Dark Adaptation*.

NIKE AJAX:
Model designation: MIM-3; cognizant service: Army.
High altitude ground-to-air defensive missile.

NIKE HERCULES:
Model designation: MIM-14A; cognizant service: Army.
A high-altitude missile, with a primary ground-to-air mission and a
secondary surface-to-surface mission, designated to function as a
defense against aerial attack.

NIKE ZEUS:
Model designation: XLIM-49A; cognizant service: Army.
A three-stage solid propellant, command-guidance antimissile missile.
Designed to intercept and destroy hostile ballistic-missile war-heads.

Nip:
Sharp bend or turn in a line or wire. See *Freshen the nip*.

Nipple:
Short connector; a short length of tubing in a boiler.

No-bottom:
A notation appearing on nautical charts indicating that the sounding
did not reach bottom. Also, a *Leadsman's* report: "no bottom," meaning
the same.

NOL:
Naval Ordnance Laboratory, White Oak, Md.

Nonjudicial punishment:
Punishment by a commanding officer upon men and officers, imposed
without trial by court-martial. Specified and limited by the Uniform
Code of Military Justice.

Nonmilitary Vessel Categories:
Nonmilitary vessels entering a controlled port are given one of four
classifications for purpose of determining examination procedures,
they are: Hostile, Clean, Doubtful, and Suspect.

North Atlantic Current:
>   Current formed in Grand Banks area by junction of Gulf Stream and
>   Labrador Current. Flows eastward toward Europe.

Notal:
>   Not to all (nor needed), a term used in messages.

Nothing to the right (left):
>   An order to the steersman not to steer to the right (left) of the
>   given course.

Notice:
>   A specially numbered announcement or one-time directive. Not permanent.
>   Also, Notice for getting underway; required materiel and personnel
>   condition of readiness (e.g. "four hours' notice").

Notice (for getting underway):
>   Time in hours for readiness to get underway to be maintained.

Notice to airmen (NOTAM):
>   Information, issued periodically, concerning any facility or aid
>   relating to air navigation.

Notice to mariners:
>   A publication giving latest changes to navigational charts and
>   other aids.

Not-under-command:
>   Said of a ship when disabled and uncontrollable.

Now do you hear there:
>   Traditional preface to the *Word* when passed by the boatswain's
>   mate throughout the ship. Usually shortened to "now hear there (this)."

No wind position:
>   Last well-determined position of an aircraft advanced along the
>   *Heading* for the true *Air Speed*.

No-year appropriation:
>   Appropriation available for incurring obligations for an indefinite period.

Nonrated man:
>   Enlisted man in the first three paygrades who is not a petty officer.

Notional ship:
>   An imaginary, arbitrary ship used in naval logistic planning.

NOTSNIKS:
>   Former designation of probe now called *HI-HOE.*

November:
>   Phonetic word for letter N.

Nuclear Explosion Warning and Radiological Data System (NEWRADS):
>   Program to provide fleet commander with information on Radiological
>   hazards which might affect operations.

Nuclear powered Guided Missile Cruiser:
The first nuclear surface ship, USS LONG BEACH, first and only
cruiser built since World War II, and only missile cruiser so built from
the keel up. Main battery consists of *TALOS, TERRIER,* and *ASROC*
launchers. No guns in original design, but two five-inch mounts have
been added since construction. Primary function is as part of nuclear
task force built around CVAN.

Nuclear Yields:
Energy released in the detonation of a nuclear weapon, measured in
terms of the kilotons or megatons of trinitrotoluene (TNT) required
to produce the same energy release.

Very low . . . . less than 1 kiloton
Low . . . . 1 kiloton to 10 kilotons
Medium . . . . over 10 kilotons to 50 kilotons
High . . . . over 50 kilotons to 500 kilotons
Very high . . . . over 500 kilotons

Nuisance minefield:
A minefield containing too few mines to interdict traffic effectively.

Null:
A symbol in cryptography having no plain text significance. Also the
least signal where intensity varies with orientation of antenna.

Number:
See *File, Signal, Service.*

Numbered document:
See *Registered Matter.*

Number in Grade:
Precedence number assigned Marine Corps officers annually, corresponding
to lineal number, of naval officer.

Nun buoy:
Cone-shaped buoy used to mark channels; it is anchored on the right
side of the channel, as seen from a ship entering the harbor from
seaward, and is painted red. See *Red, right, returning.*

O

Oakum:
A caulking material made of old, tarred, hemp rope fiber.

Oarlock:
Device to hold oars when pulling a boat; also called rowlock.

Objective area:
Geographically defined area around the assault beaches of an amphibious operation in which Commander Attack Force directs the operation of all ships and aircraft.

Ocean Shipping Procedures (OSPRO):
A joint manual for merchant shipping control during wartime.

Occulting light:
A navigational aid in which the period of light is equal to or more than the period of darkness. See *Flashing Light.*

Octant:
See *Sextant.*

Office:
Slang: cockpit of a large airplane.

Office hours:
Marine term for *Mast.*

Office of Naval Material Command (ONM):
Since December 1963, the staff of the Chief of Naval Material concerned with supporting CNM in his role as commander of the Naval Material Support Establishment. Now more properly referred to as the Office of the Chief of Naval Material.

Officer Candidate:
Enlisted person under instruction at Officer Candidate School.

Officer conducting the exercise (OCE):
A senior officer who plans and directs the exercise without necessarily having tactical command of the forces involved.

Officer in charge (O-in-C):
Generic term describing those officers not "commanding officers" who have responsibility of directing special units or activities.

Officer in tactical command (OTC):
The senior officer present or one who has been designated by him or by a common senior to exercise tactical control.

Officer of the deck (OOD):
An officer on duty in charge of the ship representing the commanding officer. His assistant is the Junior Officer of the Watch (JOOW) or Junior Officer of the Deck (JOOD). Officer on watch under instruction is the Assistant Officer of the Watch.

Officer of the Watch (OOW):
Officer on duty in the engineering spaces.

Officer's call:
A bugle call (or word passed) for officers to take their stations.

Officer service record:
Record of the nature of the duties that an officer performs. Includes his periodic evaluation by seniors in form of fitness reports, any awards, commandations, or record of punishment or censure.

Official visit:
A formal visit of courtesy requiring special honors and ceremonies. See *Call.*

Offshore:
The region seaward of a specified depth, usually the three or five-fathom isobath.

Offshore Currents:
Nontidal currents outside the surf zone independent of shoaling or river discharge influence.

Offshore Water:
Water adjacent to land whose physical properties are only slightly influenced by continental conditions.

Offshore Winds:
Winds blowing from the land seaward.

Ogive:
The forward, curved section of a projectile.

Oil canning:
The snapping in and out of the hull plating of a ship in heavy seas.

Oiler (AO):
A tanker specially configured to replenish combatant ships of all types underway at sea. Heavily outfitted with booms and hoses rigged and ready.

Oil flat:
An oil-carrying, single-screw yard craft.

Oil King:
Petty officer aboard ship who keeps fuel oil records.

Oilskins:
Waterproof clothing.

Old-fashioned anchor:
The traditional "hook" anchor. Fitted with a stock--the axis of which was at right angles to the plane of the *Flukes,* and also at right angles to the axis of the *Shank* of the anchor. When the ship tugged at her anchor, the action of the chain was to drag the stock flat upon the bottom, and this caused the flukes to stand upright with the maximum "bite" into the ground. The *Stockless anchor* accomplished the same thing by a type of hinge built into the flukes.

Old Man:
Slang: the commanding officer of any activity. The corresponding expression for an admiral is old gentleman.

OMEGA:
A highly accurate, air, sub-surface or surface VLF world-wide navigation system using phase differences for positioning.

Omnidirection range (ODR):
A navigation system for aircraft based on radio beacons which provide true headings.

One-time code:
One that is destroyed after first use.

Onshore Winds:
Winds blowing from the sea to the land.

On soundings:
Said of a ship that is near enough to land so that soundings with a lead can be taken. Sometimes considered to be within the 100-fathom curve.

On the bow:
Said of an object somewhere ahead on one bow or the other. Stated more specifically, e.g., on the port bow. The expression "broad on the port bow" means that the object is 45° on the port bow or relative bearing 315°.

On the double:
Quickly; with speed; as: "Man your stations on the double."

On the line:
Aircraft that are operational and ready for use are said to be on the line.

On the quarter:
Said of an object somewhere astern but not directly astern. Stated more specifically, as e.g., "on the starboard quarter." "Broad on the starboard quarter" means that the object bears 135° relative.

OP:
Short title for an office or individual within the Office of the Chief of Naval Operations, when so used is always followed by a number or number and letter designation, i.e. OP 50, OP 09D, Also *Ordnance Pamphlet.*

Open purchase:
Purchase of materials in the open market, instead of by requisition through government channels.

Open water:
Water with less than one-tenth ice coverage.

Operating Forces:
Fleet, seagoing, sea frontier, and naval district forces, and such other activities and forces as may be assigned by the President or the Secretary of the Navy.

Operating ratio:
The ratio of the number of hours of operating time to total possible operating time in a given period. Down-time includes scheduled and unscheduled time out of service. Expressed as a percentage.

Operation:
A military action or the carrying out of a training or administrative measure.

Operational:
Pertaining to operations; capable of operating; in contrast to administrative.

Operational Control Authority (OCA):
Naval commander responsible for the movement of ships.

Operations analyses (research, evaluation):
The scientific study of operations to gain greater effectiveness and efficiency for future activities.

Opticalman (OM):
Petty officer who repairs and maintains optical equipment.

Optimum Ship Routing (OSR):
Ship routing technique based on consideration of currents, weather and wave conditions to reduce transit time.

Orbit:
To fly a circular path, as aircraft do about an *Orbit point* or as satellites about the earth.

Orbit point:
Geographically fixed or a moving reference point for stationing aircraft.

Order:
An order directs that a job be done but does not specify how. See *Command.*

Order of Battle:
The identification, strength, command structure and disposition of the personnel, units and equipment of any military force.

Orderly:
Messenger or personal attendant, usually for a senior officer.

Ordinary, in:
Status of a ship not in commission but maintained with a skeleton force. Obsolete term.

Ordinary tides:
Mean tides.

Ordnance:
Collective term for guns, missiles, torpedoes, bombs, and related equipment.

Ordnance Data (OD):
Information of an inspection and test nature on ordnance equipment.

Ordnance engineering duty officer (OEDO):
See *Engineering duty officer.*

Ordnance Pamphlet (OP):
A book covering the description, operation, and maintenance of ordnance equipment.

Ordnance Systems Command:
Functional command replacing Bureau of Naval Weapons in the 1966
Navy Department Reorganization. Component of *Naval Material Command.*

Originator:
The command by whose authority the message is sent.

ORION:
Model designation: P-3; cognizant service: Navy.
An antisubmarine patrol aircraft developed from the commercial Lockheed
"Electra" design. Replaces the *NEPTUNE.* Ten-crew. Prop-jet.

Orlop deck:
Lowest deck of a 4-deck ship. Obsolete term. See *Deck.*

OSAGE:
Model designation: TH-55A; cognizant service: Army.
Training helicopter. One-crew. One-student.

Osborne shackle:
Used in underway replenishment at end of first messenger line. It
carries bight of hose messenger in underway alongside fueling.

Oscar:
Phonetic word for letter O.

Otter:
A device used in minesweeping that keeps sweep wire extended laterally.

OTTER:
Model designation: U-1; cognizant services: Navy/Air Force.
A short-range, high-wing, light-utility aircraft. Has provisions for
operating on wheels, wheel-skis, or floats. Two-crew, eight-passengers.
Propeller-driven.

Outboard:
In the direction away from the center line of the ship.

Outreach:
Horizontal distance from mast or kingpost to end of boom.

Overfalls:
Turbulent water surface caused by strong currents flowing over shoals
or by conflicting currents.

Overhang:
Projection of the ship's bow or stern beyond the stem or sternpost.

Overhaul:
Repair, clean, inspect, adjust. To overtake. Also to separate the
blocks of a tackle. Opposite of *Round In.*

Overhead:
The ceiling of a compartment as viewed from the inside, e.g., "The
overhead needs painting." Also, less common, the roof, as "He is
on the overhead."

Overlap:
> Linear ground distance which is repeated in adjacent photo exposures in aerial photography.

Overlay (chart):
> Transparent sheet to be used with a chart, providing special operational or navigational information such as gunfire support stations, etc.

Over leave:
> *See Absence Without Leave.*

OVERSEER:
> Model designation: MQM-58A; cognizant service: Army.
> Classified missile.

Overt:
> In intelligence work, means open and above board. Opposite of *covert.*

Overtaking vessel:
> One that overhauls another (the overtaken vessel), approaching from more than two points abaft the beam.

Over the hill:
> Slang: To desert is to "go over the hill."

Over the side:
> Over the ship's side; in the water.

Oxygen-breathing apparatus (OBA):
> A device which supplies oxygen to men who must enter closed spaces or compartments.

P

Pack ice:
   Offshore ice moving with wind and current. May be close, open or
   drift and in form of fields, floes, blocks.

Padding:
   Words or phrases unrelated to the text of a message.

Pad eye:
   A metal ring welded to deck or bulkhead.

Padre:
   Slang: *Chaplain.*

Painter:
   A line in the bow of a boat for making fast. The corresponding line
   in the stern is the *Stern fast.* See *Bow Painter, Sea Painter.*

Pallet:
   A portable platform used in handling cargo on fork-lift trucks or slings.
   Palletized cargo is made up to fit the pallets.

Palm and needle:
   Sailor's thimble made of leather, which fits over most of his palm,
   and a large needle; used for sewing heavy canvas or leather.

Pan:
   A piece of ice varying in diameter from a few yards to several hundred
   yards, formed by the action of wind and sea on field ice.

Pancake ice:
   Pieces of newly formed ice, usually between one and six feet in diameter.

Panel:
   A large cloth used by ground personnel for visual signaling. An
   electric switchboard or instrument board.

Pant, panting:
   Series of pulsations caused by minor, recurrent explosions in the fire
   of a ship's boiler. Usually caused by a shortage of air.

Pantry:
   Place where officers' food is prepared for serving; may be wardroom,
   captain's or admiral's pantry.

Papa:
   Phonetic word for letter P.

Parade:
   An area aboard ship where the divisions fall in for muster or
   inspection. Fair weather parades are topside; foul weather parades
   below. See *All Hands Parade.*

Parallel middle body:
   That length of the ship over which the midships section remains
   constant in area and shape.

Parallel of latitude:
> A circle on the surface of the earth, parallel to the plane of the equator and connecting all points of equal latitude.

Pararaft:
> A combination parachute and one-man life raft worn by pilots.

Paravane:
> Torpedo-shaped device towed on either side of a ship's bow to deflect and cut adrift moored mines.

Parbuckle:
> Device for raising or lowering a heavy object along an incline or vertical surface. A bight of rope is thrown around a secured fastening at the level to which the object is to be raised or lowered. The two ends of the rope are then passed under the object, brought all the way over it, and led back toward the bight. The two ends are then hauled or slackened together to raise or lower the object, the object itself acting as a movable pulley.

Parcel:
> To wrap a line or wire with strips of canvas. See *Serve.*

Parking harness:
> Device fitted over the controls of a parked aircraft.

Part:
> To break, as to part a line or hawser.

Party:
> Group organized for a special task such as repair party, working party, liberty party, recreation party, etc.

Passageway:
> Corridor or hall aboard ship.

Pass a line:
> Throw or project a line. To carry a line to or around something.

Pass down the line book (PDL Book):
> A notebook for the OOD or OOW in which instructions or information of a temporary nature is recorded.

Passing honors:
> Those honors, except gun salutes, rendered by a ship when ships or embarked officials or officers pass *Close aboard.*

Passive Acoustic Torpedo PAT:
> Torpedo which homes on noise generated by its target.

Passive Active Detection and Location (PADLOC) sonar:
> The SQR-13 sonar used on surface ships.

Passive Sonar:
> Gathers its target information from the sound emanations of the target only.

Passive Underwater Fire Control Feasibility Study (PUFFS):
System used by submarines against submarines. Uses hydrophones to collect information for computer processing and localization of target.

Pass the word:
Broadcast the information.

Patching:
The plugging in or connecting of required radio frequencies in the transmitter room upon request by *Radio Central.*

Patent anchor:
A *Stockless anchor.* In the development of the stockless anchor, different designs were tried, and for a time distinction was made between the various designs. The patent anchor was one of these, but the differences today are incidental to all except hobbyists.

Patent log:
Device for measuring ship's speed through the water. See *Taffrail log.*

Patrol vessel:
Small man-of-war used for general escort and patrol duties. See Appendix A.

Patternmaker (PM):
Petty officer who constructs, repairs, and finishes wood and metal patterns used in a foundry.

Paulin:
Short for *Tarpaulin.*

Pay:
Slang: disbursing or supply officer of a ship, short for paymaster. Also, to fill the seams of a wooden vessel with pitch or other substance.

Pay clerk:
Warrant officer, usually advanced from *Storekeeper* or *Disbursing Clerk.*

Paygrade:
Level of military pay, from E-1 (Recruit) to E-9 (Master CPO) and from O-1 (Ensign) to O—10 (Fleet Admiral).

Paymaster:
General term for any disbursing officer.

Pay off:
To turn the bow away from the wind. Not used as a command.

Pay out:
To slack off or ease out a line.

Peacoat:
   The heavy topcoat worn by seafaring men in cold weather. Cut short
   well above the knees. The coat was originally made of a material
   called pilot cloth, and it is probable that the name was successively
   pilot-cloth coat, pilot coat, P-coat, and finally peacoat. Also called
   Reefer in the old Navy.

Peak:
   Topmost end of the gaff; from this point the ensign is flown while
   the ship is underway. Also, to adjust for optimum performance, as
   for a radio or radar.

Peak tank:
   Tank low in the bow or stern of a ship, usually kept empty and dry,
   but sometimes designed for carrying potable water. So-called because
   one end of the tank is at the very bow or stern and therefore comes
   to a peak.

Pelican hook:
   A quick-release device made in various sizes, ranging from anchor
   chain to boat gripes, to secure chain or cable. Released by pulling
   a toggle key or pin, or knocking off a bail. The hook has a shape
   resembling a pelican's beak.

Pelorus:
   Device for taking bearings with a ring fitted with sighting vanes
   that rotates over a gyro repeater on a stand.

Pendant:
   Length of line or wire, often fitted with an eye or block at one or both ends.

Pennant:
   Flag that is smaller at the *Fly* or outward end.

Per diem:
   Additional expense money for a person on temporary additional duty.

Perigee:
   The point at which a missile trajectory or a satellite orbit is
   closest to the center of the gravitational field of the controlling
   body or bodies.

Period of roll:
   Time it takes for a ship to roll from one extremity to the other
   side and back again. Can be used to determine *Metacentric height*,
   which is a measure of initial stability.

Periscope:
   An optical device of mirrors and prisms used to project one's vision
   over an obstacle, as in a submarine periscope.

Periscope feather:
   The spray formed by the periscope of a submerged submarine moving
   through the water at moderate to high speed.

PERSHING:
   Model designation: XMGM-31A; cognizant service: Army.
   Field-artillery missile.

Personnel accounting machine installation (PAMI):
Computer installation used in personnel administration.

Personnel allocation plan:
Allocates among naval activities the total number of officers and
enlisted men expected to be in the Navy on a prescribed date.

Personnel diary:
A daily record, by name, of all personnel assigned to an activity.

Personnel man (PN):
A petty officer who assists in the classification, training, and
interviewing of enlisted men.

Per Standard Compass (PSC):
Phrase used in describing a course, e.g., "steering 090° psc." The
"standard" compass is the most reliable magnetic compass. "Pgc,"
correspondingly, means "per gyro compass." Courses are today
whenever possible given per gyro compass.

Pert Cost:
Utilizes a common reference for estimating and controlling cost and
schedule of a program to better assess progress and more realistically
measure consequences of alternate courses available. See *Program
Evaluation and Review Technique.*

PETREL:
Model designation: AQM-41; cognizant service: Navy.
Classified missile.

Petroleum-Oil-Lubricants (POL):
A term which includes all petroleum products used by the armed forces.

Petty officer:
Non-commissioned officer in the grades of master chief, senior chief,
chief, first, second, and third class.

Petty officer of the watch:
Senior enlisted assistant to the Officer of the Deck.

PHANTOM II:
Model designation: F-4; cognizant services: Navy/Air Force.
Carrier-based, all-weather, fighter aircraft. Carries missiles and
special stores. Two-crew. Probably one of the most highly regarded
fighter aircraft ever built. Jet.

PHOENIX:
Model designation: AIM-54; cognizant service: Navy.
Air-to-air missile.

Phonetic alphabet:
Words that identify letters so that they will be clearly understood;
for example, A is Alpha, B is Bravo, etc.

Photographer:
Warrant officer, usually advanced from *Photographer's Mate.*

Photographer's mate (PH):
Petty officer who does all types of photographic work.

Photographic intelligenceman (PI):
Petty officer who identifies information from photographs.

Photograph, oblique:
Any photograph other than a vertical one. May be low (angle between camera axis and horizontal is less than 45 degrees), high (angle greater than 45 degrees), or flat (axis of camera horizontal).

Photograph, vertical:
One taken with optical axis of the camera pointed vertically downward.

Picket:
Ship or aircraft stationed away from a formation or in a geographical location for a specific purpose, such as air warning.

Picket boat:
Armed boat that performs sentry, security, and patrol duty, usually at night.

Pier:
Structure for mooring vessels which is built out into the water perpendicular to the shore line. See *Dock, Wharf.*

Pier head jump:
An immediate departure from a ship as it arrives in port or a last-minute embarkation as the ship departs, viewed with mixture of disdain, amusement, and admiration.

Pig:
The float at the end of a minesweeping cable.

Pigboat:
Slang for an old-type submarine.

Pigstick:
Small spar at top of mainmast from which the commission pennant flies.

Piling:
Wood, concrete or metal poles driven into river or sea bottom for support or protection of piers or wharves. Singular: pile.

Pilot:
An expert on local harbor and channel conditions who advises the commanding officer in moving a ship in or out of port; one who operates an airplane; a book of sailing directions.

Pilot charts:
Monthly charts of oceans showing winds, currents, and weather conditions to be expected. Issued by the Oceanographic Office of the Navy Department.

Pilot house:
The compartment in the bridge structure that contains the ship controls and from which the ship is normally controlled.

Piloting:
Navigation near land using landmarks, aids to navigation and soundings.

Pilot rudder:
> A small additional rudder forward of the propeller of a landing craft. Also called maneuvering rudder.

Ping:
> Acoustic pulse signal of an echo ranging indicator.

Ping jockey:
> Slang: *Sonarman.*

Pink lady:
> Slang: cleaning alcohol, not fit for internal use.

Pintle:
> Fitting on a rudder which secures it to the hull of a ship by fitting into a *Gudgeon.*

Pip:
> Visual indication of a target on an electronic indicator screen. Also *Blip.*

Pipe, boatswain's:
> Distinctive silver whistle used to sound calls when passing the word aboard ship or during quarterdeck honors. Also used to direct the men as when hoisting in a boat or handling cargo. Sometimes referred to as *Boatswain's call.*

Pipe down:
> A command as in "Pipe down aired bedding." An order to be silent or reduce noise.

Pipefitter (FP):
> A petty officer who works as steamfitter, plumber, etc.

Pipe the side:
> Render honors with sideboys and boatswain's pipe. See *Side Honors.*

Pipe to:
> Pass the word and pipe the appropriate call to an evolution, such as "Pipe to dinner."

Piping the side:
> Name of a boatswain's call on the pipe used during side honors.

Pitch:
> The vertical motion of a ship's bow or stern in a seaway about the *Athwartships* axis. Of a propeller, the axial advance during one revolution. See *Heaving.*

Pitometer log:
> Device for indicating speed of ship and distance run by measuring water pressure on a *Pitot Tube* projected outside the ship's hull.

Pitot tube:
> Sensing element used to measure static and dynamic pressure for ship or aircraft speed indicators.

Pivot (Pivoting) Point:
> That point about which a ship pivots when turning, usually in vicinity of bridge.

Pivot ship:
> The wing ship in a line around which a *wheel* is being made. In a convoy maneuver.

Plaindress:
> Message having its address in the heading.

Plane:
> Said of a seaplane or boat when it gains enough speed to ride on the step of the hull.

Plane captain:
> Enlisted man responsible for the material condition of his assigned airplane.

Plane director:
> The man who hand-signals the pilots for taxiing aircraft on an aircraft carrier or ashore.

Plane guard:
> A fast ship *(Destroyer)* which accompanies a carrier to pick up downed personnel. Helicopters also perform this duty.

Plane handler:
> Enlisted man who handles aircraft on a carrier flight deck. Also called plane pusher.

Plan, entry (sortie):
> Plan for the entry (sortie) of a task force to (from) a port with the greatest possible security.

Plankowner:
> Man who has been on board since ship was commissioned.

Planning and overhaul yard:
> Shipyard responsible for design work and maintenance of records of ships assigned to it for planning or overhaul. Formerly these functions were assigned to the *Home Yard*, now an obsolete term.

Plan of the day:
> Schedule of ship's activities for the day including work, training, meals, recreation, etc. Also called morning orders.

Plan position indicator (PPI):
> A radar screen that exhibits a chart-like picture of the surrounding land and sea.

Platform deck:
> Partial deck of a ship below the lowest complete *Deck.*

Plimsoll mark:
> Mark on a ship's side indicating how deeply she may be loaded under various expected sea conditions, depending on season and geographical area.

Plot:
> A diagram of ship movement (surface plot), aircraft movement (air plot), or submarine movement (underwater plot). Also, tactical and operational control center aboard ship: air plot, flag plot, etc.
> To record the course of ships or aircraft, to diagram movements.

Pneumercator:
> An instrument for measuring the level and thus the volume of liquid in tanks.

Pod:
> Group of whales. Projecting streamlined container usually located under wing of aircraft.

Pogey bait:
> Slang: candy, also soda fountain items. Same as *Geedunk.*

Point oars:
> A pulling boat order given when the boat is aground; oarsman thrust their blades forward and downward at an angle of about 30°. At the command "shove off," the crew push together, lifting the boat and forcing it back off the shoal.

Pointer:
> Man who controls a gun in elevation (range).

Point oboe:
> An arbitrary point, sometimes in motion, used in gunfire target designation and carrier aircraft operations.

Point of tow:
> Device on forefoot of a ship to which the *Paravane* wires are attached.

Points, Compass:
> The 32 directions of the compass card, equal to 11 1/4 degrees of arc each.

Points, retirement and promotion:
> Credits earned by Naval Reserve officers by attending school, serving on active duty, taking correspondence courses, etc.

POLARIS:
> Model designation: UGM-27 (Series), cognizant service: Navy. Submarine-launched two-stage ballistic missile powered by solid-fuel rocket motors and guided by a self-contained inertial guidance system. Two generations in service: A2 — range 1500 NM; A3 — range 2500 NM. Can be launched from surfaced or submerged condition.

Polar lights:
> The Aurora Australis and Aurora Borealis of the southern and northern hemispheres, respectively. Displays, usually associated with sunspot activity or magnetic storms, are seen at night only.

Police:
> To inspect and to clean up.

Pollywog:
> One who has not crossed the equator.

Polynya:
> An open water area in the pack ice other than a lead.

Pontoon:
> Steel box, 5 x 5 x 7, many of which are bolted together to form causeways, barges, etc. Loosely, any watertight structure (box, barrel, etc.) used to float something.

Pontoon barge:
   A barge made of pontoons bolted together and propelled by an engine
   driving an outboard propeller.

Pontoon causeway or pier:
   A floating, movable pier made up of pontoons bolted together. Used
   in amphibious assaults to expedite unloading.

Pool, electronics:
   A receiving, stock, and issue point for electronic materials.

Poop deck:
   A partial deck, aft above the main deck.

Pooped:
   Said of a vessel when a following sea breaks over the stern. Slang:
   tired, worn out.

Poopy bag:
   Slang: lighter-than-air-craft, a blimp.

Poopy suit:
   Slang; aviator's waterproof immersion suit.

Porpoise:
   To break the surface of the ocean; to *Broach*.

Port:
   Seagoing term for left as opposed to *Starboard* which means right. A
   coastal city accessible to sea commerce. Opening in side of ship,
   as air port, cargo port, etc.

Port capacity:
   Estimated capacity of a port or an anchorage to clear cargo in 24 hours.
   Usually expressed in tons.

Port commander:
   An officer who is responsible for and has authority over all activities
   of a port.

Port director:
   Officer who controls the water operations of a port. Now called *Naval
   Port Control Officer.*

Portfolio, chart:
   A group of charts for a specific geographical area.

Port watch or in port watch:
   Watch set when ship is in port in contrast to the underway watch.
   Also, if ship is in a watch-and-watch condition, the watches are
   usually named port and starboard.

POSEIDON:
   Model designation: UGM-73A, cognizant service: Navy. Successor
   to POLARIS. POSEIDON is outfitted with multiple warheads, each of
   which can be separately targeted. Range about 2500 NM.

Position:
   The location of an object relative to a reference point or in accordance
   with recognized coordinates as longitude and latitude.

Position angle:
 The number of degrees an object seen in the sky is above the horizon.

Position buoy:
 A marker towed astern in formation. Same as *Towing Spar.*

Postal clerk (PC):
 A petty officer who acts as navy mailman in military post offices.

Post Shakedown Availability (PSA):
 Period in the shipyard after a ship's shakedown cruise during which
 she is brought to full operational condition. Length of PSA varies with
 type of ship.

Powder hoist:
 A device to lift powder from the magazines to the gun mount, or turret.

PQM-56A:
 French supersonic ramjet target drone under evaluation.

Practical factors:
 Items a man must be able to do, in addition to what he must know, in
 order to win *Advancement in Rating.*

Pratique:
 A certification that a vessel is free of contagious disease. May
 sometimes be granted by radio.

Precedence:
 The relative order in which messages should be handled.

Presidential Unit Citation (PUC):
 An honor accorded a naval unit for distinguishing itself in combat
 or other operations. Of higher degree than *Navy Unit Commendation.*

Pressure hull:
 The cylindrical, pressure-resistant core of a submarine that encloses
 all operating spaces.

Preventer:
 Any line used for additional safety or security or to keep something
 from falling or running free.

Pricker:
 Small marlinspike.

Prime contract:
 As used by DOD, any contract entered into directly by a military
 department or procurement activity of DOD.

Prime contractor:
 Any contractor who enters into a contract with the government to
 produce, assemble or deliver specific items or material or perform
 services.

Prime meridian:
 Meridian from which longitude is measured, normally the meridian of
 the original site of the Royal Observatory at Greenwich, England.

Priming:
> The carry over of water with the steam from a boiler.

Printer (PI):
> Petty officer who does general printing work.

Prisoner at large (PAL):
> Person under arrest whose restraint to certain specified limits is morally enforced.

Privileged vessel:
> Ship having right of way under *Rules of the Road* and required to hold course and speed. The other ship, the *Burdened vessel*, must take avoiding action

Prize:
> Merchant vessel captured during wartime and retained for legal prize proceedings. The term can also be applied to a captured warship.

Prize master:
> Officer placed in command of the prize to bring it into a port. He is provided with a prize crew.

Prize money:
> Paid to enlisted men for the award to their unit of the *Battle Efficiency Pennant.* No longer paid for the capture of a *Prize.*

Proceed time:
> Time allowed between the detachment of an officer and the date he must report to his new duty station, not considering travel time and leave, if any.

Program Evaluation and Review Technique (PERT):
> A managerial technique which emphasizes the planning and control of a program's time elements by using a network diagram to coordinate parallel and sequential portions of the work.

Program For Afloat College Education (PACE):
> Cooperative College-Navy Extension Program offering up to two years of college credits. BuPers sponsored.

Program torpedo:
> Torpedo designed to follow a pre-planned course.

Progressive wave:
> Wave in which water particles are in opposite motion at high and low points of the wave and show no motion at the mid-point between.

Projectile:
> The missile fired by a gun. Major classes are penetrating, fragmenting, and special-purpose.

Projectile flat:
> Stowage space for projectiles in a turret.

Projectile hoist:
> Elevator mechanism for lifting projectiles from storage space to guns.

Propagation:
Transmission of radio frequency energy.

Propeller guard:
Protective framework over projecting propeller of a ship.

Property pass:
Written permission for an enlisted man to take private property out of a ship or station.

Proportioner:
A firefighting device that produces foam by mixing a chemical and water.

Proprietary Information:
Privately owned information not previously disclosed or made available to the public.

Prospective Commanding Officer (PCO):
Officer who is ordered to assume command of a ship. Normally used when the ship is not in commission at the time of his assignment.

Protective deck:
An armored deck. In ships fitted with more than one armored deck, the protective deck is the more heavily armored of the two, the other being the *Splinter deck,* fitted above the protective deck.

PROVIDER:
Model designation: C-123; cognizant services: Air Force/Coast Guard. Transport aircraft for airborne assault troops or paratroopers. The Coast Guard used the aircraft for aerial logistical supply of Loran stations. Two-crew, 60-troops. Propeller-driven.

Prow:
Part of the bow above the water line. Not good naval usage.

Proword:
A word or phrase in condensed form representing certain frequently used orders and instructions in voice radio communications.

Proximity fuze:
See *Fuze.*

Public reprimand:
A rare but legal form of punishment upon an officer issued pursuant to the sentence of a general courtmartial.

Public works:
Buildings, grounds, utilities, other structures, and land improvements at a naval shore activity.

Puddening (pudding):
Chafing gear used to protect, for example, a towline or a spar. Also used as a bumper along the gunwale of a rearming boat.

Pulse length:
The duration, in microseconds, of a radar transmission.

Pulse-jet:
Type of jet engine which uses a flapper valve alternately to compress and then eject air. Also called aerojet.

Punt:
Rectangular shallow boat used in painting the ship's side at and above the waterline.

Purchase:
A tackle. The mechanical advantage of a tackle.

Pure water:
A term used in nuclear operating machinery. Means water so heavily distilled as to be more pure than ordinary distilled water, of quality fit to be used in the primary loop of the nuclear plant.

Pycnocline:
Steep vertical density gradient.

Pyrotechnics:
Ammunition, flares, or fireworks used for signalling, illuminating, or marking targets.

Q

Q ship:
>   Disguised man-of-war used to decoy enemy submarines or merchant raiders.

Quadrantal correctors or spheres:
>   Two iron balls secured at either side, athwartship, of the binnacle to help compensate for ship's magnetic effect on the compass.

Quadrature:
>   The points of the first and last quarters of the moon when the moon's longitude relative to the earth is 90 degrees from that of the sun.

QUAIL:
>   Model designation: ADM-20; cognizant service: Air Force.
>   Air-launched, air-breathing bomber decoy missile.

Qualification code number (officers):
>   A 4-digit number which marks an officer as having certain basic qualifications for duty.

Quarter:
>   One side or the other of the stern of a ship. To be "broad on the quarter" means to be 45° away from dead astern, and starboard or port quarter would have to be stated to be more specific. "Quarters" refers to assigned places for military purposes, ranging from *General quarters* to living areas or quarters for muster. Also, an old term referring to surrendering. To "cry for quarter" is to ask to have one's surrender accepted. The term comes from the ancient custom of permitting a captured officer to be ransomed at one-fourth of his annual pay. To "give quarter" of course means to accept the other party's surrender.

Quarterdeck:
>   Ceremonial area of the main deck, kept specially neat and clear. The specific domain of the *Officer of the Deck* while in port. Always located near the *Accommodation ladder* or *Brow*—or the principal one if more than one is rigged. In days of sail the ship would be *Conned* from the quarterdeck.

Quartering sea:
>   A sea on the quarter. That is, waves are approaching from about 45° on one side of the stern.

Quarterly Marks:
>   Periodic evaluation (quarterly) of enlisted men in proficiency in rate, seamanship, mechanical ability, leadership and conduct.

Quartermaster (QM):
An enlisted man, who is general assistant to the *Officer of the Deck* underway or in port. A man well qualified in deck and bridge routine, intelligent and able to give meaningful support to the OOD. A Navigating Quartermaster is one designated as assistant to the ship's navigator, a position of some prestige and responsibility. The helmsman during important evolutions, such as entering port or battle stations, is almost always a quartermaster. Originally the quartermaster was the man assigned to look after troops' quarters, and the Army and Marine Corps still use the term in much of its original meaning.

Quartermaster's notebook:
A pencil log maintained by the quartermaster on watch to provide material for the *Deck Log*. It is an official document; entries may be crossed out, but not erased.

Quarters:
An assembly, as quarters for inspection or a gathering on stations as fire quarters. Government-owned houses or apartments assigned to naval personnel. Living spaces aboard ship.

Quay:
A wharf.

Quebec:
Phonetic word for letter Q.

Quenching:
The significant drop in underwater sound transmission or reception due to air bubbles trapped on the sonar dome. Roll and pitch of a ship in rough water is a primary cause.

Quick-closing:
A term descriptive of special doors and hatches that can be closed quickly to preserve watertight integrity.

R

Rack:
A framework aboard ship from which depth charges are dropped. Slang: *Bunk* or bed. "Rack out" means to nap. See *Sack.*

Racon:
Radar beacon that transmits in response to signal from ship's radar.

Radar:
Radio Detection And Ranging, an instrument for determining, by radio echoes, the presence of objects and their range, bearing, and elevation.

Radar countermeasures (RADCM):
Actions taken to reduce effectiveness of enemy radar.

Radar frequency:
P-Band, 200 mc; L-Band, 100 mc; S-Band, 300 mc; C-Band 5000 mc; X-Band, 10,000 mc; K-Band, 30,000 mc; V-Band, 50,000 mc. See *Hertz.*

Radarman (RD):
Petty officer who operates and performs routine upkeep on radar equipment.

Radar picket:
Ship or aircraft stationed at a distance to increase radar detection range.

Radar Picket Escort Ship (DER):
Escort ships modified to give increased CIC, electronic countermeasures, and electronic search facilities.

Radar reflector:
Device to increase radar target signal, used in life rafts.

Radar trapping:
Atmospheric distortion of radar signals.

Radar wind sounding (RaWin):
A determination of winds aloft by the radar observation of a balloon.

Radar Wind Sounding and Radiosonde (RaWinsonde):
Radiosonde and *RaWin* combined, an observation of temperature, pressure, humidity and winds aloft, made by electronic means.

Radioactivity Detection, Indication, And Computation (RADIAC):
Term that designates various types of radiological measuring instruments or equipment.

Radiated Noise:
Underwater sound energy emitted by ships, submarines, and torpedoes.

Radio-acoustic range finding:
Determining distance by a combination of radio and sound, radio being used to indicate the time of transmission and of reception of a sound wave.

Radio and television aid to navigation (RATAN):
An aid to navigation in which a central station transmits radar map to ship's receivers, usually UHF television.

Radio beacon:
An electronic aid to navigation that sends out radio signals for reception by a directional antenna.

Radio central:
Major radio room aboard ship. Also called *Main Radio* and "radio one."

Radio countermeasures (RCM):
Actions taken to reduce effectiveness of enemy radio.

Radio data and flight information book:
Flight planning and flight information required by air crews that is stable in nature and does not need frequent revision.

Radio direction finder (RDF):
A radio receiver with a directional antenna to determine bearings of radio signals.

Radio Electrician:
Warrant officer advanced from an electronics rating.

Radio facility chart:
Information on radio aids to navigation in graphic and tabular form for use by air crews in flight operations.

Radio frequency:
VLF, below 30 kc; LF, 30-300 kc; MF, 300-3000 kc; Hf, 3-30 mc; VHF, 30-300 mc; UHF, 300-3000 mc; SHF, 3000-30,000 mc; EHF, 30,000-300,000 mc. See *Hertz.*

Radio guard:
Ship or station assuming radio communications responsibility for another ship or station.

Radiological defense:
The means taken to minimize and control damage from radioactivity.

Radioman (RM):
Petty officer who operates and performs upkeep on radio and teletypewriter equipment.

Radio sextant:
An electronic sextant that receives radio waves emitted by the sun and other celestial bodies as compared to light waves in standard celestial navigation.

Radiosonde:
Balloon which automatically transmits meterological information to a weather station.

Radioteletype (RATT):
Radioteletype in which a radio circuit actuates a teletype machine which produces a message in printed form.

Radojet:
Device for removing the air from a condenser by means of steam jets.

Radome:
Dome on an aircraft or airship which contains radar gear.

Radmail:
Administrative messages handled by radio and by regular air or guard mail.

Raft kit:
First-aid gear secured to a life raft.

Rail(s):
Metal rods acting as life lines.

Rail loading:
Loading of boats at rail of a ship instead of when waterborne.

Rainmaker:
Coil used to condense steam from the pier. Slang: a meteorologist.

Raise:
To come within sight of, as a lookout raises land when the ship makes a landfall. To establish contact on a radio circuit.

Rake:
A fall of shot observation in range. To rake is to make such observations. Also angle that stack, masts, etc., make with the vertical.

Rakish:
Having a pronounced rake to the masts, probably more for appearance than utility. Smart, speedy appearance, but also dashing, jaunty.

Ram:
Aircraft-carried antitank rocket. Also, an underwater ice projection from an iceberg or a hummocked ice flow. In the old Navy, an armored projection of the bow below the waterline, intended for use in combat.

Ramark:
A radar lighthouse that transmits independently of a ship's radar. See *Racon.*

Ram-jet:
Type of jet engine which uses inlet air velocity as compressor.

Rammer:
Part of gun mechanism that seats the projectile.

Ramp:
Hinged forward section of a landing ship or craft over which its cargo is unloaded when craft is beached.

Range:
> To lay out chain in even rows. An area for shooting, as a rifle range
> or a sea area for ship's gunnery. When safe for firing, a range is
> said to be clear, the opposite being fouled. Also, the distance to
> the target; two or more objects on shore, marked on chart, indicating
> safe course or marking distance as for a measured mile.
> See *Range, navigational.*

Range alongside:
> To come close aboard, abeam, of another vessel.

Range finder:
> An instrument to measure range or distance to the target. Optical
> range finders are either stereoscopic or coincidence type. Radar
> provides most accurate range finding.

Rangekeeper:
> Instrument which automatically receives and computes information
> necessary to fire the guns. A *Computer* does a similar job for bombing.

Range light:
> A second, sometimes optional, white light which with the masthead
> light forms a range which reveals the course of the vessel.

Range, navigational:
> A pair of lights or day beacons used to mark a line of definite bearing.
> When on the line, a navigator reports the range closed; when off the
> line, the range is open.

Range tables:
> Elements of the trajectories of specific guns and projectiles, compiled
> in convenient form.

Rank:
> Relative position of officer or petty officer within a particular
> *Grade.* See *Grade* for usage.

Rate:
> Level of proficiency within a *Rating.* Radioman, third class is a
> rate. Also means a privilege or to deserve, e.g., "he rates liberty."
> A chronometer's rate is the number of seconds it gains or loses daily.
> See *Rating.*

Ratey:
> Slang: presumptuous; impertinent.

Rat guard:
> A conical metal shield secured around mooring lines to prevent rats
> from coming aboard.

Rating:
> General grouping of enlisted personnel according to military skills,
> i.e. boatswain's mate, photographer, etc. See Appendix B.
> See *Rate.*

Rating badge:
> Insignia of rating and rate worn by petty officers.

Ration:
> An allowance for provisions in money or kind, for one man for one day.

Rations:
Food. May be abandon ship, flight, aircraft, emergency, landing
party, travel, or leave rations.

Ratline:
Three-strand, tarred hemp used for *Snaking* on destroyers, formerly
seized to shrouds to form ladders.

Rat tail:
Tapered braid that finishes off a *Stopper*.

RAVEN:
Model designation: H-23; cognizant service: Army.
Small helicopter for liaison and observation operations.
One-crew, two-passengers.

Raydist:
An accurate electronic system of navigation using range information
from two portable stations. Used principally in surveying.

Raymond releasing hook:
Quick-release hook used on boat falls.

Reach rod:
A long handle by which valves can be operated from a distance.

Reactivate (activate):
To restore a preserved ship to service. Slang: unzipper or de-mothball.

Reactor:
The energy source of a nuclear power plant, consisting of nuclear
material, a moderator, a heat-transfer medium, pressure vessel, and
shielding, plus associated parts and mechanisms.

Readiness, conditions of:
Comprehensive term which includes: material—what closures are made;
engineering—what is maximum speed ship can make at once;
armament—what and how many guns are manned.

Readiness for sea period:
Number of days, at end of vessel's overhaul, for loading ammo,
fueling, calibrating, testing, cleaning, painting, and stowing gear.

Ready:
Report made by a gun station when enough men are there to fire the
guns. See *Manned and Ready*.

Ready room:
Compartment on carriers where pilots gather for briefing and to stand by.

Ready service ammunition:
Ammunition at gun and ready for use.

Rear admiral:
Rank senior to commodore in the Navy; the junior rank among admirals.

Rear commodore:
Navy or Merchant Marine officer designated as convoy commander if
the *Convoy Commodore* and *Vice Commodore* are lost.

Rearming boat:
   Boat with padded *Gunwales* formerly used to service seaplanes.

Receipt:
   Communication indicating that a message has been received.

Receiving station (RecSta) (RecShip):
   An activity to receive, process, house, mess, clothe, pay, and
   transfer transient enlisted personnel.

Reclama:
   A request to superior authority to reconsider its decision or its
   proposed action.

Recognition:
   Process of determining friendly or enemy character of a ship, plane,
   or other object or person.

Recoil system:
   That system, usually hydraulic, which absorbs the force of the gun
   as it is driven back in recoil by the explosion.

Recreation committee:
   Enlisted men, appointed or elected, who make recommendations
   concerning welfare and recreation activities.

Recreation council:
   Board of officers and enlisted men who administer the welfare and
   recreation activities of ship, squadron, or station.

Recruit:
   Newly enlisted man, still in basic training.

Red Cross flag:
   The *Distinctive mark* of a hospital ship. Also flown by boats and
   shore activities engaged in medical service.

REDEYE:
   Model designation: XMIM-43; cognizant services: Army, Navy, Marine Corps.
   A weapon which uses an infrared-seeker and an electromagnetic guidance
   device to seek out and destroy low-flying enemy aircraft. The weapon
   can be carried and launched by one man.

REDHEADED ROAD RUNNER:
   Model deisgnation: MQM-42; cognizant service: Army.
   Classified missile.

Red lead:
   Slang: catsup. Red anticorrosive priming paint.

Red, right, returning:
   An expression used to remind navigators that red buoys are on the
   right-hand side of the channel when returning to port from seaward.

Reducer:
   A coupling or fitting that connects two pipes or hoses of different sizes.

Reduction gear:
>Gear used to reduce the economical high speed of a ship's turbine to the necessarily slower shaft and propeller speed.

Reef:
>Rock or coral extending so near surface of the water that boats or ships can not pass over safely.

Reefer:
>Short, blue woolen coat worn by midshipmen and enlisted men. Fresh-provision cargo ship or a refrigerated compartment. See *Peacoat.*

Reef knot:
>Same as *Square knot,* except that one of the ends is pulled back through the knot as in a bowknot. To shake out reefs, the topmen need only pull the end so treated, which immediately releases the knot.

Reeve:
>To pass through or lead a line or wire; Past tense is rove.

Reference points (harbor):
>Lettered geographical points on which sortie and entrance plans of a harbor are based.

Reference position:
>The OTC's announced estimate of his navigation position. Usually signaled daily to the formation.

Reference Station:
>Tide or current station for which constants have been determined which is used for comparison of simultaneous observations at other stations.

Refit book:
>A complete submarine material maintenance check-off list, compiled at the end of a war patrol in preparation for the next one.

Regimental combat team (RCT):
>Task organization of troops for amphibious operations.

Registered matter:
>Classified matter to which a number is assigned and which is accounted for at prescribed intervals. Documents numbered for administrative convenience only are *Numbered Documents.*

Registry:
>Merchant ship's certificate showing ownership and nationality.

Regular:
>Member of the regular Navy as distinguished from the reserve components.

Regulation clothing:
>Articles of uniform prescribed by Uniform Regulations and sold as *Small Stores.*

REGULUS:
>Model designation: RGM-6/15; cognizant service: Navy. Submarine-launched air-breathing surface-to-surface guided missile. Submarine must be surfaced to launch. Now obsolete.

Relative bearing:
>The direction of an object relative to the ship's head, expressed in degrees or by *Points.*

Relative plot:
>Diagram representing the positions of ships or aircraft, relative to each other and not be true (compass) direction.

Relay:
>To forward a transmission through an intermediate station; the message so forwarded.

Release:
>To authorize the transmission of a message.

Relieve:
>To relieve a man on watch or on duty is to take his place. To change, as "relieve the watch, relieve the wheel and lookout."

Relieving tackle:
>Tackle to reduce strain on a piece of equipment as on a steering engine during heavy weather.

RELLA:
>Multi-purpose air-launched probe.

Remote Underwater Manipulator (RUM):
>A seabed recovery vehicle.

RENAE:
>A weather satellite.

Repair officer:
>The head of the Repair Department of a tender or repair ship.

Repair party:
>Group of specialists organized to control damage and make repairs throughout the ship during battle.

Repeater:
>Flag used to repeat another in a hoist, now called *Substitute.*

Repeater, gyro:
>Remote compass driven by a master gyro.

Replenishment group:
>Fleet oilers, supply, and ammunition ships and assigned screen.

Replenishment at sea:
>The process or procedure of supplying fuel, food, stores, ammunition, and personnel to fleet combatant units while underway.

Reporting point:
>Geographical location relative to which the position of an aircraft is to be reported.

Report, to place on:
>To record a man's name for appearance before his commanding officer on a charge of infraction of rules or regulations under *Uniform Code of Military Justice.*

Reports, lookout:
When sighting land, lookout says "Land ho." A vessel or light
elicits "Sail ho" or "Light ho." Proper reply is: "Where away?"
On every bell during the night, the lookouts port and starboard.
report: "Port sidelight, main truck light, bright lights, sir"
and "Starboard sidelight, masthead light, bright lights, sir."
Acknowledgment is "Very well."

Reprogramming:
Process of revising previously established programs or previous
budget estimates.

Request mast:
Process by which men can submit requests to Commanding Officer or
Executive Officer.

Requisition:
Formal, written request for stores, supplies, arms, or personnel.
Also, a purchase authorization which may be charged to bureau funds.

Rescue and assistance party:
Group of specially qualified men sent off the ship with special
equipment to assist in rescue, firefighting, and salvage operations.
Formerly call *Fire and Rescue Party.*

Rescue basket:
Device for lifting an injured or exhausted man out of the water.

Rescue breathing gear:
Face-fitting device that provides oxygen for use in smoke or gas.
See *Gas Mask.*

Rescue chamber:
A two-compartment diving bell, transported to the scene of a submarine disaster by a submarine rescue vessel. The bell can make a
watertight seal with the submarine's *Escape hatch* and *Escape trunk*
and can then be hoisted to the surface with rescued personnel. See
Deep-Submergence Rescue Vehicle.

Rescue Combat Air Patrol (RESCAP):
Air patrols which cover rescue submarines and rescue aircraft. Subdivisions are SUBCAP *(Rescue Submarine Combat Air Patrol)* for
lifeguard submarines and BIRDCAP *(Rescue Aircraft Combat Air Patrol)*
for aircraft on rescue duty.

Reserve buoyancy:
The watertight nonsubmerged volume of a ship. If a ship is damaged
and takes on water, she sinks deeper until once again in equili-
brium between weight and displaced volume. Obviously, if there is no
further volume to displace water in such a case, she will sink beneath
the surface. A submerged submarine is in neutral buoyancy; no further
submergence can increase the submerged volume. When she is surfaced,
the volume of her now empty ballast tanks is of course her reserve
buoyancy, and this exactly equals her additional displacement when
submerged.

Reserve fleet:
Group of naval vessels in an inactive status, organized into *Naval
Ship Maintenance Facility.* Slang: *Mothball fleet.*

Reserve Officer Candidate program (ROC):
Program for commissioning, as reserve ensigns, those college students who take certain summer courses at Navy schools.

Reserve Officers Training Corps program (ROTC):
Program in which student officers at various colleges and universities take naval training and may be commissioned and ordered to active duty upon graduation.

Reserve on board:
Classified publications not effective until made so by proper authority.

Responsibility:
The obligation to carry out an assigned task successfully. The obligation for the proper care and custody of property or funds. See *Accountability.*

Restrict:
To keep on board: a man may be restricted because of misconduct or illness.

Restricted area:
Ocean area or airspace in which there are special restrictive measures to prevent interference between friendly forces, e.g., joint zones, *blind bombing zones, Submarine Havens,* danger areas, etc.

Restricted data:
All data concerning the design, manufacture or utilization of atomic weapons or the production or use of special nuclear material.

Restriction:
Restraint similar to *Arrest* but not involving relief from military duties.

Retirement:
Planned tactical withdrawal, as of a task force for replenishment.

Retract:
To back off a beach, as a landing craft retracts.

Retraining command:
Activity which confines and at the same time rehabilitates men sentenced by courts-martial to long imprisonment.

Retreat:
Bugle call or word passed that means fall out (disband) from a formation e.g. "Retreat from inspection". Also sounded at evening colors.

Reveille:
Arousing the ship's company in port for work and breakfast. At sea, idlers are called, and the expression reveille is not properly used.

Reverberation:
Sound scattering toward its source. Major types are surface and bottom, from surface and bottom respectively and volume, from air bubbles or suspended solids in the water.

Reverbration Index:
Valuation of the ability of echo-ranging equipment to distinguished target echo from reverbration.

Reverse slope:
Terrain that because of intervening high ground can only be reached by high-angle fire.

Reversing thermometer:
Thermometer designed to separate its mercury column on sudden inversion. By calculation, temperature at the point of inversion can be determined from its reading.

Reviewing authority:
A commander in the chain of command who reviews the sentence of a court-martial.

Rhino barge (ferry):
A self-propelled lighter made up of *pontoons* bolted together.

Rhumb line:
A line on the earth's surface making the same angle with all meridians. It is a straight line on a Mercator projection chart.

Ride:
A vessel rides to her anchor and may ride out the storm there.

Ride the vents:
An expression used in older submarines whose ballast tanks were equipped with flood valves or Kingston valves. The condition of being ready to dive with flood valves open for entry of water as soon as main vents are opened permitting entrapped air to escape. Modern submarines have ballast tanks open to sea at the bottom and always are "riding the vents."

Ridge rope:
The backbone line or wire of an awning.

Riding lights:
Lights required for a ship at anchor, in contrast to *Running Lights.*

Rig:
To devise, set up, arrange. An arrangement or contrivance. General description of a ship's upper works; to set up spars or to fit out.

Rig for red:
An order to permit only red lights, particularly within a submarine, to provide quick dark adaptation for those who may have to use their eyes suddenly at night.

Rigging:
The ropes, lines, wires, turnbuckles, and other gear supporting and attached to stacks, masts and topside structure. *Standard Rigging* is more or less permanently fixed. *Running Rigging* is adjustable, e.g., cargo handling gear.

Right-handed:
Twisted from left to right or clockwise; yarn and rope are usually right-handed.

Righting moment:
>   The force which tends to right or move back to an upright position
>   a vessel which is heeled over.

Right-laid:
>   Lay of line or wire rope in which the strands spiral in a clockwise
>   direction (as one looks along the line). Same as *right handed.*
>   See *Left-laid.*

Rig ship for visitors:
>   Word passed to all hands to have ship prepared for expected visitors.
>   This involves closing off restricted areas, stationing sentries, providing
>   guides, etc.

Rig in:
>   To unship and stow, as a boat boom or accomodation ladder is rigged in.

Rip:
>   Turbulent water produced by conflicting currents.

Rip current (tide):
>   Localized surface flow of water away from the beach and out to sea,
>   constituting a menace to those swimming in surf.

Rise and shine:
>   To get up, go to work, get going.

Riser:
>   A vertical pipe leading off a larger one, e.g., firemain riser.
>   Also, lines from parachute harness to the shrouds.

Roadstead:
>   Off-shore anchorage with good holding ground and usually some
>   protection from the sea.

Roaring forties:
>   Area between 40° and 50° south latitude in which are encountered
>   the prevailing or stormy westerlies. This area develops very high
>   seas because of an absence of land masses and consequent unlimited
>   *Fetch.*

ROCKAIR:
>   An instrumented sounding rocket.

Rocket designation system:
>   See Appendix D.

Rocket mount:
>   Device for launching rockets.

Rocket ship (LSMR):
>   Landing ship used in close support of the leading assault waves
>   during an amphibious landing. Capable of heavy and rapid rocket firing.

Rocket sondes:
>   Rocket sent aloft to register and transmit weather data.

ROCKEYE:
>   Free-fall bomb cluster with rocket power for dispersal.

Rocks and Shoals:
>   Extracts from the Uniform Code of Military Justice periodically
>   read aloud to all hands.

Rodmeter:
>   The sword or part of a pitometer log that projects from the ship's
>   hull.

Roger:
>   Used in voice radio, meaning "I have received your transmission."
>   Not to be confused with *Wilco.*

Roger dodger:
>   Slang: "affirmative;" "yes;" "O.K.;" "will do."

Roll:
>   Side-to-side motion of a ship about its longitudinal axis. See
>   *Swaying.*

Roller chock:
>   A *Chock* fitted with a roller to permit easy passage of line or wire.

Roller path:
>   A precision-machined circular roller surface upon which the roller
>   bearings of a turret, mount, or director describe a circular path
>   as it rotates. The inclination of a roller path is of paramount im-
>   portance to director fire. See *Inclination diagram.*

Rolling chock:
>   Anti-rolling bilge keel.

Roll-on/Roll-off:
>   Method of cargo handling in which cargo is loaded into vehicles that
>   drive on and drive off the ship.

Romeo:
>   Phonetic word for letter R.

Room to swing a cat:
>   A very old naval expression referring to the amount of space required
>   to swing a cat-of-nine-tails. If there is not room to swing a cat,
>   it means in naval terms that the ceiling or *Overhead* is very low.

ROOSTER:
>   Model designation: PWN-7; cognizant service: Air Force.
>   A rocket-borne falling-sphere system used to obtain wind and density
>   data.

Root valve:
>   One located where a branch line comes off the main line.

Rope:
>   Term used for special items such as *Manrope* and bellrope, wheel
>   rope, and *Wire rope. Line* is used in a general sense for all cordage
>   and for such special ones as mooring line, heaving line, shot line,
>   etc. Strips of metal foil used in radar countermeasures are also
>   called rope.

Rope Yarn Sunday:
Any afternoon, except a week-end, that is free of work. Usually Wednesday afternoon is rope yarn Sunday if no work is scheduled at sea or if liberty is granted in port.

Rose box:
The strainer at the foot of the suction pipe of a bilge pump.

Rotary current:
A tidal current flowing continually but changing direction through all compass points during a tidal cycle. Flows clockwise in the northern hemisphere and counter clockwise in the southern hemisphere.

Rotating band:
Strip of metal around a projectile for sealing the bore, positioning the rear of the projectile, and imparting rotation.

Rough log:
Original, pencil-written and legal version of the ship's log.

Round in:
To bring the blocks of a tackle closer together. Opposite of *Overhaul.*

Round line:
Three-stranded, right-handed small stuff, used for fine seizing.

Round turn:
To take a turn around a bitt or bollard to check a strain or weight. To "bring up with a round turn" is nautical phraseology for a call-down or reprimand. Literally, it means a complete twist in the anchor chains at the hawse when two anchors are down in a *Moor.*

Rouse in:
To haul in; especially by hand.

Rouse out:
Arouse; break out; bestir; e.g., "Rouse out the duty boat's crew"; "Rouse out the starboard chain."

Route:
To forward a message by a prescribed path and method.

Routing:
Process of determining the path or method of forwarding a message or of directing a ship, formation, or convoy.

Rove:
Past tense of *Reeve.* Likewise, *Hove* is the past tense of *Heave.*

Rudder:
A flat surface rigged vertically astern used to steer a ship, boat, or aircraft.

Rudder post:
The after post of the stern frame to which the rudder is hung. Also called sternpost.

Ruffles and flourishes:
>The roll of the drum (ruffles) and short burst of music (flourishes) that make up one of the honors rendered to high ranking military and civil officials.

Rules of the Road:
>Regulations designed to prevent collision of ships at sea and in inland waters.

Runner:
>Line fastened at one end to a fixed object, such as an eyebolt, and rove through a single block. It has an eye on its other end to which a tackle is *Clapped on.* The term is also loosely applied to any line rove through a block.

Running bowline:
>Bowline made over the standing part of its own rope so that it forms a free-sliding noose.

Running fix:
>Geographical position determined by two lines of position obtained by observations at different times. First line is advanced by dead reckoning.

Running lights:
>Required lights carried by a vessel or aircraft underway between sunset and sunrise. See *Riding Lights.*

Running mate:
>A line officer whose eligibility for promotion results in a certain staff officer's eligibility for promotion is known as the staff officer's running mate.

Running rigging:
>See *Rigging.*

S

Sabot:
> A bushing, used in firing subcaliber projectiles or missiles. It
> falls away as the assembly leaves the muzzle or missile launcher.

SABRE:
> Model designation: F-86; cognizant service: Air Force.
> Fighter aircraft. One-crew. Jet.

SABRELINER:
> Model designation: T-39; cognizant service: Navy/Air Force.
> A sweptback, low-wing, trainer. Engines are mounted on pylons on
> each side of fuselage just aft and above the wing trailing edge.
> Primary mission is flight training and maintenance of flying pro-
> ficiency on multi-engine jet aircraft. Two-crew, four-passengers.
> Jet.

Sack:
> Slang: *Bunk* or bed. To "sack out" is take a nap. See *Rack.*

Saddle:
> Device used to support a fuel hose when fueling ships underway.
> Also see *Skids, Boat.*

Sagging:
> Distortion of a ship's hull in which the keel droops downward in the
> middle. Opposite of *Hogging* in which keel is bent downward at the ends.

Sail:
> A large piece of fabric, usually canvas, by which the wind can be
> used to drive the vessel. The part of a modern submarine extending
> above the main deck or hull, housing the periscope supports, various
> retractable masts, and the surface conning station or bridge.

Sail area:
> The vertical hull surface of a ship upon which the wind exerts force.

Sailer:
> A boat or ship propelled exclusively by sails (archaic).

Sail ho:
> See *Reports, lookout.*

Sailing Directions:
> Books issued by the Navy Department to supplement charts of the world.
> They contain descriptions of coast lines, harbors, dangers, aids
> to navigation, and other data which cannot conveniently be shown on
> a chart.

Sail locker:
> Stowage for awnings, cots, and related gear aboard ship.

Sailor:
> An officer or man who has spent time on the sea and is accustomed to
> the ways of the sea and the ways of ships.

Sail nomenclature:
>   In a *Full-rigged ship* the sails on each mast are, from bottom
>   to top, known as:
>>   On the *Foremast,* foresail; foretopsail; foretopgallant;
>>   fore royal; fore skysail.
>>   On the *Mainmast,* mainsail; maintopsail; maintopgallant;
>>   main royal; main skysail.
>>   On the *Mizzenmast,* spanker--a *Fore-and-aft* sail with
>>   gaff and boom; mizzen topsail; mizzen topgallant; mizzen royal;
>>   mizzen skysail.
>   The topsails were so large that in the 19th century it became usual
>   to split them horizontally into upper and lower topsails.

Sally ship:
>   Evolution aboard ship in which crew runs from side to side together,
>   causing ship to roll slowly. Used to extricate ship in ice or aground
>   or to determine ship's period of roll, a measure of her stability.

Saltwater service system:
>   Series of pipes that provide saltwater for flushing and firefighting
>   aboard ship.

Salty:
>   Nautical; seagoing; sometimes means raffish, cocky, unconventional,
>   earthy.

Salute, gun:
>   A number of blank shots fired to greet some personage or to celebrate
>   an occasion.

Salute, hand:
>   A gesture of mutual respect exchanged between persons in military
>   service (except prisoners). Usually accompanied in the Navy by a
>   greeting, as "Good morning, Sir."

Saluting battery:
>   Guns used to fire a salute.

Saluting ship or station:
>   One so designated by the Secretary of the Navy as being capable of
>   rendering such an honor: in general, only major warships and large
>   naval activities.

Salvage:
>   Cast off, discarded material. To save or rescue material that has
>   been discarded, wrecked, sunk, or damaged.

Salvage group:
>   In an amphibious operation, a naval task organization designated
>   and equipped to rescue personnel and to salvage equipment and
>   materiel.

Salvage money:
>   Money divided by crew of ship that has salvaged another and brought
>   it into port to be sold. No longer paid to naval personnel.

Salvo:
>   One or more shots fired simultaneously by the same battery at the
>   same target.

Salvo latch:
Device to prevent unintentional opening of the breech of a loaded gun, until after the gun has been fired.

SAMARITAN:
Model designation: C-131; cognizant service: Air Force.
Transport aircraft arranged to handle cargo, passengers, or litter patients. Two-crew, 29-passengers or 27-litters plus attendants. Propeller-driven.

Samson post:
Vertical timber on the forward deck of a boat used in towing and securing. Sometimes used as synonym for *King Post.*

Sand table:
Device for constructing a scale model of an amphibious assault landing beach used for training purposes.

Sandblower:
Slang: short man. Low-level flight, or an aircraft designed for same.

Santa Ana:
A violent, dry offshore wind, common to coastal southern California.

SARAH:
Radar-guided version of *SIDEWINDER.*

Save-all:
Net spread under cargo handling operations between ship and pier.

Savoir:
Slang: brainy or clever man.

Scale:
Undesirable deposit, mostly calcium sulfate, which forms in the boiler tubes of naval boilers.

Scaling hammer:
Hand or power tool for removing paint and rust from metal plating.

Scanning:
Sonar echo-ranging system employing a constantly transmitted outgoing signal over the angle of search.

Scarfing:
Adhesively or mechanically locking two members (wood, metal, plastic) together to form a single long one with no sacrifice in strength.

Scarp:
Bank cut into the shore by surf.

Schooner:
A *Fore-and-aft* rigged sailing vessel, originally and still typically having two masts, although multimasted schooners were tried for a short time late in the days of sail. See *Fore-and-aft sail.*

Scope:
Number of fathoms of chain out to anchor.

Scouting:
> A mission involving search, patrol, tracking, or reconnaissance by a surface ship, submarine, or aircraft.

SCORPION:
> Model designation: F-89; cognizant service: Air Force.
> Fighter aircraft. Two-crew. Jet.

Scour:
> The movement of bottom sediments from their resting place by currents or wave motion.

Scow:
> Large, open, flat-bottom boat for transporting sand, gravel, mud, etc.

Scram:
> A nuclear-power term indicating that some difficulty in reactor operation has arisen causing automatic or deliberate activation of reactor protective features shutting it down. To scram is to lose all reactor power suddenly, necessitating elimination of the difficulty and then carrying on a programmed restart.

Scramble:
> Emergency launching of fighter aircraft. In cryptography, to mix at random.

Scramble nets:
> Cargo or disembarkation nets rigged over the side for picking up survivors.

Scraper:
> Hand tool used to scrape paint and woodwork.

Screamer:
> A magnetic device attached to the hull of a target submarine, to transmit sound for location of the sub by ASW forces.

Screen:
> Ships stationed to protect a unit, as an antisubmarine screen. To examine and evaluate, as screening of applicants.

Screw:
> Propeller of a ship.

Screw current:
> A movement of water caused by turning of the propeller.

Screwing:
> Dangerous rotary motion of ice floes caused by wind and ice pressure.

Scudding:
> Driving before a gale. Scudding under bare poles means with all sails down or furled, all upper yards lowered, and the rest secured.

Scull:
> To propel a boat by working an oar from side to side over the stern; to propel oneself in the water by working hands and forearms in a figure-eight motion.

Scullery:
> Compartment in a ship where general mess dishwashing is done.

Scupper:
> Fittings along the waterways on the weather decks and below that lead water over or through the side.

Scupper lip:
> Extension to prevent scupper discharge from running down the ship's sides.

Scuttle:
> Small, quick-closing access hole. To sink a ship deliberately.

Scuttlebutt:
> Shipboard drinking fountain: Slang: rumor or gossip.

Sea:
> A wave generated locally by wind action. Depending on the wind and fetch, seas are generally unsymmetrical in slope, have steep crests and show white caps.

Sea anchor:
> Device, usually of wood and/or canvas, streamed by a vessel or boat in heavy weather to hold the bow up to the sea. Also called a *Drogue.*

Sea bag:
> Canvas bag in which an enlisted man transports his gear.

SEA BAT:
> Model designation: SH-34; cognizant service: Navy.
> Similar to CHOCTAW except modified to perform miscellaneous utility missions. Four-crew.

Seabed:
> Bottom of the sea, beyond the *Continental shelf.*

Seabee (CB):
> Naval Construction Battalion. ACB stands for Amphibious Construction Battalion and MCB for Mobile Construction Battalion.

Sea breeze:
> Breeze blowing off the sea towards the land, caused by land heating more quickly as sun rises. See *Land breeze.*

Sea buoy:
> The buoy farthest to sea of those marking a channel or entrance. Often called a farewell buoy or departure buoy.

Sea chest:
> Sailor's trunk; intake between ship's side and sea valve or seacock.

Seacock:
> Valve in the ship's hull connected to the sea.

Sea daddy:
> Slang: an older man who takes a recruit or young officer in hand and teaches him his trade or profession.

Sea dog:
 An old *sailor.*

Seadopod:
 Surface barge-mounted capsule maintained at sea bottom pressure to house divers engaged in bottom work. Men are delivered to work site by a Submersible Delivery Capsule.

Seadrome:
 Area designated and marked for the safe operation of seaplanes on the water.

Sea duty:
 Assignment afloat in ships, aircraft, or overseas bases or on foreign stations.

SEAFARER:
 SZ-1B ASW blimp.

Sea frontiers:
 Essentially defensive commands closely corresponding to Army Defense Commands. Also function as operational commands for forces assigned by CNO.

Seagoing:
 Capable of going to sea. Salty or nautical in nature. See *Seaworthy.*

Seagull:
 Slang: chicken served in the general mess; girl of poor reputation.

SEA HORSE:
 Model designation: H-34; cognizant service: Navy.
 Similar to *CHOCTAW* modified extensively for operation in Antartica under extreme range and high gross-weight conditions in remote and primitive polar areas. Two-crew.

SEA KING:
 Model designation: H-3; cognizant service: Navy.
 Turbine-powered helicopter for all-weather ASW work. Single five-bladed rotor, retractable landing gear and amphibious hull. Four-crew.

SEA KNIGHT:
 Model designation: CH-46A; Cognizant service: Navy, Marine Corps.
 Helicopter used by the Marine Corps for troop and cargo movement. Two tandem three-bladed rotors. Three-crew, 17 troops.

SEALAB:
 An undersea laboratory development program.

Sea ladder:
 Metal rungs welded to the ship's side above the waterline. See *Jacob's Ladder.*

Sea lawyer:
 An argumentative person: one who too frequently questions orders and regulations.

Sea legs:
Adaptation to the motion of a vessel in a seaway.

Seaman (SN):
Enlisted man in paygrade E-3 who does general deck and boat duties. Any man who is familiar with ships and the sea.

Seaman Apprentice (SA):
Rate to which a man is advanced upon completion of recruit training.

Seaman guard:
Enlisted men who perform guard duty in the absence of Marines.

Seaman Recruit (SR):
Rate that a recruit holds while at a recruit training activity.

Seaman's eye:
The ability to judge distances and maneuvers at sea. To have a good seaman's eye was the ambition of all professional sailors. Officers prided themselves on their possession of this quality, and to impugn a brother officer on this score was an insult of mortal dimensions.

Seamount:
An isolated mountain structure rising from the bottom of the sea to a point near the surface. One having a flat top is a tablemount.

SEA MAULER:
Model designation: RIM-46; cognizant service: Navy. Antiaircraft missile defense system for ships.

Sea painter:
Line led from well forward on the ship to a boat alongside, to which it is secured on the near bow with a loop and toggle. Not to be confused with *Bow painter,* which is secured to the stem of the boat and which cannot be used for towing the boat alongside.

Sea power:
The ability of a country to use and control the sea and to prevent an enemy from using it.

SEA RANGER:
Model designation: TH-57; cognizant service: Navy. Trainer helicopter; has single two-bladed main rotor, turboshaft engine, skid-type gear, dual flight controls, and seats for five personnel including crew.

Search and Attack Unit (SAU):
Two or more ships or aircraft teamed for coordinated search and attack on submarines.

Searchlight Sonar:
Echo-ranging system using the same narrow beam pattern for transmission and reception.

Sea return:
Interference on radar screen caused by reflections from the sea.

Sea room:
Far enough from land for unrestricted maneuvers. Also, enough room between ships for maneuvering.

Sea slick:
> Surface area markedly different in appearance from surrounding water, usually caused by plankton.

SEASPRITE:
> Model designation: H-2; cognizant service: Navy.
> High-performance turbine-power helicopter to accomplish general utility tasks. Two-crew, two-passengers.

SEA STALLION:
> Model designation: CH-53; cognizant service: Navy.
> Assault helicopter to be employed primarily in the movement of cargo and equipment, and secondarily in the transportation of troops, in amphibious assault and subsequent operations ashore; six-bladed main rotor. Three-crew.

SEA STAR:
> Model designation: T-1; cognizant service: Navy.
> A two-place, low-wing aircraft for training operations. Provisions for carrier use. Two-crew. Jet.

Sea state:
> Numerical or written description of sea roughness.

Sea stores:
> Cigarettes and other luxuries sold at sea and abroad free of federal tax.

Seavey/Shorvey:
> A Bureau of Personnel system for sea-shore rotation. "Vey" is short for survey.

Seaway:
> A moderate to rough sea.

Seaworthy:
> Capable of putting to sea and meeting any usual sea condition.

Secchi disc:
> A white, black, or varicolored disc, usually about a foot in diameter, that measures water transparency.

Secondary conn:
> Conning station for use if the main conn (the bridge) is damaged.

Second dog watch:
> The watch from 1800 (6 PM) to 2000 (8 PM). Also called the last dog watch.

Secret:
> Information or material whose disclosure would endanger national security or cause serious injury to the interests or prestige of the U.S.

Section:
> Applied to ships or naval aircraft, a tactical subdivision of a division. Normally, one-half of a division in the case of ships, and two aircraft in the case of aircraft. Sub-division of a division of men.

Sector center:
> The true or relative bearing of an ASW search sector.

Sector, geographic (relative):
One limited by bearings from a fixed or moving point.

Sector width:
The width in degrees of a search sector.

Secure:
To make fast in a permanent sense as to "Secure the forward hold
for sea". Well-fastened or safe. To cease or stop, e.g. "Secure
from fire drill." To quit, give up, or knock off.

Seiche:
Periodic wave oscillation (rise and fall of the water's level) whose period
varies from a few minutes to less than tidal period, found in enclosed
bodies of water or superimposed on tide-induced waves in open ocean.
Caused by harmonic vibration in response to storm or tidal wave
disturbances at sea. Pronounced "sayshe."

Seize:
To bind with a small rope.

Seizing stuff:
Small Stuff.

Selection board:
Panel of officers who review records and recommend for promotion.
Used for all grades above that of lieutenant, junior grade. Also
called promotion board.

Self-sustaining:
Said of a nuclear reactor when it is producing enough power to run
all associated auxiliaries and hence the load on the ship's auxiliary
power equipment, such as diesel engines, battery, has been removed.
This phrase is generally used during start-up procedure.

Semaphore:
Rapid method of short range visual communications between ships,
using hand flags.

Semi-diurnal:
Having a period of cycle of approximately half of a lunar day, roughly
12.42 hours.

SEMINOLE:
Model designation: U-8; cognizant service: Army.
A low-wing cantilever aircraft. For command transport and utility
missions. One-crew, five-passengers. Propeller-driven.

SEMPER:
Anti-missile missile concept.

SENECA:
Model designation: H-41A; cognizant service: Army.
A four-place helicopter with two-bladed rotor, skid-type landing
gear. One-crew, three-passengers.

Senior Officer Present Afloat (SOPA):
The senior line officer of the Navy, on active service, eligible for
command at sea, who is present and in command of any unit of the operating
forces afloat in the locality or within an area prescribed by competent
authority.

Sennet, sennit:
>Braided cordage made from rope yarns or spun yarn, plaited by hand. There are many varieties such as rounded sennet, square sennet, flat sennet, French sennet, etc. Used for mats, *Stoppers, Manropes,* etc. and may have ornamental functions. See *Fancy work, Square knotting, Coxcombing, McNamara Lace.*

Sequence number:
>Number assigned a ship by the Unit Commander to indicate its position in the line.

SERGEANT:
>Model designation: MGM-29; cognizant service: Army. A field artillery all-inertial-guidance missile.

Serial:
>Unit of personnel or material numbered for ease of reference in unloadings ships during an amphibious assault.

Serial number:
>One of a consecutive group of numerals assigned a specific piece of correspondence for identification purposes. Not to be confused with the *Service number* assigned each enlisted man, although sometimes men or officers use term serial when they mean *Service, Signal, Lineal,* or *File number.*

Serve:
>To wrap with continuous, contiguous round turns. Wire rope is *Wormed, Parcelled,* and served.

Service ammunition:
>That used for combat, as distinct from target ammunition.

Service craft:
>Naval craft too small to be commissioned, yet fully operational, and usually commanded by enlisted men, are "in service." See Appendix A.

Service craft designations:
>See Appendix A.

Service Force-(SERVFOR):
>A naval task organization which performs logistic support of Fleet units.

Service line:
>Logistic support vessels formed on a line to conduct replenishment.

Service medal:
>Medal for service in specific campaign or theater of operations.

Service message:
>Brief message incidental to the correction, verification, or handling of another message, or the exchange of information between stations.

Service number:
>Record identification number for Navy and Marine Corps enlisted and for Marine Corps officers. See *File number,* and *Serial number.*

Service rating:
>See Appendix B.

Service record:
> Document recording an enlisted man's conduct, performance of duties, tests, etc.

Service schools:
> Schools offering advanced technical training for enlisted men.

Service stripe:
> Sleeve marks worn by enlisted men and women to denote length of service. Each stripe denotes 4 years. Slang: Hash Mark.

Serving:
> Additional protection over *Parceling* consisting of continuous round turns of *Small stuff.*

Setback:
> The force of inertia which tends to move certain fuze parts to the rear as the projectile is fired. Used to arm a fuze.

Set (of a current):
> The direction towards which the water is flowing. A ship is set by the current. Note that a southerly current and a north wind are going in the same direction.

Set taut, set up:
> To remove the slack; to tighten. An order to take in all the slack on running gear before heaving in.

Set the watch:
> To establish the regular routine of watches on a ship or station.

Set the course:
> To give the helmsman the desired course to be steered.

Settle:
> To sink deeper into the water.

Sextant:
> Navigational device used to measure the angular distance between two objects, usually between the earth's horizon and a celestial body. A similar instrument is an *Octant*. See *Radio sextant.*

Shackle:
> U-shaped metal fitting, closed at the open ends with a pin, used to connect wire and chain. Also to encode a message on voice radio.

SHADDOCK:
> A 200-mile range Soviet surface-to-surface missile.

Shadow zone:
> Region in which sound refraction limits effectiveness of echo-ranging sound signals.

Shaft alley:
> The space in a ship through which the propeller shafts extend from engine room to propeller.

Shakedown:
>Period of adjustment, clean up, and training for a ship after commissioning
or a major overhaul. After commissioning, a ship also makes a shakedown
cruise, usually including a visit to several foreign ports.

Shank:
>The central shaft of an anchor to which the *Flukes* are attached.

Shape:
>Small structure or object, of various descriptions and colors, dis-
played aloft by a vessel fishing, dredging, at anchor, etc.

Shark chaser:
>Small bag of shark-repelling matter usually attached to life jackets.

SHAWNEE:
>Model designation: H-21; cognizant service: Army.
Helicopter with two three-bladed rotors in tandem and turning in
opposite directions. Employed for assault and support missions.
Two-crew, 20-passengers. See *WORKHORSE.*

Sheave:
>The pulley in a *Block.* (Pronounced shiv.)

Sheer:
>Excess of *Freeboard* of a ship forward or aft over that amidships. Longitudinal
curvature of the main deck between bow and stern with low point amidships.

Sheer off:
>To steer away from; to bear off.

Sheer plan:
>Drawing of the ship showing the vertical sections of the hull form
at various sections from amidships to the outer hull as viewed from
amidships, superimposed on one drawing. *Lines drawing.*

Sheet:
>A line that regulates the angle at which a sail is set in relation
to the wind. See *Three sheets to the wind,* and *Sheet home.*

Sheet anchor:
>The main or heaviest anchor, formerly carried in the *waist* of a
sailing ship. Sometimes the term was used interchangeably with *Bower,*
but bower came into more general use with large steel ships which no
longer carried an extra anchor in the location of what would have been
their waist. Long after the *Stockless anchor* came into general use,
the sheet anchor, or bower, continued to be of the *Old-fashioned*
type because of its greater holding power for the same weight.

Sheet home:
>To extend a *Square sail* by hauling upon the *Sheets* until it is
set as flat as possible. A term used most frequently when the sail
is first set, or when *Reefs* are shaken out.

Shelf:
>The area of sea bottom from point of permanent immersion to the point
where steep descent to great depths occurs. The seaward line is usually
regarded as 100 fathoms or 200 meters. See *Continental Shelf.*

Shell:
> Projectile fired from a ship's gun. Originally the word distinguished an explosive projectile from a solid *Round shot,* since the shell was hollow and full of gun powder. The Battle of Sinope in 1853 was the first instance when shells were used in combat, and a numerically superior Russian fleet totally annihilated a Turkish fleet equipped with only solid shot. Today, shell refers to projectiles from large guns, all of which are loaded with explosive charges. Also, the casing of a *Block* with which the *Sheave* revolves.

Shellback:
> One who has crossed the equator.

Shell room:
> Projectile stowage in a ship's turret.

Sheriff:
> Slang: *Master at arms.*

Sheriff's badge:
> Slang: Command Insigna worn by line officers.

Shift colors:
> To shift the ensign and *Jack* between the steaming and in port positions, and vice versa.

Shifts:
> Work periods in shipyards. First shift (daylight shift) is morning and afternoon; second (swing) shift is late afternoon and evening; third (graveyard) shift is from midnight to breakfast.

Shift the rudder:
> Command to the steersman to apply the same amount of rudder in the opposite direction.

SHILLELAGH:
> Model designation: MGM-51; cognizant service: Army.
> A direct-fire, command to line-of-sight guided missile.

Ship:
> Any large sea-going vessel. Specifically, in days of sail, a vessel with a bowsprit and three masts, entirely *Square-rigged,* except that the lowest sail on the after-most mast, or *Mizzenmast,* was *Fore-and-aft* rigged and called the *Spanker.* Also called a *Full-rigged ship.* In days of sail each type of rig had its own name, such as *Brig, Schooner, Sloop, Snow, Brigantine, Hermaphrodite brig, Bark* or *barque, Barkentine, Topsail schooner.* A *Sloop-of-war* was a full-rigged ship mounting guns on only a single deck. Also, to set up, to secure in place, e.g., ship the rudder. To enlist or re-enlist, as to ship over. To take something aboard, as to ship a sea, or to send freight.

Ship Alteration (ShipAlt):
> Authorization to make an alteration on specific machinery or on specific parts of particular ships.

Shipboard:
> Pertaining to a ship.

Ship characteristics:
    All qualities and features that permit a ship to accomplish her mission.
    Includes *Complement,* their battle stations, and all material for
    fighting the ship.

Ship designations:
    See Appendix A.

Shipfitter (SF):
    Petty officer who works in sheet metal, piping, steel plate, etc.

Shiphandling:
    The art and skill of directing the movements of a ship in formation,
    tactics, and maneuvers, in restricted waters, or in docking and mooring.

Ship Improvement Guide (SIG):
    A catalog of all items, maintained by the ship's Characteristics Division,
    submitted for inclusion in the Class Improvement Plan.

Shipmate:
    Person with whom one has served, particularly at sea.

Ship-of-the-line:
    The battleship of the days of sail. Mounted guns on three or more
    decks. Slow and cumbersome, but very heavily built and designedly
    fit to "lie in the line of battle." Thus, a "line-of-battle-ship,"
    and the term gradually became simply "battleship."

Ship over:
    To re-enlist.

Shipper:
    An activity which has cognizance over cargo prior to its delivery to
    a carrier.

Shipping:
    Ships, usually qualified as to usage as: assault shipping, support
    shipping, etc.

Shipping board clamps:
    U-shaped fittings, threaded and provided with an end piece that is
    secured with two nuts. Used to join wire or to make a temporary eye.

Shipping-over chow:
    Any particularly good meal, supposedly served to encourage re-enlist-
    ment.

Ship rider:
    Member of a Fleet Training Group who goes to sea in a ship to assist
    in its shakedown or refresher training.

Ship's bell:
    Struck every 30 minutes to mark passing of time. Also used to sound
    fog signals and as a fire alarm.

Ship's Clerk:
    Warrant officer advanced from *Journalist, Personnel Man, or
    Yeoman.*

Ship's company:
　　All hands; everyone on board.

Shipshape:
　　Neat, orderly, as a ship should be.

Shipshape and Bristol Fashion:
　　Neat, clean, and implies all rigging coiled and flemished down,
　　everything in perfect condition as it should be. Term implies a
　　condition superior to merely shipshape.

Ship's orders:
　　Written directives upon specific subjects signed by the CO and having
　　the authority of lawful regulations.

Ship's organization book:
　　Administrative and organizational guide for a particular ship, based
　　on a standard issued by the type commander.

Ship's secretary:
　　Officer who assists the executive officer with ship's correspondence.

Ship's service:
　　The ship's retail store.

Ship's Serviceman (SH):
　　Petty officer who performs general ship's service duties such as clerk,
　　barber, cobbler, tailor, etc.

Ship's store:
　　Carries supplies for health, comfort, and personal cleanliness of the crew.

Ship Systems Command:
　　Functional command replacing Bureau of Ships in 1966 Navy Department
　　reorganization. Component of *Naval Material Command.*

Ship-to-shore movement:
　　Debarkation of troops from assault shipping to landing area.

Shipyard:
　　Shipbuilding and repair facility *Naval Shipyard* is one maintained
　　by the Navy.

Shoal:
　　An area of shallow water. Shallow.

Shoaling effect:
　　The change in a wave as it proceeds from deep to shallow water; its
　　length decreases and its height increases.

Shoe:
　　Fitting from which paravanes are towed, on the stem of a ship. More
　　generally, a protecting member under keel or bottom of ship.

Shole:
　　Flat plate to distribute the force under the end of a *Shore.*

SHOOTING STAR:
> Model designation: F-80, T-33; cognizant services: Navy/Air Force.
> Originally a single-place jet fighter aircraft with high performance
> for the time when it was new. Since modified into a high-performance
> jet trainer. Two-crew. Jet.

Shoot the sun:
> Measure the sun's altitude with a sextant.

Shoran:
> An accurate short-range navigation system often used for aerial
> surveying and mapping. Utilizes pulse transmissions, transponders,
> and a receiver.

Shore:
> Portable wooden beam used in damage control. To shore up is to brace up.

Shore boat:
> Civilian operated harbor passenger boat, also known as *Water Taxi*.

Shore duty:
> Assignment ashore in U.S. or possessions.

Shore Establishment:
> All activities of the *Naval Establishment* not included in the *Operating
> Forces* or in the *Navy Department*.

Shore fire-control party (SFCP):
> Specially trained unit for the control of naval gunfire in support
> of troops ashore.

Shoreline:
> The junction of land and sea at low tide unless otherwise specified.

Shore patrol (SP):
> Personnel ashore on police duty.

Shoring:
> Process of placing props against structure or cargo to prevent sinking,
> sagging, or movement in a seaway.

Short arm inspection:
> Slang for medical inspection for venereal disease, now rare.

Short blast:
> Whistle, horn, or siren blast of about one second's duration.

Short-handed:
> Without enough people to do the job properly.

Short stay:
> Said of an anchor when it has been hove in just short of breaking ground.

Short timer:
> Person nearing the end of his enlistment, service, or tour of duty.

Shot:
> A length of anchor chain, usually 15 fathoms.

Shot line:
>Light nylon line used in line-throwing gun.

Shoulder mark:
>Device indicating rank worn on an officer's overcoat and the jacket or coat of summer uniforms. Also called shoulder board.

Shove off:
>Slang: depart; leave; go. Proper naval usage as in "Shove off, coxswain, on the bell and make the liberty landing and return."

Show a leg:
>An expression used in rousing out sleeping men. "Rouse and shine" has been corrupted to "Rise and shine." The call "Show a leg" is derived from the days when seamen's "wives" were allowed to sleep on board ship. See *Son of a gun.* Women who put out a stockinged leg for identification were not required to turn out at first call, although their men were. The term bears no relation to "shake a leg" which is a nonnautical phrase meaning to *Bear a hand,* or hurry.

SHRIKE:
>Model designation: AGM-45; cognizant services: Navy/Air Force. Air-to-surface tactical missile used for destruction of radiation targets.

Shrouds:
>Lines or wires that give *Athwartships* support to a mast. Also lines attaching parachute canopy to the jumper's harness.

Shuttle:
>Device on an airplane catapult which transmits motion to the airplane.

Sick bay:
>Infirmary or first-aid station aboard ship.

Sick call:
>A call (and *Word*) passed daily aboard ship for those who require medical attention to report to *Sick Bay.* A scheduled time each day at all medical facilities when patients may be seen without appointment.

Side arms:
>Pistols or revolvers.

Side boy:
>Non-rated men stationed in two ranks at the gangway upon the arrival or departure of important officers or officials for whom *Side Honors* are being rendered. Number varies from two to eight.

Side cleaners:
>Men detailed to scrub the sides of the ship.

Side honors:
>Ceremonious greeting of important officers and officials as they come aboard ship. May include piping the side, side boys, the ship's band and guard, and gun salutes.

Side lights:
>The red and green, 10-point, port and starboard, running lights required of all ships by the *Rules of the Road.*

SIDEWINDER:
Model designation: AIM-9; cognizant services: Navy/Air Force.
A supersonic, air-to-air homing weapon.

Sierra:
Phonetic word for letter S.

Sight:
An accurately timed observed altitude of a heavenly body.

Sight the anchor:
To heave an anchor up far enough to see that it is clear, then again
let go. Necessary where holding ground is very soft; anchor may sink
beyond easy recovery.

Signal:
Short message using one or more letters, characters, flags, visual
displays, or special sounds. Any transmitted electrical impulse.

Signal book:
The standard publication governing flag communications between naval
vessels. Formerly called the General Signal Book, now Allied Naval
Signal Book.

Signal bridge:
Area of navigating bridge adjacent to *Flag bags,* used by signalmen.
Not a part of *Flag bridge,* but taken over by the flag when the
ship is employed as a *Flagship.*

Signal flags:
All flags used in visual communications.

Signal number:
Old term for officer's precedence number. Replaced by *Lineal number*
and *Number in grade* (Marine Corps)

Signal record book (log):
A record of all general signals transmitted or received.

Silence:
Command given by any member of a crew who observes a serious
casualty that requires immediate attention.

Silent running:
Condition of quiet operation of machinery in a submarine to deny
detection by an enemy listening for noise.

Silica gel:
Moisture absorbent chemical used in tanks, voids, magazines, etc.

Sill:
Submerged elevation separating two ocean basins.

Sill depth:
Greatest depth at which there is free horizontal communication between
two ocean basins.

Sill of a dock:
The timber or beam at the entrance gate of a drydock over which a
vessel must pass.

Sing out:
> To announce or call out.

Single Service Procurement:
> Procurement of designated supplies or services by one Military Department to satisfy its own requirements or those of other Departments on agreement by the Departments concerned or on assignment by DOD.

Single up:
> A command given preparatory to unmooring a ship from a wharf or pier. Means to take in the double sections of line between the ship and the pier, leaving her moored by only single strands of line to the *Bitts, Bollards,* or *Cleats.*

Single whip:
> A tackle using a single fixed block.

Sinuating:
> Series of curving variations from the base course steered by a ship. See *Evasive steering.*

SIOUX:
> Model designation: H-13; cognizant services: Army/Navy/Coast Guard. A light single-rotor helicopter, designed for liaison, observation, and evacuation missions. One-crew, two-passengers.

Siren:
> High-pitched, noise-making device used aboard ship when an emergency (collision, grounding, etc.) is imminent.

Sister hooks:
> Pair of hooks which fit together to make a closed ring.

Sister ships:
> Ships built on the same design. Sometimes used loosely to refer to ships in the same employment or organization.

Situation report (SitRep):
> A special report, generally of informal nature, required to keep higher authority advised. Prescribed under certain predictable circumstances, but may also be required at any time.

Skeg:
> Continuation of the keel aft under the propeller and supporting the rudder post.

Skids, boat:
> Fittings on deck designed to hold and support a boat, composed of *Saddles* making up a cradle and *Gripes* to hold the boat down.

SKIPPER:
> Anti-satellite weapon system concept using vertical launched space mines. Same as *EARLY SPRING.*

Skipper:
> Slang: the commanding officer.

Skip zone:
> Area between ground waves and sky waves in which no radio waves are received.

Skivvy:
Slang: underwear.

SKYHAWK:
Model designation: A-4; cognizant service: Navy.
Small, light, high-performance carrier-based attack aircraft. Delta wing. One-crew.

SKYHOOK:
System for rescue of personnel from the sea or isolated areas by aircraft. Also, large unmanned balloon sent aloft to record meteorological data. Also, slang: A skyhook is a mythical gadget sometimes wished for by sailors to handle awkward or heavy items.

SKY KNIGHT:
Model designation: F-10B; cognizant service: Navy.
Carrier-based fighter aircraft, generally used for special missions. Two-crew. Jet.

Skylark:
A distinctly nautical expression meaning to play or to have fun, "to have a lark." Derived from the practice of young sailors laying aloft and sliding down the back stays. Thus, to engage in horseplay, noisy banter, or friendly scuffling.

SKYMASTER:
Model designation: C-54; cognizant service: Navy/Air Force.
Four-engine transport aircraft. Five-crew, 44 passengers. Propeller driven.

Sky pilot (slang):
Chaplain on board ship, sometimes also called *Padre*.

SKYRAIDER:
Model designation: A-1; Cognizant services: Navy/Air Force.
Multipurpose aircraft, land-based or carrier-based. Had great versatility as an attack bomber or utility aircraft. Production had to be reopened because of Vietnam War, in the early stages of which it was the most popular and effective aircraft for close air support. Two-crew. Propeller-driven.

SKYRAY:
Model designation: F-6; cognizant service: Navy.
A single-place, high-performance, delta-wing, carrier-based, all-weather intercepter fighter aircraft. One-crew. Jet.

SKYTRAIN:
Model designation: C-47, C-117; cognizant service: Navy/Army/Air Force.
All-purpose transport-type aircraft. This is the famous old C-47, or DC-3 in its commercial version, both designations having virtually passed into the language. Propeller-driven, of course. Served over a 30-year period. Two-crew, 24-passengers.

SKYWARRIOR:
Model designation: A-3; cognizant service: Navy/Air Force.
Carrier-based high-performance attack aircraft. Three-crew. Jet.

Sky waves:
Radio waves reflected by the ionosphere.

Slack:
Ease out, as a line. The loose part of a line that takes no strain.

Slack water:
Period of no tidal motion between flood and ebb.

Sled:
Towed surface gunnery target, smaller and faster than a raft.

Sleeve:
Fabric tube towed by an airplane, used as an antiaircraft target.

Slew:
To rotate rapidly, as a gun director slews to get on a new target.

Slice:
An average logistic planning factor used to obtain estimates of requirements for personnel and materiel. A personnel slice generally
consists of the total strength of the stated basic combatant element,
plus its proportionate share of all supporting and higher headquarters
personnel.

Slide:
The sleeve part of the mount which directly supports the gun.

Slings:
Gear for hoisting something aboard, e.g., boat slings.

Slip:
To part from an anchor by unshackling the chain. The lost motion in
a propeller. A narrow stretch of water between two piers.

Sloop:
Sailing vessel with a single mast, rigged *Fore-and-aft.* See *Cutter.*

Sloop-of-war:
A *Full-rigged ship* mounting her main battery on only a single
deck, as distinguished from a *Frigate,* which mounted guns on
two decks. Smaller than a frigate, and faster.

Slop chute:
A chute hung over the side of a ship for the discharge of garbage.
Slang: anyone who is dirty and disorderly in appearance or habits.

Slops:
Ready-made outfits furnished to seaman on board who were inadequately
clothed. The slops-chest was a locker belonging to the officer who
sold articles of clothing to crew members, charging it against their
wages. Since such an officer--usually the ship's purser—sometimes
considered his slops-chest as a device to augment his income, his
stock had a tendency to be of poor quality and very expensive, and the
whole institution was much resented even when honestly run. Obsolete.

Sludge:
Sediment in fuel oil tanks.

Slush down:
To treat standing rigging with a preservative.

Small arms:
Rifles, shotguns, pistols, and carbines.

Small craft warning:
> Red pennant indicating weather conditions unfavorable or dangerous for small craft operations.

Small stores:
> See *Clothing and Small Stores.*

Small stuff:
> Small cordage aboard ship such as 12-thread stuff, marline, seizing stuff, or spun yarn.

Smart:
> Neat; shipshape; efficient; military; quick.

Smoker:
> Shipboard entertainment including food, boxing, humorous skits and movies. Same as *Happy Hour* when used at sea.

Smoke-pipe:
> Stack on a ship.

Smokestack:
> Slang: to pretend to be drunk.

Smoking lamp:
> A lamp aboard old ships, used by men to light their pipes; now used in phrase "The smoking lamp is lit," to indicate when men are allowed to smoke. Today it is entirely a figurative term.

Smooth-bore gunner:
> Officer who specializes in gunnery duties, although not a post-graduate student of ordnance and gunnery.

Snake out:
> To break out specific items of cargo.

Snaking:
> Netting rigged between the *Housing Line* and the *Footline* or *Waterway Bar* to prevent objects on deck from going overboard.

SNAP-7:
> System for Nuclear Auxillary Power; uses atomic power for lighting of buoys.

Snatch block:
> Single-sheaved block with a hinged strap. It can be quickly opened to take the bight of a line, thus not requiring the end of the line to be led through the block. A great convenience for handling line on deck.

SNIFFER:
> Airborne equipment for detection of exhaust gasses from a snorkeling submarine.

Snipe:
> Slang: a man of the engineering department. See *Black gang.*

Snooper:
> An aircraft that is shadowing or observing.

Snorkel:
> Device used by a submarine to enable it to draw air from the surface while submerged. Also to operate submerged with snorkel showing.

Snow:
> A three-masted square-rigger with, however, a large lateen sail on the mizzenmast. A rig common to the American Revolution era. Pronounced to rhyme with "cow."

Snow blink:
> A bright white glare on the underside of clouds, produced by the reflection of light from a snow-covered surface.

SNOWFLAKE:
> General term applied to requests from DOD for additional justification, information, or comment on budget items during preparation of the budget. Specifically, in the latter stages of this preparation, when deadlines are short and the demands are many.

Snub:
> To stop a running line suddenly by taking a turn and holding.

Snug down:
> To make preparations to weather a storm at sea.

Solar still:
> An item of survival equipment which distills fresh water using the energy of sunlight.

Soldier:
> Slang: To loaf on the job. One who loafs. Note, however, that to address an Army man or a Marine as "Soldier," or to use the word in reference to him, is a term of approval.

Solo:
> To fly or operate an aircraft with sole and complete responsibility therefor.

Soluble washer:
> Device used to delay the arming of a mine after planting.

SONAR:
> Sound Navigation And Ranging. Underwater sound equipment for submarine detection and navigation.

Sonar man (SO):
> Petty officer who manipulates and performs routine upkeep on underwater detection and attack gear.

Sonic depth finder:
> Device measuring time for a sound signal to reach bottom and return, giving reading in terms of depth.

Sonobuoy:
> A small sound receiver-transmitter normally dropped from aircraft to detect submarine noises and transmit them to the plane.

Son of a gun:
>Technically, a child born on board ship alongside one of her broad-
side cannon. The spaces between guns on the broadside were regular
berthing spaces, and the term recalls the old days when sailors were
sometimes permitted to have their wives live on board. The result of
the custom, of course, was an occasional birth--and, circumstances
being as they must have been, the term implied questionable paternity.
An old saying was that a true "man-o-war's man was begotten in the
galley and born under a gun." Because of the romantic nautical
toughness ascribed by the title, to be a son-of-a-gun quickly lost
its opprobrious connotation.

Soogey moogey:
>Solution of strong soap, lye, etc., for cleaning paintwork. Rarely
used now.

Soot blower:
>Soot removal device using a steam jet to clean the firesides of a
boiler while in use.

Sortie:
>To depart; the act of departing. A naval force sorties from a port.

Sound:
>To measure depth of water at sea or the depth of a liquid in a ship's
tanks. Result is a sounding. A whale sounds when it dives. Also to
blow, as a bugle.

Sound absorption:
>The change of sound into some other form of energy, usually heat, as
it passes through a medium or strikes a surface.

Sound channel:
>A natural phenomenon at mid-depth which forms a wave guide permitting
the transmission of sound over great distances through the sea.

Soundhead:
>The container for transmitting projector and receiving hydrophones.

Sounding Fixing And Ranging (SOFAR):
>An underwater distress signal whose location is determined by measuring
its different times of reception at several stations where, by
triangulation and time differential calculation, position can be established.

Sounding patrol:
>Duty men who periodically sound the ship's tanks and report the results
to the OOD.

Sound-powered telephones:
>Telephones that generate own power by the sound vibrations of the voice
moving in the field of a magnet.

Southeast Asia Management Information Center (SEAMIC):
>Special office established within the Navy to handle requirements to
Viet Nam.

SOUTHERN CROSS:
>Project analyzing the communications requirements of ships to determine
how these requirements can be met with minimum equipment and at minimum
cost.

Spademan:
 Man who operates the rammer on a 5'' gun.

Span:
 Line made fast at both ends with a tackle, line, or fitting made fast to
 its bight. Wire rope stretched between davit heads to which lifelines
 are secured.

Spanner:
 Wrench with fixed jaws designed for coupling hoses.

Spar:
 Long, round stick of wood or steel, frequently tapered at one or both
 ends, generally associated with masts or rigging.

Spar buoy:
 Type of buoy which looks like a stick floating upright.

Spares, equipment:
 Those to be retained with equipment to which they pertain.

Spares, tender:
 Spare parts placed on tenders or at advanced bases

SPARROW:
 Moden designation: AIM-7;
 cognizant services: Navy/Air Force.
 A solid-fuel radar homing air-to-air missile with a high-explosive
 warhead.

Speak:
 To communicate with a vessel that is in sight.

Special devices:
 Term covering synthetic training aids, teaching aids, research in
 human engineering, tactical evaluation, and training methods.

Special duty officer:
 An officer who specializes, for example in public information, but
 usually does not command.

Special money:
 Pay drawn at times other than pay day.

Special sea detail(s):
 Men assigned duties in connection with getting underway, mooring, and
 anchoring. They relieve or are relieved by the regular sea detail.

Special Services:
 Activities involving the welfare and recreation of personnel.

Special Services Officer:
 One who is responsible for recreational activities.

Specialty mark:
 The design or insignia, part of a petty officer's rating badge, that
 indicates his rating.

Special weapons:
 Those involving nuclear or atomic energy.

Specific Operational Requirement (SOR):
>Prepared by CNO telling the Chief of Naval Material of the need for some particular operational capability. This is the final document in requirements documentation and normally marks the transition from research to system development.

Specified Command:
>A command which has a broad continuing mission and which is established and so designated by the President through the SecDef with the advice and assistance of JCS. Normally composed of forces from one Service. See *Joint Command*.

Speed:
>Speeds ordered are commonly one-third, two-thirds, standard, full, and flank. One-third and two-thirds are fractions of standard speed; full speed is designated speed slightly—usually about one-eighth—more than standard; flank speed is as fast as the ship can go. For going astern, the common speeds are one-third, two-thirds, full, and emergency. In the merchant service, half-speed is used instead of one-third and two-thirds, and a similar system is followed by the British Navy.

Speed, base:
>The resultant speed along the base course during evasive steering.

Speed cones:
>Yellow conical shapes, hoisted at the port and starboard yardarms to indicate engine speed to ships astern. No longer used in U.S. Navy.

Speed key:
>Special telegraph key for sending code at high rate. Also called a *Bug*.

Speed letter:
>Priority form of abbreviated correspondence sent by mail.

Speed light:
>Red or white, steady or flashing, light on the mainmast that indicates the speed the ship is making to other ships in company. No longer used in U.S. Navy.

Speed, normal:
>Speed at which ships are to proceed if a signaled speed has not been ordered. A reference speed used by U.S. Navy which corresponds to *Speed, Standard.*

Speed, operational:
>The highest speed at which ships will be required to proceed during a particular period or operation.

Speed, signaled:
>The speed at which the guide of a group of ships has been ordered to proceed.

Speed, standard:
>Speed prescribed as standard for that type of ship, commonly 15 knots.

Speed, stationing:
>Speed slower than operational speed used for economy reasons when maneuvering or changing station.

Spider:
Portable magnifying glass on a compass.

Spin stabilize:
To stabilize a missile in flight by having it rotate around its long axis.

Spit:
Small point of land or a long, narrow shoal, usually sand extending outward from shore.

Spit kit:
Spittoon; ashtray. Also derisive term for small, unseaworthy vessel.

Splash boards:
Boards rigged on stern of small craft to keep water out of cockpit.

Splash line:
In night *Underwater Demolition Unit* operations, the point of the enemy beach at which swimmers enter the water from rubber boats.

SPLASHNIK:
Buoy for wave measurement by telemetry. Information on its vertical motion is sent to ship or shore.

Splice:
To join two lines or two parts of a line by unlaying them and inter-twining their strands.

Splice the main brace:
To have a drink. The main brace was one of the most important ropes in the old sailing navy, a piece of rigging upon which much of the strength of the masts depended. When it became necessary, for whatever the reason, to repair the main brace, completion of the demanding job carried with it a reward of an extra ration of rum or grog.

Splinter deck:
One fitted with armor. See *Deck, Protective deck.*

Splinter screen (shield):
Light metal armor around bridge and gun stations on a ship. Designed for moderate protection only against bomb and shell fragmentation.

Split plant operation:
Subdivision of engineering plant of a ship into two or more independent units for purposes of damage control. Usually each main engine or turbine is driven by the steam from one fireroom.

Spoiler board:
Boards lashed across the leading edges of aircraft wings to destroy lift when aircraft are secured in windy weather.

Sponson:
Projecting structure, platform, or short wing on hull of ship or aircraft.

Sponsor:
The woman who christens a ship at its launching.

Spot:
> To observe the fall of shot. A gunnery correction to range, deflection, or fuze range. To station aircraft on a carrier's decks. The location of aircraft on deck, e.g., a flight deck spot. To move cargo or cargo handling gear.

Spotting board:
> Miniature flight and hangar decks with aircraft models used to plan aircraft carrier spotting of aircraft. Also, a synthetic fall of shot trainer used to instruct gunnery spotters.

Spread:
> Multiple salvo of torpedoes fired ahead, at, and astern of a target to insure a hit.

Spring:
> Mooring line that makes an acute angle with the ship and the pier generally leading aft from bow, forward from quarter. To turn a vessel alongside a pier with a line.

Spring range:
> The average semi-diurnal range of tides at *Syzygy*.

Spring rise:
> The mean height of high water above chart datum at *Syzygy*.

Spring stay:
> See *Triatic stay*.

Spring tidal currents:
> Tidal currents of increased velocity during *Syzygy*.

Spring tides:
> The increased range of tides occurring when the moon and the sun are in phase.

Sprinkling system:
> Emergency water system for putting out fires and keeping boundaries cool in all types of magazines containing explosives or pyrotechnics, rockets, etc.

Spud:
> A post or pile used to secure a dredge or scow.

Spur shore:
> Wooden spar used to hold vessel clear of a pier.

Squadron:
> Administrative or tactical organization consisting of two or more divisions of ships. Also, administrative unit of aircraft, for tactical purposes divided into divisions and sections.

Squall:
> Short but intense windstorm.

Square:
> To straighten, as "square your hat."

Square away:
　　To straighten, make shipshape, or to get settled in a new job or home.
　　Also to inform or admonish someone in an abrupt or curt manner.

Square knotting:
　　Hobby of making belts, watch bands, etc., out of knotted cord.
　　See *Sennet, coxcombing.*

Square rigger:
　　A sailing ship the majority of whose sails are *Square sails.*
　　Distinguished from such ships as *Schooner, Sloop, Lateen-rigged.*

Square sail:
　　A sail cut into a square or rectangular shape and mounted on *Yards*
　　which extend equally on both sides of a mast. The standard sail of a
　　Square rigger. Distinguished from a *Fore-and-aft sail.*

Squatting:
　　The change of trim and overall lowering of a ship's stern in the
　　water at high speed.

Squawk-box:
　　Inter-office or -station voice communication unit; *Intercom.*

Squealer rings:
　　The rings in the glands of a turbine that have the smallest clearance.
　　Their rubbing is an audible alarm signal for stopping the turbines.

Squib:
　　Miniature electrically fired explosive, used in rockets as an igniter
　　or on a *Sand Table* to represent bomb and shell bursts.

SQUID:
　　Forward-launched ASW weapon developed by the British Navy.

Squilgee:
　　Wooden, rubber-shod deck dryer. Pronounced squeegee. Also squillagee.

SRAM:
　　Model designation: AGM-69A;
　　cognizant service: Air Force.
　　A short-range air-to-surface attack missile. Design details are classified.

Stability:
　　Ability of a ship to right itself after being heeled over.
　　See *Metacenter, Metacentric height.*

Stability board:
　　Visual representation, used by damage control personnel, of liquid
　　loading, location of flooding, effect on list and trim, etc.

Stabilize:
　　Maintain on horizontal plane by means of a gyro mechanism.

Stable element:
　　Gyro mechanism that stabilizes an instrument, such as a gun sight,
　　against the roll and pitch of a ship.

Stack:
>A large pipe extending above the main deck to exhaust smoke and gas from the boilers. Also the assembled electronic components of sonar gear are referred to as the "sonar stack".

Stack cover:
>Canvas cover for stack when not in use. Also called a *Watch Cap.*

Stack wash:
>Air turbulence astern of a ship due to stack gases.

Stadimeter:
>Instrument for measuring distance to objects of known heights by mechanical solution of a right triangle. Commonly used to measure distance to other ships in formation.

Staff:
>Personnel without command function who assist a commander in administration and operation.

Staff officers:
>Those who perform staff functions such as doctors, chaplains, dentists, civil engineers, supply officers, and medical service officers, as distinct from *Line Officers.*

Stage:
>Platform hung over the side from which men can work, paint, etc.

Staging:
>Processing, in a specific area, of troops in transit from one area to another.

Staging area:
>Place where an amphibious expedition has final training.

Stanchion:
>Vertical metal post aboard ship.

Stand:
>Brief period of no change in water level at high or low tide.

STANDARD:
>Model designation: RIM-66/67; cognizant service: Navy.
>A surface-to-air weapon with surface-to-surface capability for shipboard use. See *Standard Missile.*

Standard commands:
>Official phrases used in such activities as gunfiring, shiphandling, etc.

Standard compass:
>The magnetic compass used by the navigator as a standard. PSC means per standard compass. A direction, or course, by the standard compass (psc) differs from the true direction by the amount of the *compass error.* See *Gyro compass.*

Standard Missile:
>Improved version of *TARTAR* and *TERRIER* for launch from either type launcher, surface-to-air.

Standard rudder:
  That amount (number of degrees) required to cause a ship to turn with
  standard *Tactical Diameter*. Full rudder is usually maximum rudder
  less a few degrees to avoid possibility of jamming the rudder.

Standard speed:
  Usually, 15 knots. See *Speed,* and *Speed, standard.*

Standard stock:
  That material listed in the catalog of Navy Material—general stores
  section.

Standard terminology:
  Words, terms, and phrases used in official directives. Those in Naval
  Warfare Publications (NWP) are considered the standard for all other
  publications.

Standard Written Agreement (SWAG):
  Contract signed by reserve officers going on voluntary active duty.

Stand by:
  To wait. To substitute for someone who has the day's duty. A substitute. A preparatory expression, e.g., "Stand by; commence firing."

Stand from under:
  Literally, to get out and away from danger. Also to avoid wrath of
  a superior.

Standing lights:
  Dim red lights throughout interior of ship.

Standing order:
  A semi-permanent order or directive.

Standing part:
  That part of the tackle| that is made fast. The part on which
  power is applied is the *Hauling Part.*

Standing rigging:
  Heavy ropes, usually made of wire nowadays, that support spars or
  masts and are permanently secured.

Stand out:
  To depart from port or harbor and take a course to seaward.

STAR I:
  One-man submarine and test vehicle.

Starboard:
  Directional term for right, as opposed to port, which means left.

Star finder:
  Mechanical or graphic device for identifying celestial bodies.

STARFIGHTER:
  Model designation: F-104; cognizant service: Navy.
  Single-place, light, high-performance fighter aircraft. One-crew. Jet.

Star gauge:
  Device for measuring accurately the bore diameter of a gun.

STARLIFTER:
Model designation: C-141; cognizant service: Air Force.
A large long-range transport aircraft. Six-crew, 154-troops or
123-paratroops, or 80-litters plus eight-medics. Jet.

Star shell:
Projectile which detonates in the air and releases an illuminating
parachute flare.

Star tracker:
A light-sensing device properly gimballed and electronically controlled
to detect and maintain the line of sight to a star. When mounted
on a stable platform, it becomes an automatic *Sextant.*

Stateroom:
An officer's living space aboard ship.

Station:
To assign. A post of duty, as a battle station. A position in a formation
of ships. A naval activity. In ship's plans an engineering "section"
perpendicular to the keel is sometimes called a "station."

Station bill:
Listing of crew's drill stations.

Station keeping:
The art of keeping a ship in its proper position in a formation
of ships.

Stay:
Wire supporting a mast fore and aft.

Steady as you go or steady as she goes:
An order to steersman to mark the ship's head at the moment of the
order, return to that heading, and steer that course. Command used
frequently while conning the ship.

Steam drum:
See *Drum, steam.*

Steam fog:
Fog formed when water vapor is added to air that is much colder than
the vapor's source; most commonly, when very cold air drifts across
relatively warm water.

Steam lance:
Device for using low-pressure steam on deck to remove ice.

Steelworker (SW):
Petty officer who erects steel structures.

Steep to:
Said of a coast or shore that rises abruptly from the water.

Steerageway:
The lowest speed at which a ship can be steered.

Steering engine:
> The machinery that turns the rudder.

Steersman:
> The man who steers the ship, same as helmsman.

Steinke hood:
> Bonnet placed over an individual's head enclosing an air pocket and permitting him to escape from a submarine sunk at moderate depth. Fitted with a transparent plastic visor for vision.

Stem:
> The foremost vertical member in a ship's hull, that part of the hull farthest forward.

Sterilizer:
> Device for making a mine harmless after a certain period.

Stern:
> The aftermost section of a ship.

Stern anchor:
> Any *Anchor* carried aft. May be used for a *Stream anchor* or, as in certain amphibious ships of World War II whose special configuration made them ride better stern-to than bow-to, it may be the ship's principal anchor.
> Ships designed to beach themselves to land troops and equipment (e.g. the World War II LST) needed a stern anchor to hold themselves in position and to withdraw off the beach when their mission was completed, in a manner similar to *Kedging*. See *Kedge anchor*.

Sternboard:
> The commencement of motion astern. See *Sternway*.

Stern fast:
> Stern line used to secure a boat.

Stern hook:
> Member of a boat's crew who stands aft and makes the stern of the boat secure.

Sternpost:
> Steel casting which forms the aftermost member of the ship's frames. In a boat, it is the equivalent wooden member. Opposite of *Stem*.

Stern tube:
> Circular bearing for the propeller shaft when it emerges from the ship. Also, a stern torpedo tube.

Sternsheets:
> Space in an open boat, at the stern, not occupied by *Thwarts*. Since most boats have a stern thwart, the sternsheets is the space just forward of this stern thwart, between it and the stern-most regular thwart.
> See *Foresheets*.

Sternway:
> Progress astern. Opposite of *Headway*.

Steward (SD):
> Petty officer who supervises running of officer's mess, including cooking.

Steward elbow:
> Special fitting used at end of hose where it enters fuel trunk during underway fueling.

Stewardsman (TN):
> Enlisted man in paygrade three who performs general duties in officer's messes. Addressed always as Steward.

Stock:
> The cross bar of an *Old-fashioned anchor.*

Stockage objective:
> Maximum quantities of material maintained to sustain current operations.

Stockless anchor:
> An anchor without a stock, so that it can be housed right up into its own *Hawse* and secured merely by putting a *Stopper* on the chain. The *Old-fashioned anchor* was very difficult to secure for sea because of the stock. When ships became very large and required much heavier anchors, it became impracticable to use them. The stockless anchor was a natural development. See *Anchor.*

Stopper:
> Short length of line wrapped around a line in order to stop it from running, e.g., boat-fall stoppers. A chain stopper is a portion of a ship's anchor gear consisting of a short length of chain with one end secured firmly to the deck and the other end fitted with a heavy *Pelican hook* or clamp. When a ship is anchored, the strain is taken by the stopper so that the *Capstan* and *Anchor engine* can be used for other purposes or secured.

Stops:
> Short pieces of line used to secure a sail or clothing that is rolled up. See *Clothes stop.*

Storekeeper (SK):
> Petty officer who performs clerical and manual duties in the supply department.

Stores:
> Supplies.

Storm:
> Meteorological disturbance; literally, a wind of 56 to 65 knots.

Stove:
> Broken in; smashed. Generally used with the word "in," as "the sea stove in the bulkhead."

Stow:
> To put away; to store.

Stowage factor:
> Number of cubic feet that cargo will occupy in a vessel.

Stowage plan:
Paper showing location of all cargo on board.

Straddle:
A *Salvo* in which some of the shots are seen to fall beyond the
target and some short of it, or some right and others left. The mean
point of impact is thus on or near the target. Splashes beyond the
target are known as "overs," and those short of it are "shorts."
Minimum dispersion is of course desired, and thus a "straddle"
generally insures that at least some of the projectiles are hitting.

Straggler:
See *Unauthorized absentee.*

Strakes:
Continuous lines of fore and aft planking or plating in a boat or ship.

Strand:
Part of a line or rope made up of yarn. To go aground.

Strap:
A ring of wire or line, made by splicing the ends together, used for
handling weights, etc. Also, a metal band such as those used to secure
the lead ballast in a submarine.

Strategic minefields:
Calculated to reduce and impede the enemy's warmaking ability by
destruction of his seaborne communications.

Strategy:
The basic overall plan by which a naval commander intends to accomplish
his mission. Not to be confused with national strategy, with which
it must of course be compatible.

STRATOCRUISER:
Model designation: C-97; cognizant service: Air Force.
Transport aircraft with pressurized cabin, five-crew, 60-passengers.
Propeller-driven.

STRATOFORTRESS:
Model designation: B-52; cognizant service: Air Force.
A high-speed, high-altitude, land-based heavy-bomber aircraft.
Has high swept wings, eight main wheels retracting into fuselage,
and small outrigger wheels at wing tip. Eight-crew. Jet.

STRATOFREIGHTER:
Model designation: KC-97; cognizant service: Air Force.
Cargo version of *STRATOCRUISER.* Five-crew. Jet.

STRATOJET:
Model designation: B-47; cognizant service: Air Force.
Multi-engine, midwing bomber aircraft. Four-crew. Jet.

STRATOLIFTER:
Model designation: C-135; cognizant service: Air Force.
A long-range, high-performance transport. Four-crew, 75-troops in
normal seating, 126-troops in high-density seating, or 44 litters
and 48 ambulatory patients with six attendants, or equivalent cargo.
Jet.

STRATOLINER:
Model designation: VC-137; cognizant service: Air Force.
Administrative transport aircraft. Seven-crew, 49-passengers. Jet.

STRATOTANKER:
Model designation: KC-135; cognizant service: Air Force.
A modified *STRATOLIFTER* equipped with a flying boom for
aerial refueling of other aircraft. May be used as a cargo and/or
troop transport. Four-crew, 80-troops. Jet.

Stream:
Bay, river, or fairway, e.g., anchored in the stream. To extend a flag or
line out to its length, in air or water as appropriate.

Stream Anchor:
A small *Anchor* dropped off the stern or quarter to prevent a
ship from swinging to a current. Now rare.

Strike:
A combat flight against ground or ship targets. Also means to work
for, as in the expression: "He is striking for Chief." See *Striker.*

Strike below:
Take below decks, as stores are struck below after being brought aboard.

Strike for:
To learn the trade of, as a man may strike for yeoman.

Striker:
An apprentice or learner.

Strip ship:
Process of removing inflammable and superfluous material from a ship
when war or emergency is imminent. See *Clear ship.*

Strongback:
Spar between the davits against which a whaleboat is griped in. A
damage control bar or beam, shorter than a shore. Also, a supporting
girder for a hatch cover.

Strut:
The bracket supporting a ship's propeller shaft outside of the hull.

Stuffing box:
Device to prevent leakage between a moving and a fixed part in a ship,
particularly where a moving part comes out through the hull.

Stuffing tube:
Packed tube making a watertight fitting through a bulkhead for a
cable or small pipe.

Styx:
A 20-mile Soviet surface-to-surface missile.

Subcaliber:
Pertaining to a much smaller caliber gun mounted on or in a larger
gun for practice purposes.

Sublittoral zone:
Subdivision of the Littoral System of the Benthic Division including waters 50 to 200 meters in depth.

Submarine (SS):
Warship designed for under-the-surface operations. Attack submarines have the primary mission of locating and destroying ships, including other submarines. Missile submarines have primarily the mission of attacking land targets. See Appendix A.

Submarine chaser (PC) (SC):
Small (100'-200') patrol vessel. See Appendix A.

Submarine Combat Air Patrol (SUBCAP):
One of the variations of *Rescue Combat Air Patrol,* over a submarine.

Submarine Emergency Buoyancy System (SEBS):
Gas generator emergency deballasting system to permit rapid surfacing of a submarine.

Submarine emergency identification signals:
Black or green smoke—torpedo has been fired. Yellow—sub is coming up. Red—sub is in danger.

Submarine escape lung:
See *Steinke hood.*

Submarine haven:
Ocean area restricted to use by submarines. See *Moving havens.*

Submarine marker buoy:
Buoy released from a sunken submarine that floats to surface and marks the spot for salvage and rescue.

Submarine patrol areas:
Stretch of water with specific geographical limits, assigned to a submarine as her area of action. Essentially the same as *Submarine patrol zones* except more permanent in nature and associated with probable focal points of enemy traffic.

Submarine patrol zones:
Restricted sea areas established for the purpose of permitting submarine operations unhampered by the operations of or possible attack by friendly forces.

Submarine radio rescue buoy:
Device released from sunken submarine which can rise to surface and broadcast an emergency signal.

Submarine rescue chamber:
Device lowered to a disabled submarine and fitted over an *Escape hatch,* in which a small number of men each time may be brought to the surface.

Submarine sanctuaries:
Restricted areas established for the conduct of noncombat submarine or antisubmarine exercises. They may be either stationary or moving and are normally designated only in rear areas.

Submarine striking force:
A group of submarines formed for a specific offensive action against the enemy. In modern context they would probably have missile-launching capabilities. U.S. SSBNs could be considered such a striking force today, or could be formed into several different submarine striking forces for different specific objectives.

Submarine rocket (SUBROC):
Model designation: UUM-44A; cognizant service: Navy. Submarine-launched rocket. Can be fired from a submerged torpedo tube.

Submariner:
Officer or man assigned to duty in submarines. Acceptable pronunciation in U.S. Navy is "submarine-er," not "sub-mariner."

Submerged Ordnance Recovery Device (SORD):
Surface-manipulated, closed-circuit television-guided snare for recovery of sunken ordnance.

Submersible pump (portable):
Watertight electric pump that can be lowered into a flooded compartment in order to pump it out.

Subsistence (allowance):
Money paid in lieu of food furnished. For officers only, unless there is no general mess. See *Commuted Rations.*

Substitute:
Flag used to repeat another flag in the signal hoist, formerly called *Repeater.*

Subsurface currents:
Currents flowing below the surface. Normally they have different speed and set from surface currents.

SUITCASE:
Portable command center for use on bridge of surfaced submarine, about the size of a portable typewriter; designed to replace several bridge instruments.

Sundowner:
An extremely strict officer. The term nowadays carries a connotation of sadism in the application of the rules. See *Martinet* for the same meaning without the sadistic implication. Derived from the ancient regulation that officers and men of a ship in commission must spend the night on board and must in fact be back aboard by sundown. A captain who insisted on observance of this regulation after it had outlived its purpose was called a "sundowner."

Sun over the yardarm or sun over the foreyard:
An expression meaning that it is about time for the first drink.

SUPER CONSTELLATION:
Model designation: C-121; cognizant service: Air Force. High-speed transport aircraft with unusual airfoil-shaped fuselage. Similar to *CONSTELLATION*, except has increased fuselage length and different engines. Four-crew, four-relief crew, 72-troops, or 47-litters plus two-attendants. Propeller-driven.

SUPERFORTRESS:
Model designation: B-29/B-50; cognizant service: Air Force.
An improved version of the World War II B-29 superfortress. B-50
did not see service during World War II. Now long retired.
Propeller-driven.

SUPER GENIE:
Model designation: AIR-2B; cognizant service: Air Force.
A missile.

Superheaters:
Heating units to raise the temperature of saturated steam to gain
greater efficiency.

Super High Frequencies (SHF):
3,000-30,000 megacycles or megaHertz (mHz).

SUPER JOLLY:
Model designation: HH-53B; cognizant service: Air Force.
Similar to *SEA STALLION* except reconfigured to accomplish combat
crew-recovery missions. Also armed with three 7.62 mm miniguns.
Six-crew.

SUPER SABRE:
Model designation: F-100; cognizant service: Air Force.
A low, thin, sweptback wing, single-place supersonic fighter jet with
afterburner. One-crew. Jet.

Superstructure:
All structure above the main deck of a ship. May be split or all in
one group.

Superstructure deck:
A partial deck above the *Main deck.* See *Deck.*

Supply Systems Command:
Functional command created in 1966 Navy Department reorganization,
replacing Bureau of Supplies and Accounts. Component of the *Naval
Material Command.*

Surf forecasting:
Technique of predicting size and nature of surf. Important for amphibious
operations.

Surface Effects Ship (SES):
An air cushion or hover ship.

Surface reverberation:
A form of sound scattering, generally called *Reverberation.*

Surge:
To hold a line taut on a winch drum without hauling in. To slack off
a line or let it slip slowly around a fitting. Also, the horizontal
water motion accompanying a *Seiche.*

Surging:
Motion of a ship in which it is displaced forward and aft alternately,
usually when moored. See *Yawing.*

Surveillance Area:
> The outer limits of the AAW area, where search, detection, and tracking are accomplished.

Survey:
> Official procedure in expending accountable material from books or records. May be a special, formal, or informal survey. To survey an area is to explore and chart it.

Surveying ship (AGS):
> Ship that conducts surveys and makes charts on board.

Surveyor (SV):
> Petty officer who surveys roads, airfields, ditches, etc.

Suspect Nonmilitary Vessel Category:
> Vessel of doubtful classification, whose movements are controlled or believed to be controlled by a hostile nation, or within the past six months has touched a port of such nation.

Sverdrup:
> A unit of volume transport equal to one million cubic meters per second.

Swab:
> Mop.

Swallow:
> The larger opening in a *Block*, between the sides, through which the fall leads or the line reeves.

Swallow float:
> Tubular buoy adjustable so it will remain in water of certain density level to drift with the water mass so it can be tracked to determine current velocity.

Swamp:
> To fill with water, as a boat may do in heavy seas. The boat might or might not sink as a result.

SWAMP:
> Landing force support system development.

Swash:
> The rush of water up onto the beach following the breaking of a wave.

Swash plates:
> Metal plates in steam drums, oil tanks, etc. to prevent the surging of liquid with motion of the ship.

Swaying:
> Motion of a ship in which it is displaced laterally as distinct from rolling. See *Roll*.

Sweep:
> Minesweeping operation. May be either a clearance or exploratory sweep. A rotating radar antenna is also said to sweep.

Sweepers:
> Those who sweep down: "Sweepers, start your brooms; clean sweep down fore and aft."

Sweeping, mine:
  See *Minesweeping.*

Swell:
  Wind-generated waves which have advanced into a calmer area and are
  decreasing in height and gaining a more rounded form. The heave of
  the sea.

Swept channel:
  Area that is kept clear of mines.

Swing ship:
  To steam on various courses to determine a curve of compass error
  (Deviation).

Swivel:
  Metal link with an eye at one end, fitted to revolve freely and thus
  keep turns out of a chain. See *Mooring swivel.*

Sword arm:
  The device, containing a *Pitot Tube,* that is lowered beneath the
  hull when the ship is clear of port or anchorage. See *Pitometer log.*

System:
  A term brought into the Defense Department vocabulary in 1961 to denote
  the entire complex of equipment and procedure by which a desired
  objective is accomplished. There can be subsystems within larger
  systems. For example there can be a *Sparrow* missile system as a
  part of an *Aircraft system* which is itself a portion of an aircraft-
  carrier system.

Syzygy:
  The two opposite points in the orbit of the moon when it is in con-
  junction or opposition to the sun. Points of the new and full moon.

T

Tab:
> Part of an OpOrder or OpPlan.

Tablemount:
> See *Seamount.*

Table of organization (TO):
> In Marine Corps, a list of number, ranks and duties of personnel.

Tack:
> **Lower** forward corner of a *Fore-and-aft* sail. The direction relative
> to the wind in which a sailing vessel goes, either on the port or
> starboard tack depending on the direction from which the wind
> strikes the sails, port or starboard. To tack is to come about or
> change tacks, thus a sailing boat tacks or zigzags up wind. Distance
> a boat sails on a port or starboard tack is called a tack.

Tackle:
> Any arrangement of line and blocks to gain a mechanical advantage.
> Pronounced TAY-kle.

Tackline:
> Short length of line used in a flaghoist to increase the normal distance
> between flags. Separates two signals on the same hoist, or may have
> a special meaning. Derogatory term for a man, meaning "six feet of nothing."

Tactical air control:
> The direction of aircraft in close support of amphibious troops, exercised
> from aboard ship or from the beach. Personnel are organized into tactical
> Air Control Squadrons and Groups *(Tacrons), (Tacgrus).*

Tactical Air Control Center:
> The principal air operations installation (land or ship-based) from which
> all aircraft and air warning functions of tactical air operations are
> controlled.

Tactical Air Control Group:
> *Ship-based* - An administrative and tactical component of an amphibious
> force which provides aircraft control and warning facilities afloat for
> offensive and defensive missions within the tactical air command area
> of responsibility.

Tactical Air Navigation (Tacan):
> A form of secondary radar used in air navigation.

Taffrail:
> A rail at the stern of a ship.

Taffrail log:
> Device that indicates the speed of a ship through the water. It is
> trailed on a line from the *Taffrail* and consists of a propeller-
> like rotator and a recording instrument.

Tactical Command Ship—(CC):
> One designed to serve as a command ship for a fleet/force commander.
> It is equipped with extensive communication equipment.

Tactical diameter:
>   Perpendicular distance between path of a ship on the original course
>   and the path of the ship when steadied on new course after having
>   turned through 180 degrees with a constant rudder angle. Standard
>   tactical diameter is that prescribed by competent authority.

Tactical Range Recorder—(TRR):
>   Equipment used in evaluation of visual presentation of ranging echoes
>   from an underwater target.

Tactics:
>   The employment of units in battle. Must be distinguished from
>   *Strategy.*

Tag, identification:
>   Metal tag worn by all personnel when directed, recording their name, file
>   or service number, blood type and religious affiliation (optional). Slang:
>   *Dog Tag.*

Tag line:
>   Line used to steady a load being swung in or out.

Tail block:
>   A block with a tail of rope instead of a hook.

Tailhook:
>   The hook lowered from the after part of the carrier aircraft which
>   engages the *Arresting gear* upon landing. Slang: A "tailhooker"
>   is a Navy aviator qualified in carrier operations.

Tail on:
>   Order to lay hold of a line and haul away.

Tailor-mades:
>   Slang: non-regulation enlisted men's uniforms.

Take a strain:
>   To apply tension on a line, wire, or chain. Take an even strain: relax.

Take a turn:
>   To pass a line around a cleat or bitts and to hold it, check it, or ease it.

Take charge:
>   To assume command or direction of. To become uncontrollable, as a
>   vehicle might take charge on the deck of a rolling ship if not secured.

Take in:
>   Command to take aboard a designated mooring line or lines. See *Cast Off.*

Talker:
>   Usually *Telephone talker.* A man assigned to pass on orders and information
>   to and from his station, usually by telephone.

Tally-ho:
>   Sight contact with his target by a fighter pilot.

TALON:
>   Model designation: T-38; cognizant service: Air Force.
>   Trainer aircraft. Two-crew. Jet.

TALOS:
Model designation: RIM-8; cognizant service: Navy.
Surface-to-air, high-altitude air-breathing guided missile, fired from surface warships.

Tango:
Phonetic word for letter T.

Tanker:
Ship that transports fuel to a base or service squadron. An *Oiler* fuels other ships at sea or at an anchorage.

Tank top:
Top side of tank section or double bottom of a ship.

Taps:
Bugle call sounded as last call at night for all hands to turn in.

TAR:
Designates a Naval Reserve officer or enlisted man on active duty in the Training and Administration of the Naval Reserve.

Tar:
General name for a sailor of the old school. Derived from the old custom of a sailor tarring his trousers as well as other wearing apparel in order to make them waterproof.

Tar down:
To coat standing rigging with tar.

Tare:
An allowance for the weight of a container.

Target angle:
Relative bearing of the firing ship from the target measured from the bow of the target to the right through 360 degrees. See *Angle on the bow.*

Target bearing:
True compass direction of a target from the firing ship.

Target-grid method:
Standard shore bombardment procedure.

Target indication:
Information on targets available.

Tarpaulin (Tarp):
Any flat piece of canvas used for a cover.

Tarpaulin muster:
Collection of funds aboard ship for some common purpose such as to assist a shipmate's widow. Now rare.

TARHE:
Model designation: CH-54A; cognizant service: Army.
Helicopter that can lift heavy cargo. Has one main lifting rotor, dual controls, and limited authority controls for the aft-facing pilot during winch operations. Has single-point hoisting system plus four-point load-leveling capability.

TARTAR:
Model designation: RIM-24; cognizant service: Navy.
Shipborne, surface-to-air missile with solid-propellant rocket engine.

Task element:
Component of a Task Group organized for specific tasks. Assigned a 4-digit number, such as TE 58.11, making it subordinate to CTG 58.1.

Task fleet:
Mobile command of ships and aircraft necessary for a specific, major, continuing task.

Task force (TF):
Major component of a task organization capable of large-scale combat or support operations. Usually assigned a 2-digit number, such as 58, making it TF 58.

Task group (TG):
Component of a task force organized for specific tasks. Assigned a 3-digit number such as TG 58.1, by CTF 58.

Task Organization:
Fleet, Force, Group, Element, Unit: Standard operational organization format for U.S. Navy. Example: for Fifth Fleet, Task Fleet is 5th Fleet.

Task Force	-- a major component of	5th Fleet	-- TF 58
Task Group	-- component of	TF 58	-- TG 58.1
Task Element	-- component of	TG 58.1	-- TE 58.13
Task Unit	-- component of	TE 58.13	-- TU 58.13.3

Commanders are designated CTF 58, CTG 58.1, CTE 58.13, CTU 58.13.3.

Tattoo:
Bugle call sounded just before *Taps* as signal to prepare to turn in.

Taut:
Tight, without slack. Well-disciplined, as a taut ship.

Taximen:
Plane handlers who assist in the taxiing of aircraft.

Teleman (TE):
A petty officer who performs communications, clerical and cryptoboard duties.

Telemetering system:
Measuring, receiving, and transmitting instruments carried by a test missile together with receiving and recording instruments at a control system.

Telemetry:
Science involving the taking of measurements and their transmission to detached stations where they can be displayed, interpreted or recorded.

Telephone talker:
Man who handles a telephone during general evolutions such as general quarters. See *Talker.*

Telescope, ship's:
Mounted scope of up to 32 power carried by ships for spotting flaghoists and other signals.

Temporary Additional Duty (TAD):
   A short assignment in addition to regular duties. Pronounced "tee-ay-dee."

Tend:
   To attend, as a diver's air line. To extend, as anchor chain tends forward. To act as a tender for; to service.

Tender:
   Logistic support and repair ship such as a destroyer tender (AD).

TERN:
   Norwegian-designed, antisubmarine, ahead-thrown rocket comparable to *WEAPON ALFA*. Designed for installation in ships of 500 to 1,000 tons.

TERRA:
   Shipborne shore bombardment missile. Also referred to as **TRSSM**.

TERRIER:
   Model designation: RIM-2; cognizant service: Navy
   A surface-to-air weapon for shipboard use. Launched by a solid-fuel rocket booster and propelled by a solid-fuel rocket sustainer.

That's high:
   Order to cease hauling or hoisting on a line.

Thermocline:
   An ocean layer of rapidly changing temperature in comparatively small change of depth. Layer refracts sound waves causing a serious submarine detection problem.

Thief sample:
   Sample of oil or water taken from a ship's tank for analysis.

Thieving paste:
   A chemical coating on a sounding rod which reveals the level of the oil or water.

Thimble:
   Metal ring grooved to fit inside a grommet or eye splice.

Thole pin:
   Pin fitting into gunwale of a boat, carrying a rope grommet for use as a rowlock.

THOR:
   Model designation: PGM-17; cognizant service: Air Force. Missile.

Three M:
   Standard Navy Maintenance and Material Management System, (SNMMMS).

Three sheets in, or to, the wind:
   Well under the influence of liquor. Metaphoric reference, of course, is a sailing ship in disarray, with *Sheets* flying in the breeze.

Throttleman:
   Man in engineroom who handles the throttles and thus controls the speed of the ship.

Thrums (Thrumming):
Short yarns sewed to canvas to make chafing gear called thrum mat or *collision mat.*

THUNDERCHIEF:
Model designation: F-105; cognizant service: Air Force.
Single-place, mid-wing, high-performance, fighter-bomber aircraft. One-crew. Jet.

THUNDERFLASH:
Model designation: RF-84F; cognizant service: Air Force.
Similar to *THUNDERSTREAK* except equipped with an elongated nose section incorporating photographic equipment. Air intake ducts are relocated in the wing-root leading edge. One-crew. Jet.

THUNDERSTREAK:
Model designation: F-84F; cognizant service: Air Force.
Single-place fighter aircraft. Air intake duct in the nose.
One-crew. Jet. See *THUNDERFLASH;*

THUNDERJET:
Model designation: F-84G. cognizant service: Air Force.
A later version of THUNDERSTREAK, unaccountably given a new popular name even though the plane is merely a modification of its predecessor. Improved operational characteristics may have been the reason.

Thwarts:
The cross seats or planks in a boat just below the *Gunwales.*

Tidal bore:
Wave created when tidal pressure overcomes river current in a restricted area. The bore moves upstream against the current.

Tidal current:
Current caused by rise and fall of tides.

Tidal day:
Period of a complete tidal cycle, as determined by *Lunar day.*

Tidal predictions:
Time predictions for occurrence of high and low waters published by the Department of Commerce for stations throughout the world.

Tidal prism:
Total amount of water that flows in and out of a harbor as a result of tide.

Tidal range:
Total rise (or fall) from low water to high water or vice versa.

Tidal wave:
A tremendous wave, an abberation of nature, that sweeps across an area and generally does great damage. The correct term for such waves is Tsunami. They are considered to result from submerged earthquakes or volcanic action and have no relation to tidal action.

Tide:
The vertical rise and fall of the ocean level caused by the gravitational force of the moon and the sun. Rising tide is a flood tide, falling tide is an ebb tide.

Tide race:
  A very rapid tidal current in a narrow channel or passage.

Tide rips:
  Turbulent water produced by opposition to tidal currents.

Tide tables:
  Coast & Geodetic Survey publications giving data, including time and height, on tides at various locations.

Tie downs:
  Fittings to secure aircraft on deck.

Tier:
  A layer of anchor chain in a chain locker.

Tie-tie:
  Cloth straps that tie together, as on a kapok life jacket.

TIGER:
  Model designation: F-11; cognizant service: Navy.
  High-performance fighter, sweptback wings. One-crew. Jet.

Tiller:
  Casting or forging attached to rudder stock. Lever that turns the rudder on a boat.

Time charter:
  Lease of a vessel in which the owner operates, equips, and maintains the ship.

Time, Greenwich mean (civil):
  Mean or civil time at the meridian of Greenwich and universally used in almanacs as well as in worldwide communications.

Time, mean or civil:
  Time measured by the average rate of the sun's apparent movement.

Time, Navy:
  Expressed in 4 digits, 0000-2400 based on 24 hour day; e.g., 1430 is 30 minutes after 2 o'clock P.M.

Time orderly:
  Messenger whose duty it is to strike the hour and half hour on the ship's bell.

Time, sidereal:
  Time measured by the rotation of the earth with respect to the stars. Useful mainly in locating stars for navigational use.

Time, standard or zone:
  Mean or civil time fixed for zones, generally 15° in width for both land and ocean areas with some arbitrary redesignation for convenience.

Tincan (can):
  Slang: destroyer.

Tin fish:
  Slang: torpedo.

TINY TIM:
Air to ground rocket.

TITAN:
Model designation: HGM-25; cognizant service: Air Force.
A two-stage, radio-inertial-guided ICBM.

Toggle:
Pin fitted into an eye or ring used to secure gear and to permit quick release.

TOM CAT:
Special picket destroyer that operates with a fast carrier task force.

Tomming:
To brace from above, as shores may be used in a cargo hold.

Tompion:
A plug that fits into the bore of a gun at the muzzle to keep out dirt
and spray. Pronounced TOMP-kin.

Ton:
A unit of measurement or weight. Units of weight: Short ton. . .2000 lb;
long ton. . .2240 lb; metric ton. . .2205 lb (1000 kilograms). Units of
volume: measurement ton (ship ton). . .40 cubic ft; register ton. . .100
cubic ft.

Tongue of the Ocean:
Deep natural basin in the Bahamas running more than 100 miles along
the eastern shore of Andros Island. Site of the Atlantic Undersea
Test and Evaluation Center (AUTEC).

Tonnage:
Gross register—entire cubic capacity of a ship expressed in register tons.
Net register—cubic capacity, less certain non-cargo spaces, expressed
in register tons. Displacement—weight of a ship in long tons either with
cargo, fuel, water, etc. (loaded), or without (light). Deadweight cargo—
difference between displacement loaded and displacement light.

Tons per inch immersion:
The number of tons necessary to increase a vessel's mean draft one inch.

Top:
A platform on a mast. In sailing ships this was usually located at the
juncture of the lower mast and the topmast (i.e., about one-third of the
height of the entire mast, which was usually made of three sticks attached
together in such a way that the upper two could be lowered down to the
deck upon necessity). Sharpshooters were detailed to the tops (often
called "fighting tops") during battle. Such a sharpshooter killed Horatio
Nelson at Trafalgar in 1805, and James Lawrence of USS CHESAPEAKE
in the battle with HMS SHANNON in 1813. A modern warship has only
one "fighting top," a bulky structure called the *Foretop* which contains
fire control equipment and is built integrally into the highest point of an
extremely strong, usually a tripod, foremast. Tops in other masts, if any,
are of secondary importance and are rarely at the highest points of
their masts. See *Foretop, Maintop, Mizzentop, Masthead.*

Top hamper:
General term for superstructure and rigging. Masts, spars, antennas,
etc., are known collectively as a ship's top hamper.

Top off:
>To fill up, as a ship tops off in fuel oil before leaving port.

Topping lift:
>Tackle made up of one or more blocks around which run one or more parts of fiber or wire rope connecting the end of a boom to its mast or post. Thus a boom may be used as a derrick, being raised or lowered to a suitable position.

Topsail:
>One of the principal sails of a *Square-rigged* ship. The lowest sail on any mast which can be spread from an upper and a lower *Yard*. See *Sail nomenclature*.

Topsail schooner:
>Two-masted sailing vessel with essentially a *Schooner* rig except that the *Fore-and-aft* sails on the *Foremast* are not quite so high, leaving room on the mast for two or three square *Yards* from which one or two *Topsails* can be carried.

Topside:
>Above, in a ship, referring to the *Deck* above, as distinguished from *Overhead,* which refers to the ceiling of a compartment. The topside or topsides means the upper deck or decks; any deck or area which is exposed to the weather is considered topside.

Top up:
>To raise a boom with its *Topping Lift.*

Torch pot:
>See *Combustion chamber.* The chamber or pot in a steam torpedo where air, fuel, and water are mixed together and ignited to produce steam to drive the torpedo engine.

TORNADO:
>Model designation: B-45; cognizant service: Air Force. Multi-engine, midwing bomber aircraft. Four-crew. Jet.

Torpedo:
>Self-propelled underwater explosive weapon designed to be aimed or to seek a target, and detonated by contact, sound, or magnetic force. Various types identified by Mark and Mod numbers. Slang: fish or tin fish.

Torpedo, MARK-14, 16, and 18:
>Conventional nontarget-seeking torpedoes for submarines. MK-14 is steam, MK-16 is navol, Mk-18 is electric.

Torpedo, MARK-37:
>Submarine- or surface-fired acoustic homing torpedo.

Torpedo, MARK-39:
>A submarine torpedo, wire-guided.

Torpedo, MARK-43:
>Lightweight homing ASW torpedo for surface ships and aircraft. Became obsolescent in 1965.

Torpedo, MARK-44:
>Homing ASW torpedo for surface ships and aircraft.

Torpedo, MARK-46:
  Advanced active acoustic homing ASW torpedo for launch from fixed wing
  aircraft, helicopters, or from surface ships' torpedo tubes or *ASROC.*
  MOD O uses solid rocket-fueled hot gas propulsion system. MOD 1
  is advanced version using liquid propellant.

Torpedo, MARK-48:
  Wire guided ASW torpedo

Torpedo range:
  Distance torpedo can run with its available fuel supply.

Torpedo retriever:
  Fast boat for recovering practice torpedoes.

Torpedo run:
  Actual distance torpedo travels to target.

Torpedo tube:
  Device for launching torpedoes from a ship or submarine.

Torpedo tube shutters:
  Movable fairings on outboard end of submarine torpedo tubes whose
  closure preserves the streamlined form of the hull.

Torpedoman's Mate (TM):
  Petty officer who performs upkeep and repair of torpedoes and ASW
  ordnance.

Torsionmeter:
  Device for measuring the twist in the propeller shaft from which the
  horsepower developed by the turbine is calculated.

Toss oars:
  An order to raise oars from rowlocks to a vertical postion, blades
  fore and aft, with handles resting on bottom of boat.

Tow:
  Any vessel being towed. To pull along through the water.

Tow glider:
  AA gunnery target.

Towing bridle:
  See *Bridle.*

Towing light:
  Two or three vertical white lights required by the *Rules of the Road*
  of a vessel towing.

Towing spar:
  Wooden device towed astern by ships in formation in low visibility to
  assist in station keeping. Also called *Fog Buoy* or *Position Buoy.*

Towing winch:
  Special winch, used by large tugs in towing, which compensates for
  variation in the tension on the towline.

TRACER:
>Model designation: E-1; cognizant service: Navy.
>A high-wing transport aircraft equipped for Airborne Early-Warning operations. Four-crew. Propeller-driven.

Tracer:
>A message sent to ascertain reason for nondelivery of a prior message. Also, a projectile trailing smoke or showing a light for correction in aim; most usually employed in machine-gun ammunition.

Track:
>To mark the course of a target on a radar scope or plotting board. To follow a target, noting course and speed, as a patrol aircraft tracks a convoy. Also, the course made good over the ground.

Track angle:
>Angle between the target course and the reciprocal of the torpedo course measured from the bow of the target to the right, through 360 degrees, or to port or starboard through 180 degrees.

TRACKER:
>Model designation: S-2; cognizant service: Navy.
>ASW search and attack aircraft. Carrier-based. Four-crew. Propeller-driven.

Tracking:
>Observation of a mobile object to report its composition, location, course, and speed.

Track spacing:
>The distance between tracks of successive searches or the distance between adjacent sweeping units in a simultaneous search.

Tractor:
>Term referring to landing ships and craft; as the "tractor group" of a task force moving to the objective area. Also an aircraft that tows targets for AA practice.

TRADER:
>Model designation: C-1; cognizant service: Navy.
>All-weather instrument flight trainer and light transport aircraft. Two-crew, nine-passengers. Propeller-driven.

Trades or Trade Winds:
>Those generally steady winds from the NE in the Northern Hemisphere and SE in the Southern Hemisphere in the lower latitudes so important for commerce in the days of sail. They are caused by the normal flow of air from the poles towards the sun-heated equator deflected by the rotation of the earth.

Tradevman (TD):
>Petty officer who operates and maintains training devices.

Train:
>Service or logistic support ships attached to a fleet.

Trainer:
>Man who controls gun or mount in horizontal movement (deflection or train).

Train in and secure:
Put away equipment and cease present exercises.

Training:
Major activity on all levels which includes battle, on the job,
orientation, first-aid, and safety training, as a few examples.

Training aid:
Material (audio or visual) to facilitate the learning process.

Training bill:
Schedule and outline of training for a particular unit of men.

Training Center:
An activity that instructs newly enlisted personnel in naval duties
and customs.

Training cycle:
Period between successive ship overhauls.

Trajectory:
The path of a projectile, missile, or bomb in flight.

Transducer:
Device for conversion of energy from one form to another, e.g. electrical
to mechanical or acoustic.

Transfer:
Distance gained by a ship at right angles to original course when turning.
The movement of enlisted men from one duty assignment to another.

TRANSIT:
A navigational satellite.

Transit Navigation Satellite:
A development to provide an all-weather global system by which the
positions of surface craft, submarines, and aircraft can be accurately fixed.

Transom:
Planking or steel plates across the stern of a boat or a ship. A settee
or sofa aboard ship.

Transponder:
An automatic transmitter which emits a signal when interrogated by
another signal.

Transport area:
Station area for the transports that debark troops during an amphibious
assault.

Transport division (squadron):
The attack transports and cargo ships that carry and land a regimental
combat team. Several divisions organized to carry a reinforced infantry
division comprise a transport squadron.

Transport group:
Subdivision of an amphibious attack force comprising the assault
transports and cargo ships.

Trapping:
Atmospheric distortion of radar signals.

Trials, machinery:
> Tests of main propulsion machinery of a ship. May be builders, acceptance, post repair, standardization, or tactical.

Triatic stay:
> Wire from foremast to after stack or mast of a ship. Also *Spring stay.*

Trice:
> To haul up, as to trice up all bunks, which means to push up all bunks and secure them there.

Trick:
> Steersman's watch is known as a trick at the wheel.

Trick wheel:
> Steering wheel in the steering engine room or emergency steering station of a ship.

TRIDENT:
> Model Designation: UGM96A, cognizant service: Navy. New sea-based strategic system consisting of three-stage, solid-propellant missiles with aided inertial guidance, a quieter submarine, and a CONUS support complex. Initial operational capability 1978 with TRIDENT submarines carrying ICBM range missiles operating from Bangor, Washington. Eventual replacement for POLARIS/POSEIDON.

Trim:
> The fore and aft inclination of a ship—down by the head or down by the stern. Sometimes used to include list. To trim a submarine is to adjust water in the variable ballast tanks, or trim tanks, to establish neutral buoyancy. Also means shipshape; neat.

Trim tanks:
> Forward and after variable ballast tanks of a submarine. Known as "forward trim" and "after trim."

Trip:
> To let go, as to trip a pelican hook.

Triplane target:
> Towed sonar target used in training of ASW ships.

TROJAN:
> Model designation: T-28; cognizant service: Navy/Air Force. A two-place primary training aircraft. Two-crew. Propeller-driven.

Tropic range:
> Same as *Great Tropic Range.*

Trough:
> The hollow between two waves.

Truck:
> The highest part of a mast.

True air speed:
> Rate of motion of aircraft relative to the air.

True bearing:
> Direction of an object relative to true instead of magnetic north.

True heading:
> Horizontal direction in which an aircraft or ship is heading, relative to true north.

Trunk:
  Space aboard ship used for ventilation, access, etc.

Trunnions:
  The major supports of a gun which provide the axis about which the gun
  rotates in elevation. Tilt of trunnions introduces range and deflection
  errors.

Try cocks:
  Small cocks or faucets on the steam drum used to verify the water
  level if the *Gauge Glass* fails.

Tsunami:
  See *Tidal wave.*

Tumble:
  To lose stability, as a gyroscope tumbles.

Tumble home:
  The convex curve of a boat's or ship's side toward the centerline, above
  the waterline. The opposite of *Flare.*

Turbine:
  Multi-bladed rotor, driven by steam or hot air, which, in turn, drives
  a propeller or a compressor.

Turbo blower:
  Also called low-pressure blower. A blower used to complete evacuating
  water from submarine ballast tanks after submarine has been brought
  to the surface by compressed air, and opened to the atmosphere. A
  far more economical way of completing the surfacing procedure than by
  using the precious high-pressure air.

Turbo-jet:
  Type of engine which uses a turbine-driven compressor.

Turbo-prop:
  Aircraft engine in which a gas turbine drives a propeller and also
  provides thrust with tail pipe exhaust.

Turk's head:
  An ornamental collar on an oar, rail, spar, etc., braided from small line.

Turnbuckle:
  Metal appliance consisting of a thread and screw or pair of screws
  with eyes, capable of being set taut or slacked and used for setting
  up *Standing rigging* or other gear.

Turn count masking:
  Practice of changing propeller revolutions at random to prevent
  submarine from estimating speed of attacking ship.

Turn in:
  Go to bed. To turn in all standing is to do so fully clothed.

Turning circle (of a ship):
  That path followed by a ship with constant rudder angle when turning.

Turn out:
  To awake and get up.

Turn to:
Go to work.

Turn (together):
A maneuver in which all ships turn simultaneously to a new course.

Turn turtle:
To capsize.

Turret:
Loosely used—means the armored enclosure for the guns of a man-of-war, tank, or aircraft. Gun mounts, which are only protective houses around smaller guns, are frequently erroneously called "turrets." A true turret has a great amount of rotating mechanism extending below the visible portion on the main deck, inside an armored *Barbette,* and is used only for heavy guns, six-inch or larger.

Turret guns:
Those 6" and larger mounted in a turret.

TUSCARORA, USS:
A mythical ship, claimed to have had 17 decks and a straw bottom.

'Tween deck:
Any deck in the hold of a ship between the tank tops and the main deck.

Twilight:
The period before sunrise and after sunset during which light is reflected from the sun. The four kinds, depending on angular distance of sun below the horizon, are: civil at 6 degrees; observational at 10 degrees; nautical at 12 degrees; astronomical at 18 degrees.

Two-blocked:
Hoisted all the way up. See *Close Up.*

Two-fold purchase:
A tackle both blocks of which contain two sheaves.

TWX:
Commercial teletypewriter exchange service.

Type:
Class into which ships are divided because of their basic characteristics. For example, destroyers of a fleet are under an administrative commander who is a type commander.

Type Command:
An administrative subdivision of a fleet or force into ships or units of the same type, as differentiated from a tactical subdivision.

TYPHON:
Model designation: RIM-50/RIM-55;
Cognizant service: Navy.
Development discontinued. A shipborne surface-to-air missile.

Typhoon:
See *Hurricane.*

U

Ultra high frequencies (UHF):
(300-3,000 megacycles. See *Hertz*.

Unauthorized absentee (UA):
The proper all-inclusive term for a man absent from his command without authority. Replaces old terms straggler, absentee, and absent without leave (AWOL).

Unbend:
To untie, loosen, cast adrift.

Uncle:
Phonetic word for letter U.

Uncover:
To remove the hat.

Undercarriage:
Landing gear of an airplane.

Underfoot:
Said of an anchor when it is directly under ship's forefoot.

Under hack:
Restriction to specified limits; a nonjudicial punishment of an officer awarded by his commanding officer (slang).

Undertow:
The seaward current caused by surf breaking on a beach. For each wave, as it breaks and carries water forward, there is a corresponding flow of water along the ground seaward, following the movement of water within a wave, which is essentially a circular movement. In heavy surf, the flow of water landward must find a way to return to the sea, and often a distinct and rapid current perpendicular to the shoreline can be felt and perceived, This current is usually narrow and a swimmer can escape it by swimming parallel to the beach.

Underwater Demolition Unit (UDU):
Team of specially trained men who do reconnaissance and demolition work along the beaches just prior to an amphibious assault.

Underwater Mechanic (UM):
Petty officer who performs underwater repair and salvage duties.

Underway:
Said of a vessel when she is not made fast to the ground (by anchor, grounding, or mooring) or to the shore.

Underway replenishment group:
A task group organized to provide logistic replenishment of ships underway by transfer-at-sea methods.

Uniform Code of Military Justice (UCMJ):
Enacted by Congress for all Armed Services. For the Navy it replaces the Articles for the Government of the Navy. Traditionally known as *Rocks and Shoals*.

Uniform of the day:
> Prescribed by the CO or by the SOP. To be worn at all times except when working uniform is authorized.

Union:
> The inner, upper corner of a flag if it has a distinctive design. The union of the flag of the United States, for example, is the blue field with fifty white stars on it. It is significant of the union of the states into a single country. See *Jack* or *Union Jack*.

Union Jack:
> Flag flown at the bow of a ship moored or anchored, consisting of the union of the national flag. Also flown in the boat of a high civil official and at a yardarm during a general court-martial or court of inquiry.

Unit:
> Refers to a command unit. May be a single ship or aircraft, or a group of ships or planes under a single commander. The important point is that the unit behaves like one. If split into two or more component parts, each such part becomes a unit in its own right, until the irreducible individual man, aircraft, or ship is reached.

United States Armed Forces:
> A collective term for the regular components of the Army, Navy, Air Force, and Coast Guard in time of war. See *Armed Forces*.

United States Naval Ship:
> A ship owned by the U. S. Navy, but not commissioned as a part of the Navy. Normally manned with civilian crews and operated by the *Military Sea Lift Command*.

United States Navy Regulations:
> Principles for the guidance of the Naval Establishment, particularly the duties, responsibilities and authority of all offices and individuals, issued by SecNav and approved by the President.

Unit of fire:
> A unit of measure for ammo supply, representing a specified number of rounds per weapon.

Universal time:
> Greenwich Mean Time, as measured for Greenwich, England.

Unlay:
> To untwist and separate a rope's strands.

Unload through the muzzle:
> To fire in a safe direction in order to empty a gun of its charge.

Unship:
> To remove from place; to take apart.

Up anchor:
> The order to weigh anchor and get underway.

Up and down:
 Said of an anchor chain when the anchor is under the forefoot. See
 Underfoot.

Up behind:
 An order to cease hauling and to slack a line quickly.

Uprush:
 The rush of water onto the foreshore after the breaking of a wave.

Uptakes (exhaust trunks):
 Large enclosed passages for exhaust gases from boilers to the stacks.

Upwelling:
 A mass of cold, dense sea water that rises up from the depths of the ocean
 to the surface.

Utilities Man (UT):
 Petty officer who installs and maintains heating, water, power, and
 sewage equipment.

UTE:
 Model designation: U-21; cognizant service: Army.
 Unpressurized, cantilever low-wing utility aircraft. Performs utility
 missions in the combat zone. Supports commanders and staff in
 command and control functions. Two-crew, ten-troops. Prop-jet.

V

Van:
The forward part or group of a formation of ships, opposite of rear.

Vang:
Line used to steady or support a boom or spar. Also called a *Guy*.

VANGUARD:
Series of scientific satellite launches carried out in 1950's.

Variable Time (VT) fuze:
Fuze which is actuated by the reflection of self-generated radar emissions from the target as the projectile passes near it. Also called *Proximity fuze*.

Variation:
Magnetic compass error caused by the difference between the geographic and magnetic poles expressed in degrees east or west.

Vector:
An aircraft's course or heading. To direct; to give a course to.

Veer:
To let out or pay out chain or line. Also, when the wind changes direction clockwise or to the right, it is said to veer. See *Haul*.

Vent:
Valve in a tank or compartment used primarily to permit air to escape.

Ventilation system:
Series of air supply and exhaust lines to all parts of the ship.

Vertical envelopment:
A tactical maneuver in which troops, either air dropped or air landed, attack the rear and flanks of a force, in effect cutting off or encircling the force.

Vertical replenishment (VERTREP):
Vertical replenishment in which helicopters are used by supply ships to resupply the fleet while underway.

VERTOL:
Vertical takeoff and landing.

Very good; very well:
Response by a senior to a report by a junior.

Very High Frequencies (VHF):
30-300 megacycles. See *Hertz*.

Very High Frequency Omnidirectional Range (VOR):
VHF Omnidirectional range used principally in air navigation. It provides a magnetic bearing from ground stations. When combined with Distance-Measuring Equipment, DME, this system produces bearing and distance establishing a fix.

Very High Frequency Omnidirectional Range and Tactical
Air Navigation (VORTAC):
> A military designation for an omnidirectional range station including
> Tactical Air Navigation, Tacan, a distance-measuring system.

Very Low Frequencies (VLF):
> 10-30 kilocycles. See *Hertz.*

Very's pistol:
> Device for firing small pyrotechnics into the air as signals.
> Commonly called Very pistol.

Vessel:
> By U.S. statutes, includes every description of craft, ship, or other
> contrivance capable of use as a means of transportation on water.

Vice admiral:
> The rank between admiral and rear admiral. See *Admiral.*

Vice Commodore:
> See *Commodore.* Second in command of a convoy.

Victor:
> Phonetic word for letter V.

VIGILANTE:
> Model designation: A-5, RA-5C; cognizant service: Navy.
> Supersonic all-weather attack aircraft, carrier-based. Primary
> mission is tactical reconnaissance, and the most common version
> is the RA-5C, which carries reconnaissance equipment in a ventral
> fuselage fairing. Jet.

VIKING:
> Single-stage Navy research rocket.

VIPER:
> Model designation: XAGM-80A; cognizant service: Air Force.
> Classified missile.

Virtual PPI Reflectoscope (VPR):
> A navigational radar fitted to the PPI of a radar for comparing the
> PPI picture with a chart of the area.

Visible:
> Capable of being seen on a dark clear night at sea. Legal definition
> of navigational light, generally combined with the distance at which
> visible.

Visit and search:
> A visit upon private vessels to determine their nationality, character
> of their cargo, nature of employment, etc.

Visiting:
> Routine visiting is for friends and relatives of the crew at specified times.
> General visiting is for the general public on holidays, etc.

Visit, official:
> See *Official visit.*

Visual Omnidirectional Range (VOR):
>   A navigation system, principally for aircraft use, providing a readout of direction from a transmitting station.

Vital Area:
>   The area within the destruction area occupied by forces or objectives to be protected. It extends beyond range of enemy bomb or short-range air-to-surface missile release points.

Voice tube:
>   Tube for voice communication within the ship. Now generally replaced by telephones.

Void:
>   Empty compartment below decks.

Volume reverberation:
>   Type of sound scattering; general term is *Reverberation.*

VOODOO:
>   Model designation: F-101;
>   cognizant service: Air Force.
>   Single-place, sweptback mid-wing aircraft designed as an escort and penetration fighter. One-crew. Jet.

Voyage repairs:
>   Emergency work needed by a ship which will not affect its operating schedule.

W

Waist:
Amidships portion of ship; the part of the deck between forecastle and poop. Rarely used now.

Wake:
The disturbed water astern of a moving ship.

Wake light:
Dim light at stern directed down on wake to assist following ships to keep station.

Walk back:
An order to keep a line in hand or on the capstan, ready to hold it or resume hoisting, but to walk it back, i.e., ease it backward. "Walk back handsomely" means to walk back slowly and carefully, ready for instant emergency. Usually used in connection with hoisting a boat by hand.

Walkback:
Improper functioning of *Arresting Gear* which causes the airplane to be pulled backward along the flight deck after its forward motion is stopped.

Walk back the cat:
Expression meaning to start all over again or to retire to a previously held position and start a process or procedure again.

Walkways:
Space adjacent to flight deck aboard an aircraft carrier.

WALLEYE:
Television-guided air-to-surface bomb.

Wall knot:
Knot formed in the end of a line by looping each strand around the one behind it and passing its end through the loop of the strand in front.

Wardroom:
The compartment where officers gather to eat and to lounge aboard ship.

Warhead:
Forward section of a torpedo that carries the explosive. For training shots, an exercise head is fitted.

WARNING STAR:
Model designation: C-121; cognizant service: Navy. Development of *CONSTELLATION* and *SUPER CONSTELLATION*. Special search airplane with bottom and top radar antenna. 26-crew.

Warp:
To haul a ship ahead by a line or anchor along a pier or dock. Also, to change the heading of a ship by putting out a kedge anchor and hauling the bow or stern around.

Warping head:
  Revolving vertical cylinder, part of a *Windlass*.

Warping tug:
  A special tug made up from pontoon sections and used by an
  amphibious construction battalion during an amphibious assault.

Warrant officer:
  An officer, senior to CPO's and junior to all commissioned
  officers, who derives his authority from a warrant issued by the
  Secretary of the Navy.

Wash-deck hose:
  Special hose connected to a fireplug, used for washing down the
  decks.

WASP:
  Sounding rocket. Army WASP is an antipersonnel air-to-surface
  40 mm rocket.

Watch:
  Duty period at sea, normally 4 hours long. A day's watches are:
  First watch 2000-2400, mid watch 0000-0400, morning watch 0400-
  0800, forenoon watch 0800-1200, afternoon watch 1200-1600, first
  dog watch 1600-1800, second dog watch 1800-2000. A buoy is said
  to "watch" when it is floating in its proper position and attitude.

Watch and watch:
  See *Heel and Toe*.

Watch cap:
  Stack cover, usually of canvas. Also an enlisted man's blue knitted cap.

WATCH DOG:
  Special picket destroyer with a carrier task force.

Watch officer:
  An officer regularly assigned to duty in charge of a watch or
  of a portion thereof; for example, the officer of the deck, OOD,
  or the engineering officer of the watch, EOOW or sometimes simply
  OOW. A qualified watch officer is one to whom his commanding officer
  entrusts the ship without reservation during a night watch with ships
  darkened.

Watch, quarter and station bill:
  List showing the duties and billet assignments of all enlisted
  men. Opposite the men's names are listed their battle, cleaning,
  and emergency stations, etc.

Water breaker:
  Container for fresh water.

Water drum:
  See *Drum, water*.

Waterline:
  Point to which ship sinks in water; line painted on hull showing
  point to which ship sinks when properly trimmed. See *Plimsoll mark*.

Waterlogged:
>Filled or soaked with water but still floats; or, a thing that
>normally floats, now so soaked with water that it does not; e.g.,
>a waterlogged timber might or might not float. A waterlogged boat,
>or ship, is scarcely afloat.

Water sky:
>Dark streak on sky caused by reflection of leads, polynyas, and open water.

Water taxi:
>*Shore boat.*

Watertender:
>Man in charge of a fireroom, responsible to keep the level of
>water in the boilers at the right height, and to supervise the
>entire watch to the end that the boilers remain at maximum
>efficiency. The watertender was in his heyday during days of the
>coal-fired boilers, when his function was an art highly prized and regarded.

Watertight closure log:
>Log recording the special openings made of the watertight closures
>by permission of the OOD.

Watertight door:
>A door that is strongly made and fitted with special closure
>equipment, *Gasket* and *Dogs,* so that when it is closed
>water cannot pass through it in either direction even if
>accompanied by considerable pressure.

Waterway:
>The gutter under the lifelines to carry off deck water through the scuppers.

Waterway bar:
>See *Lifelines.*
>Sometimes used in place of the *Footline.*

Wave height:
>Vertical distance between wave trough and wave crest, usually expressed
>in feet. Significant height is average of the highest third of all waves.
>Occasionally, at statistically predictable intervals, waves form that are
>very much higher than average.

Wave off:
>Signal from LSO of a carrier to "pull up and try again."

Wave period:
>Time interval between passage of two consecutive, identical wave
>segments by a given point, normally expressed in seconds.

Wave refraction:
>Tendency of a wave to swing so it parallels the shore. Caused by
>lower portions of the wave slowing as they "feel" bottom.

Wave Velocity:
>Vector quantity specifying the speed and direction of a wave.

Way:
>A ship's movement through the water, as "the ship has way on."

Waterspout:
　　A tornado-like phenomenon occurring over water in which very low
　　pressure in center sucks up water.

Way enough:
　　An order to finish the stroke, toss and boat the oars; indication
　　that there is sufficient speed to accomplish a maneuver.

Ways, building:
　　Inclined skids leading into the water upon which a ship is built.
　　When it is time to launch her, the regular supports under the hull
　　are replaced with structures, also called skids, designed to slide down
　　the inclination and support the hull upright until it enters the
　　water. The ways are carefully greased, and at the last moment, just
　　after the christening ceremony, the final holding devices are
　　removed or cut and down she goes.

WEAPON ALPHA:
　　Model designation: RUR-4; cognizant service: Navy;
　　Similar to *ASROC.* An earlier version.

Weasel:
　　Vehicle capable of operating on snow.

Weather:
　　Towards the wind, opposite of lee. To expose to the elements. To
　　survive, as to weather a storm. Exposed, as weather deck. See *Windward.*

Weathercocks:
　　Said of a ship that comes up into the wind readily.

Weather deck:
　　Top-most deck of a ship, or any exposed deck. See *Deck.*

Weather eye:
　　To keep a weather eye is to be on the alert. Also: to keep a weather eye out.

Weather helm:
　　Carrying a little rudder to keep the ships's head up to the
　　weather. Necessary if the ship tends to fall off to leeward.

Weaving:
　　A form of zigzag steered by ships. Also, sinuous course steered
　　by aircraft in which two or more aircraft turn toward each other
　　for mutual support.

Web belt:
　　Broad, woven, cotton belt, fitted with eyelets for carrying canteen,
　　pistol, etc. Part of landing party uniform and worn as badge of
　　office by enlisted sentries, messengers, orderlies and others.
　　Sometimes called a duty belt.

Wedge cleat:
　　See *Cleat.*

Weekend warrior:
　　Member of Naval Reserve.

Weigh:
>To lift the anchor off the bottom in getting underway.

Weigh-off:
>An airship maneuver, preparatory to landing, to determine proper condition for landing.

Well deck:
>That part of the weather deck having some sort of superstructure both forward and aft of it. See *Deck.*

Wet down:
>Slang: to celebrate. A newly promoted officer wets down his new stripe.

Whaleboat:
>Small double-ended boat.

Wharf:
>Structure parallel to the shore line to which ships moor for loading, unloading, or repairs.

Wharfage:
>Charge for use of berthing space.

Wheel:
>To alter course in such a manner that all ships of a convoy remain in the same relative position.

Wheelhouse:
>Pilothouse; the topside compartment where on most ships the OOD, helmsman, quartermaster of the watch, etc., stand their watches.

Whelps:
>Projections on the periphery of the *Wildcat* drum that fit the anchor chain and pull it by a sort of gear-tooth action.

Where away?:
>Answering call requesting location of object sighted by lookout.

Wherry:
>Light, handy, pulling boat with a transom stern.

Whip:
>To wrap, as the end of a line is whipped with small stuff. Also, a tackle used to lift minor weights.

Whiskey:
>Phonetic word for letter W.

Whistle, ship's:
>A noisemaker, normally using steam or air, usually attached to the forward stack of a ship.

White hat:
>Slang: Enlisted man.

Whiteout:
> Optical phenomenon occurring at high latitudes when neither shadows,
> horizon or clouds are discernable, sense of depth and orientation is
> lost and only very dark, nearby objects can be seen.

Wide berth:
> At a considerable distance.

Wilco:
> Term indicating receipt and understanding of a voice radio message.
> Used only when asked to acknowledge. Means "will comply." Not to
> be confused with *ROGER,* which means only "message received."

Wildcat:
> That part *(Drum)* of an anchor windlass that engages and moves the
> anchor chain. Also called a chain grab. See *Whelps.*

Williamson turn:
> Maneuver used to recover a man lost overboard. Put rudder over
> towards man, shift rudder at 70 degrees from original heading, steady
> on reciprocal of original heading, and ship should return to place where
> man went over.

Williwaw:
> Violent squall characteristic of mountainous coasts, particularly the
> Aleutian Islands.

Winch:
> An electric, hydraulic, or steam machine aboard ship used for hauling
> in lines, as in boat and cargo lifting. Fitted with a horizontal
> *Gipsy* or a vertical *Warping head.*

Winch-head:
> A gipsy. See *Winch.*

Wind angle:
> Angle between direction from which wind is blowing and the line of
> sight.

Wind drift:
> Drift motion of the water caused by wind pressure on the sea surface.

Windlass:
> Machine primarily used for handling an anchor chain with a drum
> called a *Wildcat* or *Chain Grab* fitted with *Whelps* that
> engage the links. Also fitted with a *Warping Head,* a revolving
> concave vertical cylinder similar to a *gypsy* and used for hauling in lines.

Windsail:
> Canvas wind catchers fitted with canvas tubes to lead fresh air
> below decks.

Wind scoop:
> Metal scoop fitted into a port to direct air into the ship for
> ventilation.

Wind ship:
> To turn a ship end for end, usually with lines at a pier, although
> it may also be done with prepared anchors and cables. Thomas
> Macdonough did this with conspicuous success at the Battle of Lake
> Champlain, and thereby achieved victory at a crucial point in the
> War of 1812. Pronounced to rhyme with "mind."

Windward:
> Towards the wind. Similar to *Weather* but not used interchangeably.

Wind waves:
> Waves growing in height under influence of the wind.

Wing:
> Two or more squadrons (groups) of aircraft or airships. Also, the
> part of a hold to either side of the square of the hatch.

Wingman:
> A pilot who flies formation on another, on his wing.

Wire drag:
> To explore for uncharted shoals or pinnacles. A weighted wire is
> dragged at a fixed depth.

Wiredrawn steam:
> Steam that has lost pressure due to friction of ports, passages, etc.

Wire rope:
> Rope made of wire strands twisted together, as distinguished from the
> more common and weaker fiber rope. Sometimes called a "cable," or
> "wire cable."

Wishbone:
> Supporting rods for the upper accommodation ladder platform.

Women Accepted for Voluntary Emergency Service (WAVES):
> Commissioned and enlisted women serving in the Navy.

Wolf pack:
> Coordinated submarine attack group of two or more submarines.

Wooden:
> Slang: stupid; slow.

Word, the:
> News; information; *Dope.*

Work a ship:
> To handle ship by means of engines and other gear; for example, to
> work a ship into a slip using engines, rudder, and lines to docks.

WORKHORSE:
> Model designation: H-21; cognizant service: Air Force;
> Same as *SHAWNEE.* There is no explanation for maintainance of
> separate popular names by Army and Air Force in this instance. A
> twin-rotor helicopter with rotors in tandem.

Working party:
> Group of men assigned to a specific job.

Work request:
> The formal application, with detailed information, from a ship to a repair activity asking that specific work be done. Not a *Job Order*.

World grid:
> A grid dividing the world into 1,000 meter (yard) squares. Used to designate targets.

Worm:
> To fill the lays of line or wire before *Parcelling*.   See *Serve*.
> "Worm and parcel with the lay. Turn and serve the other way."

X

X-ray:
Phonetic word for letter X.

Y

Yacht ensign:
A modified *Ensign,* flown by yachts, whose dip is answered by *Men-of-war.*
May be saluted upon arrival aboard or upon departure from the yacht.

Yankee:
Phonetic word for letter Y.

Yard:
Spar attached at the middle to a mast and running athwartships;
used as a support for *Square sails.* A shipbuilding and repair facility,
as Boston Naval Shipyard.

Yardarm:
Either end of a yard.

Yardarm blinker:
White, all-around, signal lights on the mast at the ends of a small yard.
Keyed from the signal bridge.

Yarn:
Twisted fibers used for rough seizings, which may be twisted into
strands; also, a story, as to "spin a yarn," meaning to tell a
story not necessarily true.

Yawing:
Rotary oscillation about a ship's vertical axis in a seaway. Sheering
off alternately to port and starboard while at anchor is also called
yawing. An aircraft yaws like a ship. See *Surging.*

Yawl:
A small sailing craft, generally a yacht, fitted with a single tall
mast, generally called the *Main,* and with a very much shorter one
abaft of the rudder post, call the *Jigger.* Sails are *Fore-and-aft*
rigged and may be with or without a gaff boom. In appearance very
similar to a *Ketch,* except that the aftermost mast of a ketch is
forward of the rudder and most often is larger than that of the yawl.

Yeoman (YN):
Petty officer who performs clerical and secretarial duties.

Y gun:
Depth charge launching device used to propel depth charge laterally
away from the side of ship, thus enlarging size and effectiveness
of pattern.

Yielding elements:
Spring-loaded mechanisms to support the *Arresting Gear.*

Yoke:
The piece fitting across the head of a rudder, to which the ends of
the steering lines are attached. The yoke usually has two arms of
equal length across the rudder head, or the vertical rudder shaft,
and is almost always at right angles to the line of the rudder,
though in modern design it need not be. The *Helm,* or *Tiller,*
are of older derivation and are always in line with the rudder, with
a single arm.

Z

Zenith:
That point of the celestial sphere vertically overhead. See *Nadir.*

Zenith distance:
Angular distance from the zenith to a position on the celestial
sphere measured on a vertical circle.

Zerk fitting:
Small plug to which a grease gun can be applied to force lubricating
grease into important parts of machinery.

Zigzag:
Series of relatively short straight-line variations from the base
course. See *Evasive steering.*

Zinc:
Piece of metal secured to underwater body of a ship to counter
electrolysis.

ZIPPERS:
Dawn and Dusk Combat Air Patrol.

Zoo plankton:
Animal plankton as distinct from plant plankton.

Zulu:
Phonetic word for letter Z.

ZUNI:
Unguided aircraft-launched rocket, 5-inch diameter.

SHIP AND SERVICE CRAFT DESIGNATIONS

Every U.S. Navy ship and service craft is given a letter designation which broadly classifies it as to function, major capability, or specific use. In general, the letter designation for ships is followed by a hull number which precisely identifies the ship from among those bearing similar designations, and thus the combination is the equivalent of a name in itself. For example, the USS *Enterprise* is designated CVAN-65. In addition to her name in appropriate places, she carries her number on her bows, and on the flight deck in huge numerals where it may easily be read by approaching aircraft. For service craft this rule is followed in part only. Sometimes, instead of a hull number, a model designation takes its place.

Clearly, the designations are not as systematic as they might be, and they are further complicated by occasional conversion of a ship to a different type from that originally designed. In such cases the original hull number is sometimes retained and sometimes not.

The letter "N," when used as the last letter of a ship classification symbol, denotes nuclear propulsion. When used as the last letter or sometimes the next-to-last letter of a service craft classification, it indicates a non-self-propelled version of a similar craft that does have its own propulsion.

Combatant Ship Classifications

1. Warships

Battleship .... BB

Cruisers:
Heavy Cruiser .... CA
Guided Missile Cruiser .... CG
Guided Missile Cruiser (nuclear propulsion) .... CGN
Light Cruiser CL
Guided Missile Light Cruiser .... CLG

Command Ship CC

Aircraft Carriers:
Attack Aircraft Carrier .... CVA
Attack Aircraft Carrier (nuclear propulsion) .... CVAN
ASW Support Aircraft Carrier .... CVS

Destroyers:
Destroyer .... DD
Guided Missile Destroyer .... DDG
Frigate .... DL
Guided Missile Frigate .... DLG
Guided Missile Frigate (nuclear propulsion) .... DLGN

Ocean Escorts:
Escort Ship .... DE
Guided Missile Escort Ship .... DEG
Radar Picket Escort Ship .... DER

Submarines:

Submarine	SS
Submarine (nuclear propulsion)	SSN
Fleet Ballistic Missile Submarine (nuclear propulsion)	SSBN
Guided Missile Submarine	SSG

Patrol Ships:

Patrol Escort	PCE
Patrol Rescue Escort	PCER
Patrol Gunboat	PG

2.   Amphibious Warfare Ships

Amphibious Command Ship	LCC
Inshore Fire Support Ship	LFR
Amphibious Fire Support Ship	LFS
Amphibious Assault Ship (general purpose)	LHA
Amphibious Cargo Ship	LKA
Amphibious Transport	LPA
Amphibious Transport Dock	LPD
Amphibious Assault Ship	LPH
Amphibious Transport (small)	LPR
Amphibious Transport Submarine	LPSS
Dock Landing Ship	LSD
Tank Landing Ship	LST

3.   Mine Warfare Ships

Mine Countermeasures Ship	MCS
Minesweeper, Coastal (nonmagnetic)	MSC
Minesweeper, Fleet (steel hull)	MSF
Minesweeper, Ocean (nonmagnetic)	MSO
Minesweeper, Special (device)	MSS

Combatant Craft Classifications

1.   Patrol Craft

Patrol Craft (hydrofoil)	PCH
Patrol Gunboat (hydrofoil)	PGH
Fast Patrol Craft	PTF

2.   Landing Craft

Landing Craft, Assault	LCA
Landing Craft, Mechanized	LCM
Landing Craft, Personnel, Large	LCPL
Landing Craft, Personnel, Ramped.	LCPR
Landing Craft, Utility	LCU
Landing Craft, Vehicle, Personnel	LCVP
Amphibious Warping Tug	LWT

3.   Mine Countermeasures Craft

Minesweeping Boat	MSB
Minesweeper, Drone	MSD
Minesweeper, Inshore	MSI
Minesweeping Launch	MSL
Minesweeper, River (Converted LCM-6)	MSM
Minesweeper, Patrol	MSR

4.   Riverine Warfare Craft

Assault Support Patrol Boat .... ASPB
Armored Troop Carrier .... ATC
Command and Control Boat .... CCB
Monitor .... MON
River Patrol Boat .... PBR
Patrol Craft, Inshore .... PCF
Quiet Fast Boat .... QFB
Riverine Utility Craft.............................. RUC
Strike Assault Boat .... STAB

5.   SEAL Support Craft

Landing Craft Swimmer Reconnaissance .... LCSR
Light SEAL Support Craft .... LSSC
Medium SEAL Support Craft .... MSSC
Swimmer Delivery Vehicle .... SDV

6.   Mobile Inshore Underseas Warfare (MIUW) Craft

MIUW Attack Craft .... MAC

Auxiliary Ship Classifications

Destroyer Tender .... AD
Degaussing Ship.................................. ADG
Ammunition Ship .... AE
Store Ship .... AF
Combat Store Ship .... AFS
Miscellaneous .... AG
Escort Research Ship .... AGDE
Hydrofoil Research Ship .... AGEH
Environmental Research Ship .... AGER
Miscellaneous Command Ship .... AGF
Missile Range Instrumentation Ship .... AGM
Major Communications Relay Ship .... AGMR
Oceanographic Research Ship .... AGOR
Patrol Craft Tender .... AGP
Radar Picket Ship .... AGR
Surveying Ship .... AGS
Auxiliary Submarine .... AGSS
Technical Research Ship .... AGTR
Hospital Ship.................................... AH
Cargo Ship...................................... AK
Cargo Ship, Dock .... AKD
Light Cargo Ship .... AKL
Stores Issue Ship .... AKS
Cargo Ship and Aircraft Ferry .... AKV
Vehicle Cargo Ship .... AKR
Net Laying Ship .... ANL
Oiler .... AO
Fast Combat Support Ship .... AOE
Gasoline Tanker .... AOG
Replenishment Oiler .... AOR
Transport .... AP
Self-propelled Barracks Ship .... APB
Small Coastal Transport .... APC
Repair Ship .... AR
Battle Damage Repair Ship .... ARB

Cable Repairing Ship	ARC
Internal Combustion Engine Repair Ship	ARG
Landing Craft Repair Ship	ARL
Salvage Ship	ARS
Salvage Lifting Ship	ARSD
Salvage Craft Tender	ARST
Aircraft Repair Ship (aircraft)	ARVA
Aircraft Repair Ship (engine)	ARVE
Aircraft Repair Ship (helicopter)	ARVH
Submarine Tender	AS
Submarine Rescue Ship	ASR
Auxiliary Ocean Tug	ATA
Fleet Ocean Tug	ATF
Salvage Tug	ATS
Auxiliary Training Submarine	ATSS
Seaplane Tender	AV
Guided Missile Ship	AVM
Aviation Supply Ship	AVS
Auxiliary Aircraft Transport	AVT
Distilling Ship	AW
Training Aircraft Carrier	CVT
Fast Deployment Logistics Ship	FDL
Unclassified Miscellaneous	IX

Service Craft Classifications

Large Auxiliary Floating Dry Dock (non-self-propelled)	AFDB
Small Auxiliary Floating Dry Dock (non-self-propelled)	AFDL
Medium Auxiliary Floating Dry Dock (non-self-propelled)	AFDM
Barracks Craft (non-self-propelled)	APL
Auxiliary Repair Dry Dock (non-self-propelled)	ARD
Medium Auxiliary Repair Dry Dock (non-self-propelled)	ARDM
Submersible Research Vehicle (nuclear propulsion)	NR
Target and Training Submarine (self-propelled)	SST
Submersible Craft (self-propelled)	X
Miscellaneous Auxilliary (self-propelled)	YAG
Open Lighter (non-self-propelled)	YC
Car Float (non-self-propelled)	YCF
Aircraft Transportation Lighter (non-self-propelled)	YCV
Floating Crane (non-self-propelled)	YD
Diving Tender (non-self-propelled)	YDT
Covered Lighter (self-propelled)	YF
Ferryboat or Launch (self-propelled)	YFB
Yard Floating Dry Dock (non-self-propelled)	YFD
Covered Lighter (non-self-propelled)	YFN
Large Covered Lighter (non-self-propelled)	YFNB
Dry Dock Companion Craft (non-self-propelled)	YFND
Lighter (special purpose) (non-self-propelled)	YFNX
Floating Power Barge (non-self-propelled)	YFP
Refrigerated Covered Lighter (self-propelled)	YFR
Refrigerated Covered Lighter (non-self-propelled)	YFRN
Covered Lighter (range-tender) (self-propelled)	YFRT
Harbor Utility Craft (self-propelled)	YFU
Garbage Lighter (self-propelled)	YG
Garbage Lighter (non-self-propelled)	YGN
Salvage Lift Craft, Heavy (non-self-propelled)	YHLC
Dredge (self-propelled)	YM
Salvage Lift Craft, Medium (non-self-propelled)	YMLC
Salvage Lift Craft, Light (self-propelled)	YLLC
Gate Craft (non-self-propelled)	YNG

Fuel Oil Barge (self-propelled) .... YO
Gasoline Barge (self-propelled) .... YOG
Gasoline Barge (non-self-propelled) .... YOGN
Fuel Oil Barge (non-self-propelled) .... YON
Oil Storage Barge (non-self-propelled) .... YOS
Patrol Craft (self-propelled) .... YP
Floating Pile Driver (non-self-propelled) .... YPD
Floating Workshop (non-self-propelled) .... YR
Repair and Berthing Barge (non-self-propelled) .... YRB
Repair, Berthing and Messing Barge (non-self-propelled) ... YRBM
Floating Dry Dock Workshop (hull) (non-self-propelled) .. YRDH
Floating Dry Dock Workshop (machine) (non-self-propelled) YRDM
Radiological Repair Barge (non-self-propelled) .... YRR
Salvage Craft Tender (non-self-propelled) .... YRST
Seaplane Wrecking Derrick (self-propelled) .... YSD
Sludge Removal Barge (non-self-propelled) .... YSR
Large Harbor Tug (self-propelled) .... YTB
Small Harbor Tug (self-propelled) .... YTL
Medium Harbor Tug (self-propelled) .... YTM
Water Barge (self-propelled)· .... YW
Water Distilling Barge (non-self-propelled) .... YWDN
Water Barge (non-self-propelled) .... YWN

Two basic systems are used to designate the U.S. Navy's enlisted men. The simpler and newer is the paygrade system, in which the lowest ranking are at the E-1 paygrade and the highest at the E-9. If a man advances beyond E-9 he either becomes a *Warrant Officer* or is given a Commission, usually as a *Limited Duty Officer* or LDO. The older traditional system combines designation as to a man's specialty with his ranking within that specialty, e.g., BM2, Boatswain's Mate Second Class, who is at the E-5 paygrade.

There are various paths of advancement within each primary rating. For example, a seaman might want to advance through the Gunner's Mate channel, or he might choose the missile or technician channels, or he might choose the less diversified Quartermaster channel. A man interested in engineering might enlist as a Fireman Recruit in the E-1 paygrade and advance through Engineman, Electrician's Mate, Machinist's Mate or other channels.

A paygrade (E-4, E-5, E-6, etc.) within a rating is called a *rate* and reflects a level of achievement within that rating.

Paygrades

E-1 Seaman recruit, fireman recruit, airman recruit, construction recruit, hospital recruit, dental recruit, steward recruit

E-2 Seaman apprentice, fireman apprentice, hospital apprentice, dental apprentice, steward apprentice

E-3 Seaman, fireman, airman, constructionman, hospitalman, dentalman, stewardsman

E-4 Petty officer, third class (PO3)

E-5 Petty officer, second class (PO2)

E-6 Petty officer, first class (PO1)

E-7 Chief petty officer, acting appointment (CPOA)

E-7 Chief petty officer, (CPO)

E-8 Senior chief petty officer (SCPO)

E-9 Master chief petty officer (MCPO)

A *rating* is defined as an occupation in the Navy made up of duties calling for closely related kinds of skills, abilities, and aptitudes. Each rating has its own specialty mark which is worn on the left sleeve by all properly qualified men. The Navy rating structure is divided into three classifications: *general, service,* and *emergency.*

General ratings: Broad occupational fields, encompassing similar duties and functions, which require related patterns of aptitudes and qualifications and which provide paths of advancement for career development.

Service ratings: Subdivisions of certain general ratings which provide for required specialization in training and utilization of personnel.

Emergency ratings: Additional specialized ratings required in time of war.

When asked his rate, a man will sometimes simply answer "Boatswain's Mate," as an example, merely to indicate his specialty. Or he might say "Third Class," meaning he is a Third Class Petty Officer, the lowest petty officer rate, a person in the E-4 paygrade. "Boatswain's Mate Third" would be a specific and complete answer. In recent years, use of the paygrade designation alone has become more common, and it is not unusual for such a question to be answered simply by stating the paygrade, in this instance, E-4.

For illustration, following are the advancement steps for the Quartermaster rating:

Title	Symbol or abbreviation		Paygrade
Seaman Recruit	SR ⎫		E-1
Seaman Apprentice	SA ⎬ Nonrated men		E-2
Seaman	SN ⎭		E-3
Quartermaster Third Class	QM3		E-4
Quartermaster Second Class	QM2		E-5
Quartermaster First Class	QM1	⎫	E-6
Chief Quartermaster	QMC	⎬ Petty Officers	E-7
Senior Chief Quartermaster	QMCS	⎭	E-8
Master Chief Quartermaster	QMCM		E-9

Grades E-1 through E-3

The men in this group are collectively known as *nonrated.* Their titles consist of a basic name-e.g. Airman, or abbreviated AN. The Airman, or his counterpart, the Seaman (SN), is in paygrade E-3. All such ratings have two lower grades: the Recruit, paygrade E-1, abbreviated AR for Airman Recruit or SR for Seaman Recruit; and the Apprentice, paygrade E-2, abbreviated AA for Airman Apprentice and SA for Seaman Apprentice. The term Seaman, abbreviated SN, corresponds to the old Ordinary Seaman or Able-Bodied Seaman, sometimes also called AB.

A man enlisting for the first time would be brought in as a Recruit in any one of the following nonrated groups. After recruit training he would be designated an Apprentice, and after further training and qualification he would be promoted to paygrade E-3 and assume the basic title of the branch he has been in so far. At this point he will begin his training for the lowest of the petty officer ranks, which simultaneously begins his specialization.

All ratings named below are given at the E-3 level; all may be entered at the E-1 level, with "R" instead of "N" in the abbreviation.

AN	Airman
CN	Constructionman
DN	Dentalman
FN	Fireman
HN	Hospitalman
SN	Seaman
TN	Stewardsman

GENERAL RATINGS

(Grades E-4 through E-9)

AB	Aviation Boatswain's Mate
AC	Air Controlman
AD	Aviation Machinist's Mate
AE	Aviation Electrician's Mate
AFCM	Master Chief Aircraft Maintenanceman (E-9 only)
AG	Aerographer's Mate
AK	Aviation Storekeeper
AM	Aviation Structural Mechanic
AO	Aviation Ordnanceman
AQ	Aviation Fire Control Technician
AS	Aviation Support Equipment Technician
AT	Aviation Electronics Technician
AVCM	Master Chief Avionics Technician (E-9 only)
AX	Aviation ASW Technician
AZ	Aviation Maintenance Administrationman
BM	Boatswain's Mate

BR	Boilermaker
BT	Boilerman
BU	Builder
CE	Construction Electrician
CM	Construction Mechanic
CS	Commissaryman
CT	Communications Technician
CUCM	Master Chief Constructionman (E-9 only; Constructionman is also the title of the E-3 grade and is not used in intervening grades.)
DC	Damage Controlman
DK	Disbursing Clerk
DM	Illustrator Draftsman
DP	Data Processing Technician
DS	Data Systems Technician
DT	Dental Technician
EA	Engineering Aid
EM	Electrician's Mate
EN	Engineman
EO	Equipment Operator
EQCM	Master Chief Equipmentman (E-9 only)
ET	Electronics Technician
FT	Fire Control Technician
GM	Gunner's Mate
HM	Hospital Corpsman
IC	Interior Communications Electrician
IM	Instrumentman
JO	Journalist
LI	Lithographer
ML	Molder
MM	Machinist's Mate
MN	Mineman
MR	Machinery Repairman
MT	Missile Technician
MU	Musician
OM	Opticalman
PC	Postal Clerk
PH	Photographer's Mate
PICM	Master Chief Precision Instrumentman (E-9 only)
PM	Patternmaker
PN	Personnelman
PR	Aircrew Survival Equipmentman
PT	Photo Intelligenceman
QM	Quartermaster
RD	Radarman
RM	Radioman
SD	Steward
SF	Shipfitter
SH	Ship's Serviceman
SK	Storekeeper
SM	Signalman
SPCM	Master Chief Steam Propulsionman (E-9 only)
ST	Sonar Technician
SW	Steelworker
TD	Tradevman (i.e., "Training Devices Man")
TM	Torpedoman's Mate
UT	Utilitiesman
YN	Yeoman

SERVICE RATINGS

ABH	Aviation Boatswain's Mate Aircraft Handling
ABF	Aviation Boatswain's Mate Fuels
ABE	Aviation Boatswain's Mate Launching and Recovery Equipment
ATW	Aviation Electronics Technician Airborne CIC Equipment
ATR	Aviation Electronics Technician Radar and Radar Navigation Equipment
ATN	Aviation Electronics Technician Radio and Radio Navigation Equipment
AQB	Aviation Fire Control Technician Bomb Director
AQF	Aviation Fire Control Technician Fire Control
ADJ	Aviation Machinist's Mate Jet Engine Mechanic
ADR	Aviation Machinist's Mate Reciprocating Engine Mechanic
AMH	Aviation Structural Mechanic Hydraulic Mechanic
AME	Aviation Structural Mechanic Safety Equipment
AMS	Aviation Structural Mechanic Structures
ASE	Aviation Support Equipment Technician Electrical
ASH	Aviation Support Equipment Technician Hydraulics and Structures
ASM	Aviation Support Equipment Technician Mechanical
BUR	Builder Concrete
BUH	Builder Heavy
BUL	Builder Light
CYN	Communications Yeoman
CEP	Construction Electrician Power
CES	Construction Electrician Shop
CET	Construction Electrician Telephone
CEW	Construction Electrician Wiring
CMA	Construction Mechanic Automotive
CMH	Construction Mechanic Construction
ETN	Electronics Technician Communications
ETR	Electronics Technician Radar
EAD	Engineering Aids Draftsman
EAS	Engineering Aids Surveyor
EON	Equipment Operator Construction Equipment
EOH	Equipment Operator Hauling
FTG	Fire Control Technician Gun Fire Control
FTM	Fire Control Technician Missile Fire Control
GMG	Gunner's Mate Guns
GMM	Gunner's Mate Missiles
GMT	Gunner's Mate Technician
SFM	Shipfitter Metalsmith
SFP	Shipfitter Pipefitter
STS	Sonar Technician Submarine
STG	Sonar Technician Surface
SWE	Steelworker Erector
SWF	Steelworker Fabricator
UTA	Utilities Man Air Condition
UTB	Utilities Man Boilerman
UTP	Utilities Man Plumber
UTW	Utilities Man Water and Sanitation

APPENDIX C

AIRCRAFT DESIGNATION SYSTEM

This system, applicable to all the Services, is complicated and difficult to follow. It consists of the following in the order given: Status Prefix Symbol, Modified Mission Symbol, Basic Mission Symbol, Type Symbol, a hyphen, Design Number, and Series Letter. As a basic aircraft is designed and built, it will first be given its basic designation, e.g., A-7. As service indicates modifications, improvements, and adaptations, a later model might be the XEA-7E. For a full explanation of symbols, caveats, and exceptions, refer to the *Department of Defense Model Designation of Military Aircraft, Rockets and Guided Missile Book,* published semiannually by ASNPD-10, Wright-Patterson Air Force Base, Ohio, 45433.

Each aircraft, missile, or rocket also has a popular name, in addition to the official designation. All current popular names are indexed in this volume, with a brief of characteristics and the model basic designation. In building up the designation of a later modification or adaptation, not all letters in the system need be used; for example, the PHANTOM II, the famous F-4, has a photo-reconnaissance version, the RF-4B. The prototype of the plane would have been the YRF-4B, the "Y" later being lifted.

The following tables explain the meanings of the symbols.

Classification Letters

When applicable, classification letters are used to indicate that aircraft or airships are being used for experimentation or testing. When used, the classification letter will appear to the immediate left of the modified mission or the mission/type letter if the modification letter is not used. The following status prefix symbols, also called classification letters, are used:

Letter	*Title*	*Description*
G	Permanently Grounded	An aircraft permanently grounded, utilized for ground instruction and training.
J	Special Test, Temporary	Aircraft on special test programs by authorized organizations or on bailment contract having a special test configuration or whose installed property has been temporarily removed to accommodate the test. At completion of the test, the vehicle will be returned either to its original configuration or to standard operational configuration.
N	Special Test, Permanent	Aircraft on special test programs by authorized activities or on bailment contract, whose configuration is so drastically changed that return of aircraft to its original configuration or conversion to standard operational configuration, practicable or economical limits.
X	Experimental	Aircraft in a developmental, experimental stage where basic mission and design number have been designated but not established as a standard vehicle for service use.
Y	Prototype	Aircraft procured in limited quantities to develop the potentialities of the design.
Z	Planning	Designations used for identification purpose during the planning or predevelopment stage.

Modified Mission Letter

Modified mission symbols, or prefix letters, are assigned to the aircraft or airship when required by the individual services. This letter appears to the immediate left of the basic mission or type letter in the designation.

Letter	Title	Description
A	Attack	Aircraft modified to search out, attack, and destroy enemy land or sea targets, using conventional or special weapons. Also used for interdiction and close air support missions.
C	Cargo/Transport	Aircraft modified for carrying cargo and/or passengers.
D	Director	Aircraft capable of controlling a drone aircraft or a missile.
E	Special Electronic Installation	Aircraft modified with electronic devices for employment in one or more of the following roles: a. Electronic countermeasures. b. Airborne early warning radar. c. Airborne command and control including communications relay. d. Tactical data communications link for all nonautonomous modes of flight.
H	Search/Rescue	Aircraft having special equipment for performance of search and rescue missions.
K	Tanker	Aircraft having special equipment to provide in-flight refueling of other aircraft.
L	Cold Weather	Aircraft modified for operation in the arctic and antarctic regions: includes skis, special insulation, and other ancillary equipment required for extreme cold weather operations.
M	Missile Carrier	Aircraft modified for carrying and launching guided and nonguided missiles as part of the weapon system.
Q	Drone	Aircraft capable of being controlled from a point outside the aircraft.
R	Reconnaissance	Aircraft having equipment permanently installed for photographic and/or electronic reconnaissance missions.
S	Antisubmarine	Aircraft modified so that it can function to search, identify, attack, and destroy enemy submarines.
T	Trainer	Aircraft specially equipped or modified for training purposes.
U	Utility	Aircraft having small payload, utilized or modified to perform miscellaneous missions such as carrying cargo or passengers, towing targets, etc.
V	Staff	Aircraft having accommodations such as chairs, tables, lounge, berths, etc., for the transportation of staff personnel.
W	Weather	Aircraft having meteorological equipment permanently installed.

Basic Mission/Type Letters

The basic mission or type letters appear in each designation. They will always be to the immediate left of the hyphen in the designation. Only two "type" designations are used; they are marked by asterisks (*) in the listing which follows. A plane assigned the "H" type designation will carry either a modified or a basic mission letter only in addition to the type letter. The only exception to this rule is the use of the combination "R/S" symbol to indicate aircraft designed for integrated reconnaissance strike use.

Letter	Title	Description
A	Attack	Aircraft designed to search out, attack, and destroy enemy land or sea targets, using conventional or special weapons. Also used for interdiction and close air support missions.
B	Bomber	Aircraft designed for bombing enemy targets.
C	Cargo/Transport	Aircraft designed for carrying cargo and/or passengers.
E	Special Electronic Installation	Aircraft equipped with electronic devices requiring employment in the following roles: a. Electronic countermeasures. b. Airborne early warning radar. c. Airborne command and control including communications relay aircraft. d. Tactical data communications link for all nonautonomous modes of flight.
F	Fighter	Aircraft designed to intercept and destroy other aircraft and/or missiles.
*H	Helicopter	A rotary-wing aircraft designed with the capability of flight in any plan; e.g., horizontal, vertical, or diagonal.
K	Tanker	Aircraft designed for in-flight refueling of other aircraft.
O	Observation	Aircraft designed to observe (through visual or other means) and report tactical information concerning composition and disposition of enemy forces, troops, and supplies in an active combat area.
P	Patrol	Long range, all weather, multi-engine aircraft operating from land and/or water bases, designed for independent accomplishment of the following functions: antisubmarine warfare, maritime reconnaissance, and mining.

Letter	Title	Description
R	Reconnaissance	Aircraft designed to perform reconnaissance missions.
S	Antisubmarine	Aircraft designed to search out, detect, identify, attack, and destroy enemy submarines.
T	Trainer	Aircraft designed for training personnel in the operation of aircraft and/or related equipment, and having provisions for instructor personnel.
U	Utility	Aircraft used for miscellaneous missions such as carrying cargo and/or passengers, towing targets, etc. These aircraft include those having a small payload.
*V	VTOL and STOL	Aircraft designed for vertical take-off or landing with no take-off or landing roll, or aircraft capable of take-off and landing in a minimum prescribed distance.
X	Research	Aircraft designed for testing configurations of a radical nature. These aircraft are not normally intended for use as tactical aircraft.

Type symbols

Design Number

The Design number will always appear in any designation to the immediate right of the hyphen in the designation. This number is assigned sequentially to all new aircraft in each basic mission group or when an exisitng aircraft in a basic group is modified to the extent that it no longer reflects the original configuration or capability—e.g., redesign from a straight to a delta wing configuration or changing the number of engines.

Series Letter

Each basic series of aircraft begins with the letter "A"—e.g., the Corsair II is now designated the A-7A. If it is adapted in the future to uses other than attack missions without major configuration changes, these modifications will be indicated by new designations such as A-7B, etc.

POPULAR NAMES OF AIRCRAFT

Popular Name	Model Designation	Cognizant Service
ACADEME	TC-4C	Navy
AERO COMMANDER	U-4/U-9	AF
ALBATROSS	HU-16	Navy/CG/AF
AZTEC	U-11	Navy
BEAVER	U-6	AF/Army/Navy
BIRD DOG	O-1	Army/Navy/AF
BRONCO	OV-10	Navy/AF
BUCKEYE	T-2	Navy
CANBERRA	B-57	AF
CARGO MASTER	C-133	AF
CARIBOU	C-7A	AF
CAYUSE	OH-6A	Army
CHEYENNE	AH-56A	Army
CHICKASAW	H-19	AF/Army/Navy
CHINOOK	CH-47	Army
CHOCTAW	CH-34	AF/Army
COCHISE	T-42A	Army
COMMANDO	C-46	AF
CONSTELLATION	C-121A	AF/Navy
CORSAIR II	A-7	Navy/AF
COUGAR	F-9	Navy
CRUSADER	F-8	Navy
DASH	QH-50C	Navy
DELTA DAGGER	F-102	AF
DELTA DART	F-106	AF
DESTROYER	RB-66	AF
FLYING BOXCAR	C-119	AF
FLYING CLASSROOM	T-29	AF/Navy
FLYING EDSEL	F-111	AF/Navy
FREEDOM FIGHTER	F-5	AF
GALAXY	C-5A	AF
GLOBEMASTER	C-124	AF
GREYHOUND	C-2	Navy
GULFSTREAM I	C-4	CG
GULFSTREAM II	VC-11	CG
HAWKEYE	E-2	Navy
HERCULES	C-130	AF/Navy
HUEYCOBRA	AH-1G	Army
HUSKIE	H-43	AF/Navy
HUSTLER	B-58	AF
INTRUDER	A-6	Navy
INVADER	A-26	AF
IROQUOIS	UH-1	Army

Popular Name	Model Designation	Cognizant Service
JET STAR	C-140	AF/Navy
JOLLY GREEN GIANT	HH-3E	AF
KIOWA	OH-58	Army
LIFTMASTER	C-118	AF/Navy
MENTOR	T-34	AF/Navy
MESCALERO	T-41	Army/AF
MOHAWK	OV-1	Army
MOJAVE	CH-37	AF/Navy
NAVIGATOR	RC-45J/UC-45J	Navy
NAVION	U-18	AF
NEPTUNE	P-2	Navy
NIGHTINGALE	C-9	AF
ORION	P-3	Navy
OSAGE	TH-55A	Army
OTTER	U-1	AF/Navy
PHANTOM II	F-4	Navy/AF
PROVIDER	C-123	AF/Coast Guard
RAVEN	H-23	Army
SABRE	F-86	AF
SABRELINER	T-39	AF/Navy
SAMARITAN	C-131	AF
SCORPION	F-89	AF
SEA BAT	SH-34	Navy
SEAHORSE	H-34	Navy
SEA KING	H-3	Navy
SEA KNIGHT	H-46	Navy
SEA RANGER	TH-57	Navy
SEASPRITE	H-2	Navy
SEASTALLION	CH-53	Navy
SEA STAR	T-1	Navy
SEMINOLE	U-8	Army
SENECA	H-41A	Army
SENTINEL	U-19	AF
SHAWNEE	H-21	Army
SHOOTING STAR	F-80/T-33	AF/Navy
SIOUX	H-13	Army/Navy/Coast Guard
SKYHAWK	A-4	Navy
SKY KNIGHT	F-10	Navy
SKYMASTER	C-54	AF/Navy
SKYRAIDER	A-1	Navy/AF
SKYRAY	F-6	Navy
SKYTRAIN	C-47/C-117	AF/Navy/Army
SKYWARRIOR	A-3	Navy/AF
STARFIGHTER	F-104	Navy
STARLIFTER	C-141	AF
STRATOCRUISER	C-97	AF
STRATOFORTRESS	B-52	AF
STRATOFREIGHTER	KC-97	AF
STRATOJET	B-47	AF
STRATOLIFTER	C-135	AF
STRATOLINER	VC-137	AF
STRATOTANKER	KC-135	AF
SUPER CONSTELLATION	C-121	AF
SUPERFORTRESS	B-29/B-50	AF
SUPER JOLLY	HH-538/C	AF
SUPER SABRE	F-100	AF
TALON	T-38	AF

Popular Name	Model Designation	Cognizant Service
TARHE	CH-54A	Army
THUNDERCHIEF	F-105	AF
THUNDERFLASH	RF-84F/RF-84K	AF
THUNDERJET	F84-G	AF
THUNDERSTREAK	F-84F	AF
TIGER	F-11	Navy
TORNADO	B-45	AF
TRACER	E-1	Navy
TRACKER	S-2	Navy
TRADER	C-1	Navy
TROJAN	T-28	AF/Navy
UTE	U-21	Army
VIGILANTE	A-5	Navy
VOODOO	F-101	AF
WARNING STAR	C-121	Navy
WORKHORSE	H-21	AF

APPENDIX D
MISSILE DESIGNATION SYSTEM

Missiles, guided missiles and rockets are designated in a single system similar to the *Aircraft designation system.* All have popular names and are indexed herein in accordance with such names, as for aircraft. For fuller explanation, see *DOD Model Designation of Military Aircraft, Rockets and Guided Missile Book,* published semiannually by ASNPD-10, Wright-Patterson Air Force Base, Ohio 45433.

By reference to the tables of symbol meanings which follow, the MIM-3A, for example, is a Mobile, Intercept, Guided Missile, model 3A. *Nike Ajax,* the popular name for the MIM-3A, cannot be derived from the tables, but will be found indexed under "N" in the Popular Names section of this Appendix.

Status Prefix Symbols
(Classification Letters)

Letter	Title	Description
J	Special Test, Temporary	Vehicles on special test programs by authorized organizations and vehicles on bailment contract having a special configuration to accommodate the test. At completion of the test the vehicles will be either returned to their original configuration or returned to standard operational configuration.
N	Special Test, Permanent	Vehicles on special test programs by authorized activities and vehicles on bailment contract, whose configurations are so drastically changed that return of the vehicles to their original configurations is beyond practicable or economical limits.
X	Experimental	Vehicles in a developmental or experimental stage, but not established as standard vehicles for service use.
Y	Prototype	Preproduction vehicles procured for evaluation and test of a specific design.
Z	Planning	Vehicles in the planning or predevelopment stage.

Launch Environment Symbols

Letter	Title	Description
A	Air	Air launched.
B	Multiple	Capable of being launched from more than one environment.
C	Coffin	Stored horizontally or at less than a 45 degree angle in a protective enclosure (regardless of structural strength) and launched from the ground.

Letter	Title	Description
F	Individual	Carried and launched by one man.
H	Silo Stored	Vertically stored below ground level and launched from the ground.
L	Silo Launched	Vertically stored and launched from below ground level.
M	Mobile	Launched from a ground vehicle or movable platform.
P	Soft Pad	Partially or nonprotected in storage and launched from the ground.
R	Ship	Launched from a surface vessel such as ship, barge, etc.
U	Underwater	Launched from a submarine or other underwater device.

Mission Symbols

Letter	Title	Description
D	Decoy	Vehicles designed or modified to confuse, deceive, or divert enemy defenses by simulating an attack vehicle.
E	Special Electronic	Vehicles designed or modified with electronic equipment for communications, countermeasures, electronic radiation sounding, or other electronic recording or relay missions.
G	Surface Attack	Vehicles designed to destroy enemy land or sea targets.
I	Intercept-Aerial	Vehicles designed to intercept aerial targets in defensive or offensive roles.
Q	Drone	Vehicles designed for target, reconnaissance, or surveillance purposes.
T	Training	Vehicles designed or permanently modified for training purposes.
U	Underwater Attack	Vehicles designed to destroy enemy submarines or other underwater targets or to detonate underwater.
W	Weather	Vehicles designed to observe, record, or relay data pertaining to meteorological phenomena.

Vehicle Type Symbols

Letter	Title	Description
M	Guided Missile	Unmanned, self-propelled vehicles designed to move in a trajectory or flight path all or partially

Letter	Title	Description
		above the earth's surface and whose trajectory or course while the vehicle is in motion, is capable of being controlled remotely or by homing systems, or by inertial and/or programmed guidance from within. This term does not include space vehicles, space boosters or naval torpedoes, but does include target and reconnaissance drones.
N	Probe	Non-orbital instrumented vehicles not involved in space missions that are used to penetrate the aerospace environment and transmit or report back information.
R	Rocket	Self-propelled vehicles without installed or remote control guidance mechanisms, whose trajectory or flight path cannot be altered after launch. Rocket systems designed for line-of-sight fire are not included.

Popular Names of Rockets, Missiles, and Probes

Popular Name	Model Designation	Cognizant Service
ASROC	RUR-5	Navy
ATLAS	CGM-16	AF
BOMARC	CIM-10	AF
BULLPUP	AGM-12	AF/Navy
CARDINAL	MQM-61A	Army
CONDOR	AGM-53	Navy
DRAGON	XFGM-77A	Army
ENTAC	MGM-32	Army
FALCON	AIM-4	AF
FIREBEE	BQM-34	AF/Army/Navy
FOCUS I	AGM-87	Navy
GENIE	AIR-2	AF
HARPOON	XAGM-84A	Navy
HAWK	MIM-23	Army/Navy/Marine Corps
HONEST JOHN	MGR-1	Army/Navy/Marine Corps
HOUND DOG	AGM-28	AF
KINGFISHER	AQM-60A	Army
KITTY	PWN-6	AF
LANCE	XMGM-52B	Army
LITTLE JOHN	MGR-3A	Army
MACE - A	MGM-13	AF
MACE - B	CGM-13	AF
MATADOR	MGM-1	AF
MAVERICK	ZAGM-65A	AF
MINUTEMAN	LGM-30	AF
NIKE AJAX	MIM-3	Army
NIKE HERCULES	MIM-14A	Army
NIKE ZEUS	XLIM-49A	Army
OVERSEER	MQM-58A	Army
PERSHING	XMGM-31A	Army
PETREL	AQM-41	Navy
PHOENIX	AIM-54	Navy
POLARIS	UGM-27	Navy

Popular Name	Model Designation	Cognizant Service
POSEIDON	UGM-73	Navy
QUAIL	ADM-20	AF
REDEYE	XMIM-43	Army/Navy/Marine Corps
REDHEAD ROAD RUNNER	MQM-42	Army
REGULUS	RGM-6/15	Navy
ROOSTER	PWN-7	AF
SEA MAULER	RIM-46	Navy
SERGEANT	MGM-29	Army
SHILLELAGH	MGM-51	Army
SHRIKE	AGM-45	Navy/AF
SIDEWINDER	AIM-9	Navy/AF
SPARROW	AIM-7	Navy/AF
SRAM	AGM-69A	AF
STANDARD	RIM-66/67	Navy
SUBROC	UUM-44A	Navy
SUPER GENIE	AIR-2B	AF
TALOS	RIM-8	Navy
TARTAR	RIM-24	Navy
TERRIER	RIM-2	Navy
TITAN	HGM-25	AF
THOR	PGM-17	AF
TYPHON	RIM-50/ RIM-55	Navy
VIPER	XAGM-80A	AF
WEAPON ALPHA	RUR-4	Navy

APPENDIX E

ELECTRONICS NOMENCLATURE (AN) SYSTEM

Most electronic equipment has no popular name. These short titles are unclassified, whereas the actual name of the equipment may be classified. All begin with AN/, and the system is often called the AN system. Three indicator letters follow, signifying the kind of installation, type of equipment, and purpose. Thus, AN/APA-2D: AN/—listed in the Joint Electronics Type Designation System; A—installed in aircraft; P—radar; A—auxiliary assembly; 2—model number 2; D—modification D of model 2.

Equipment Indicator Letters

Installation

A- Airborne (installed and operated in aircraft).

B- Underwater mobile, submarine.

C- Air Transportable (inactivated, do not use).

D- Pilotless carrier

F- Fixed

G- Ground, general ground use (include two or more ground type installations).

K- Amphibious

M- Ground, mobile (installed as operating unit in a vehicle which has no function other than transporting the equipment).

P- Pack or portable (animal or man).

S- Water surface craft.

T- Ground, transportable

U- General utility (includes two or more general installation classes: airborne, shipboard, and ground).

V- Ground, vehicular (installed in vehicle designed for functions other than carrying electronic equipment etc., such as tanks).

W- Water surface and underwater.

Type of Equipment

A- Invisible light, heat radiating.

B- Pigeon

C- Carrier

D- Radiac

E- Nupac

F- Photographic

G- Telegraphic or teletype.

I- Interphone and public address.

J- Electro-mechanical (not otherwise covered).

K- Telemetering

L- Countermeasures

M- Meteorological

N- Sound in air

P- Radar

Q- Sonar and underwater sound

R- Radio

S- Special types, magnetic, etc., or combinations of types.

T- Telephone (wire)

V- Visual and visible light

W- Armament (peculiar to armament, not otherwise covered)

X- Facsimile or television

Purpose

A- Auxiliary assemblies (not complete operating sets used with or part of two or more sets or sets series).

B- Bombing

C- Communications (receiving and transmitting)

D- Direction finder and/or reconnaissance

E- Ejection and/or release.

G- Fire control or searchlight directing

H- Recording and/or reproducing (graphic meteorological and sound)

L- Searchlight control (inactivated, use "G")

M- Maintenance and test assemblies (including tools)

N- Navigational aids (including altimeters, beacons, compasses, racons, depth soundings, approach, and landing)

P- Reproducing (inactivated, do not use)

Q- Special, or combination of purposes

Installation	*Type of Equipment*	*Purpose*
		R- Receiving, passive detecting
		S- Detecting and/or range of bearing
		T- Transmitting
		W- Control
		X- Identification and recognition.

AN/AAR-30:
Airborne infra red system.

AN/AAS-18:
Infrared mapping system.

AN/AIC-22:
Airborne intercom for P-3A.

AN/AJA-2:
Central gyro reference system.

AN/AJB-3A:
Altitude reference and
bombing system.

AN/AJQ-14:
Inertial bomb navigation for F-111B.

AN/AKT-11:
Telemetry transmitter.

AN/ALD-2:
Airborne ECM system.

AN/ALD-5:
Electronic reconnaissance system.

AN/ALQ-78:
Antisubmarine warfare electronic
countermeasures assembly.

AN/AMT-12:
Meteorological sounding system.

AN/APA-56:
Aircraft early warning radar indicator.

AN/APA-60 or 60A:
Autopilot.

AN/APA-63 or 63A:
Autopilot.

AN/APA-125:
Standard aircraft indicator.

AN/APA-127:
Fire control group for F3H-2N.

AN/APA/128:
Fire control group for F4H-1.

AN/APA-138:
Aircraft projected optical display
system.

AN/APA-141:
Radar.

AN/APA-150:
Radar for HSS-1.

AN/APA-157:
Fire control group for F-4B and F-4C.

AN/APC-83:
Radar set for F-8.

AN/APD-7:
Side-looking radar for RA-5C.

AN&APG-22:
CW range radar.

AN/APG-43:
FM/CW radar.

AN/APG-53A:
Radar fire control system.

AN/APM-63:
Autopilot test equipment.

AN/APM-66:
Test equipment for An/APN-22.

AN/APM-82:
RF monitor.

AN/APM-83:
Spectrum analyzer.

AN/APM-84:
Radar modulator tester.

AN/APM-84A:
Radar modulator tester.

AN/APM-84B:
Radar modulator tester.

AN/APM-85:
Monitor, computer tester, dummy
load.

AN/APM-86:
Computer test set.

AN/APM-91:
Computer test set.

AN/APM-92:
Monitor, computer tester, dummy load.

AN/APM-153:
Test set for AN/APN-59.

AN/APN-22:
Microwave FM/CW altimeter.

AN/APN-23:
Active seeker.

AN/APN-54:
Radar beacon.

AN/APN-77:
Helicopter doppler navigator.

AN/APN-97A:
Doppler navigation system.

AN/APN-114:
Flare-out altimeter for missiles.

AN/APN-117:
Radar type.

AN/APN-120:
Electronic altimeter set.

AN/APN-130:
Radar type.

AN/APN-140:
Electronic altimeter.

AN/APN-141:
Low-altitude pulse radar altimeter.

AN/APN-141-V:
Pulse radar altimeter.

AN/APN-145:
Loran navigation system.

AN/APN-153:
Doppler navigation set.

AN/APQ-T1:
Mark V IFF trainer.

AN/APQ-20:
CM system.

AN/APQ-50:
Airborne radar.

AN/APQ-54:
Projectile velocity measuring equipment.

AN/APQ-60:
Missile illuminator.

AN/APQ-67:
Radar type.

AN/APQ-72:
Airborne radar for F-4B.

AN/APQ-92:
Advanced airborne research radar system for A6A.

AN/APQ-94:
Radar set for F-8D.

AN/APQ-99:
Radar set.

AN/APQ-102:
Radar type.

AN/APR-19:
Missile control receiver.

AN/APS-20:
Aircraft early warning search radar.

AN/APS-49:
Airborne rapid scan snorkel detecting radar.

AN/APS-80:
Radar set.

AN/APS-88:
Airborne radar.

AN/APS-88A:
Airborne radar.

AN/APS-96:
Airborne early warning search radar for E2A

AN/APS-109:
Radar homing and warning for F-111B

AN/APX-46:
Air-to-ground IFF for F-111B.

AN/APX-46(V):
Advanced multi-function IFF transponder equipment.

AN/APX-64:
Advanced multi-function IFF transponder equipment.

AN/AQA-1:
Sonobuoy indicator equipment.

AN/AQA-3:
Sonobuoy indicator group.

AN/AQA-4:
Sonobuoy indicator group.

AN/AQA-5:
Electronic indicator group for P-3A.

AN/AQM-2:
Test equipment for AN/AQS-2.

AN/AQM-7:
Sonar test set for AN/AQS-12.

AN/AQS-2:
Dipping sonar for blimps.

AN/AQS-4:
Dipping sonar for helicopters.

AN/AQS-4A:
Dipping sonar for helicopters.

AN/AQS-6:
Dipping sonar for fixed wing aircraft.

AN/AQS-8:
Dipping sonar for helicopters.

AN/AQS-10:
Variable depth sonar.

AN/AQS-12:
Dipping sonar for helicopter.

AN/AQS-13:
Dipping sonar for helicopter.

AN/ARA-25:
Aircraft radio set.

AN/ARA-50:
UHF/ADF communications for F-111B.

AN/ARC-23:
Radio set.

AN/ARC-38A:
Airborne radio communications set.

AN/ARC-51:
Aircraft UHF communications system.

AN/ARC-51A:
UHF radio.

AN/ARC-52:
Airborne radio for F-111B.

AN/ARC-84:
Airborne VHF communications and navigation equipment.

AN/ARC-94:
Aircraft HF-SSB communications.

AN/ARC-104:
FH-SSB airborne transceiver.

AN/ARN-52:
TACAN set.

AN/ARN-76:
Aircraft Loran C microcircuit receiver.

AN/ARR-52:
Sonobuoy receiving set.

AN/ARR-52A:
Radio receiver, P-3A, S-2E.

AN/ARR-69:
Auxiliary UHF transmitter, receiver.

AN/ARW-78:
Radio decoder.

AN/ASA-16:
Indicator group.

AN/ASA-20:
Airborne recorder.

AN/ASA-23:
Missile launch group.

AN/ASA-25:
Data display group.

AN/ASA-26:
Airborne recorder.

AN/ASA-27:
Airborne tactical data system for E-2A.

AN/ASA-31:
Target position computer group.

AN/ASA-32:
Flight control system for F-4.

AN/ASA-50:
Navigational computer group.

AN/ASB-12:
Bomb navigation system.

AN/ASE-1:
Missile launch set.

AN/ASK-2:
Wind memory computer.

AN/ASM-9:
Load simulator.

AN/ASM-12:
Load simulator.

AN/ASM-87:
Altitude simulator.

AN/ASN-19:
Navigation computer for A4E.

AN/ASN-30:
Navigation computer group.

AN/ASN-39:
Navigations system computer test set for A-4 and F-4B.

AN/ASN-41:
Navigational computer set.

AN/ASN-44:
Lightweight inertial navigation system.

AN/ASN-46:
Navigation computer for F-4B and C.

AN/ASQ-8 or 10:
Magnetic anomaly detectors for fixed wing aircraft.

AN/ASQ-13:
Advanced helicopter sonar system.

AN/ASQ-17:
Airborne receiver-transmitter.

AN/ASQ-19:
Communications-navigation-identification system for F-4B.

AN/ASQ-54:
Airborne tactical data system for E-2A.

AN/ASQ-56:
Communications-navigation-identification system for A-5A.

AN/ASQ-57:
Communications-navigation-identification system for A-6A.

AN/ASQ-58:
Communications-navigation-identification system for E-2A.

AN/ASQ-61:
Computer system for A-6A and E-2A.

AN/ASR-3:
Airborne submarine exhaust detector.

AN/ASW-20:
Automatic flight control system.

AN/ASW-21:
Automatic carrier landing system for F-111B.

AN/ASW-22:
BULLPUP automatic guidance system.

AN/AVA-1:
Analog display indicator and terrain avoidance display.

AN/AWA-6:
Hydraulic cooling group.

AN/AWG-9:
Fire control radar for F-111B.

AN/AWG-10:
Airborne radar for advanced F-4B.

AN/AWM-8:
Missile control system test set.

AN/AWM-9:
Fire control system test set.

AN/AWM-15:
Radar and fire control group test set.

AN/BAR-2:
Infra-red receiving search equipment.

AN/BAR-4:
Infra-red receiving search equipment.

AN/BLQ-3:
Low frequency acoustic jammer
for submarine countermeasures.

AN/BLQ-4:
High Frequency acoustic jammer
for submarine countermeasures.

AN/BLQ-5:
Low-frequency acoustic jammer,
submarine counter-countermeasures
equipment.

AN/BLQ-6:
High frequency acoustic echo
repeater, submarine
countermeasures.

AN/BPA-7:
Submarine antenna drive system.

AN/BPS-2:
Submarine air search radar.

AN/BPS-2A:
Submarine air search radar.

AN/BPS-3:
Submarine height finding radar.

AN/BPS-6:
Submarine air search radar.

AN/BPS-7:
Submarine height finding radar.

AN/BQA-2:
Secure submarine communications
group.

AN/BQA-3:
Computer indicator group.

AN/BQA-3A:
Computer indicator group.

AN/BQA-8:
Sonar performance computer.

AN/BQG-1:
Passive under water fire control sonar.

AN/BQG-2:
Passive underwater fire control sonar.

AN/BQG-3:
Passive underwater fire control sonar.

AN/BQG-4:
Passive underwater fire control sonar.

AN/BQM-1:
Test set for AN/BQR-3 and 3A.

AN/BQN-3:
Submarine depth sounder.

AN/BQQ-1:
Integrated search fire control sonar
system.

AN/BQQ-1A:
Integrated search fire control sonar
system.

AN/BQQ-1B:
Integrated search fire control sonar
system.

AN/BQQ-2:
Sonar system for SUBROC.

AN/BQR-2:
Submarine passive sonar system.

AN/BQR-3:
Submarine passive sonar system.

AN/BQR-7:
Passive sonar system.

AN/BQR-7A:
Passive sonar system.

AN/BQS-6A:
Aquisition sonar.

AN/BQS-8:
Integrated under-ice sonar system.

AN/BR-28:
Passive array of submarine
hydrophones.

AN/BRA-11:
Medium-high frequency communications antenna.

AN/BZN-3:
Submarine secure depth sounder.

AN/CPN-4:
Ground controlled approach
equipment.

AN/DPM-2:
Guided missile control test set.

AN/DPM-3:
　　Harness bench test set.

AN/DPM-4:
　　Seeker test set.

AN/DPM-5:
　　Illuminator test set.

AN/DPM-9:
　　Calibrator guided missile test set.

AN/DPN-15:
　　Semi-active seeker.

AN/DPN-24:
　　Missile guidance set.

AN/DPN-51:
　　Missile guidance set.

AN/DPN-60:
　　Missile guidance set.

AN/DPN-72:
　　Missile guidance set.

AN/DRW-29:
　　Radio set.

AN/DSM-15:
　　Missile launcher test set.

AN/DSM-16:
　　Servo test set.

AN/DSM-18:
　　Guided missile test set for *TALOS*.

AN/DSM-32:
　　Missile test set.

AN/DSM-60:
　　Guided missile test set for *TALOS*.

AN/FCC-55:
　　Multiplexer set.

ANFE:
　　Aircraft Not Fully Equipped.

AN/FNS-64/2:
　　Station keeping equipment.

AN/FPN-10:
　　Radar beacon.

AN/FPN-28:
　　S and X band ground controlled
　　approach equipment.

AN/FPN-29:
　　Harbor surveillance and control
　　radar.

AN/FPS-33:
　　Long-range air traffic control radar.

AN/FPS-41:
　　Meteorological radar.

AN/FPS-81:
　　Weather radar.

AN/FQQ-8:
　　Submerged sonic detection system.

AN/FQQ-10:
　　Colossus sonar set.

AN/FQS-3:
　　Shore installation sonar.

AN/FRA-49:
　　High frequency transmitter antenna
　　coupler.

AN/FRA-84:
　　Military version of standard micro-
　　wave system Type 74B.

AN/FRC-109(v):
　　Military version of standard micro-
　　wave system Type 76C.

AN/FRT-48:
　　UHF transmitter, 100,000 watt.

AN/FRT-61:
　　Low frequency transmitter,
　　100,000 watt.

AN/FRT-62:
　　Shore radio transmitter.

AN/GJQ-9:
　　Test equipment for shop mainten-
　　ance of flight control system.

AN/GMD-1B:
　　Automatic radio direction finding
　　and recording system.

AN/GYK-3:
　　Modular data processing system.

AN/GYK-3(V):
　　Modular digital data processing
　　system.

AN/MKR-6:
Telemetry receiver.

AN/MPB-1, 2 and 3:
Deep sea acoustic projector for
sonar testing.

AN/MPN-5:
Ground controlled approach equipment, S and X bands.

AN/MPS-4 and 4A:
Height finding radar.

AN/MPS-21:
Three dimensional search radar.

AN/MPS-23:
Three dimensional search radar.

AN/MPS-24:
Long range search radar.

AN/MPT-1:
CW target illumination radar.

AN/MRC-59:
Tactical communications.

AN/MRC-60:
Tactical communications.

AN/MSQ-5:
ASW aircraft checkout equipment.

AN/MSP-44:
Tracking radar, X band.

AN/MSQ-51:
Tracking and guidance radar for
drones.

AN/PDR-1:
Radiac set.

AN/PDR-22:
Radiac set.

AN/PQC-1A:
Underwater communications system
for divers.

AN/PRC-38:
Portable man-pack radio transceiver.

AN/PRC-41:
UHF pack set communications.

AN/PRC-55:
Handset radio for flight deck use.

AN/PRC-56:
Helmet radio for flight deck use.

AN/PVM-1:
Radar chronograph set.

AN/SAC-4:
Intermediate range communications
set.

AN/SLT-5:
CM jammer.

AN/SPA-4B:
Shipboard radar indicator.

AN/SPA-6:
Radar indicator.

AN/SPA-8:
Shipboard standard radio indicator
display.

AN/SPA-13:
Aircraft control computer.

AN/SPA-25:
Radar repeater indicator, 300 mile.

AN/SPA-28A:
Electrical synchronizer group.

AN/SPA-33:
Standard shipboard indicator group.

AN/SPA-40:
Range-height indicator.

AN/SPA-44:
Target illumination radar for
TERRIER.

AN/SPA-61:
Target pointing system.

AN/SPG-49:
Guidance radar, *TALOS* and
TERRIER.

AN/SPG-51:
Guidance radar for *TARTAR.*

AN/SPG-51A and B:
Guidance radar for *TARTAR.*

AN/SPG-55:
C-Band guidance radar for
TERRIER.

AN/SPG-55A, B:
  Fire control radar for *TERRIER.*

AN/SPG-56:
  Tracking and guidance radar for
  TALOS.

AN/SPG-59:
  Acquisition and guidance radar.

AN/SPM-1:
  Target transmitter.

AN/SPM-4:
  Frequency power meter.

AN/SPM-10:
  Radar test set.

AN/SPM-12:
  RF Monitor for AN/SPG-49.

AN/SPM-15:
  Radar test set for AN/SPG-51.

AN/SPM-18:
  Radar test set for shipboard
  checkout.

AN/SPN-4:
  Surface search radar.

AN/SPN-6:
  Carrier surveillance radar.

AN/SPN-8:
  Shipboard CCA radar.

AN/SPN-10:
  Automatic landing system for use
  aboard carriers.

AN/SPN-12:
  True air speed indicator system for
  LSO.

AN/SPN-21:
  Surface search radar.

AN/SPN-32:
  Loran C receiver.

AN/SPN-35:
  Radar set, CCA

AN/SPN-59:
  Indicator group.

AN/SPQ-5:
  Long range tracking and guidance
  radar for *TERRIER.*

AN/SPQ-55:
  Tracking and guidance radar for
  TERRIER.

AN/SPS-3:
  Surveillance radar.

AN/SPS-4:
  Surface and zenith search radar.

AN/SPS-5:
  Surface and air search radar.

AN/SPS-5A, B, C, and D:
  Surface search radar.

AN/SPS-6C:
  Surface search radar.

AN/SPS-7:
  Surveillance radar.

AN/SPS-8:
  Search radar.

AN/SPS-10:
  Surveillance radar, C band.

AN/SPS-10F:
  Surface search radar, C band.

AN/SPS-12:
  Surveillance radar, L band.

AN/SPS-13:
  Three dimensional search and
  height finding radar.

AN/SPS-17:
  Long-range search radar.

AN/SPS-18:
  Surface search radar.

AN/SPS-19:
  Surface search radar.

AN/SPS-20:
  Surface search radar.

AN/SPS-21:
  Surface search radar.

AN/SPS-21A or B:
  Surface search radar.

AN/SPS-23:
  Shipboard height finding radar.

AN/SPS-29:
  Air search radar for guided missile
  destroyers.

AN/SPS-30:
  Long range height finder radar for
  carriers and guided missile cruisers.

AN/SPS-32:
  Three dimensional tracking radar.

AN/SPS-33:
  Three dimensional tracking radar.

AN/SPS-34:
  Search and height finder radar.

AN/SPS-35:
  Surface search radar.

AN/SPS-37:
  Shipboard air search radar.

AN/SPS-38:
  Early warning radar.

AN/SPS-39:
  Frequency scanning search radar.

AN/SPS-40:
  Destroyer air search radar.

AN/SPS-42:
  Three dimensional electronic
  scanning radar.

AN/SPS-43:
  Air search radar.

AN/SPS-45:
  Destroyer air search radar.

AN/SPS-48:
  Three-dimensional frequency
  scanning radar.

AN/SPS-49:
  Air search radar.

AN/SPS-50:
  Air search radar.

AN/SPS-52:
  Three-dimensional electronic
  scanning radar.

AN/SPW-2:
  Tracking and guidance radar for
  TALOS.

AN/SQA-10:
  Variable depth sonar.

AN/SQA-14:
  Searchlight sonar.

AN/SQA-16:
  Searchlight sonar.

AN/SQA-19:
  Variable depth sonar.

AN/SQA-20:
  Sonar tracking display group.

AN/SQA-T3A:
  Sonar trainer.

AN/SQD-20:
  Sonar for *SEAHAWK* program.

AN/SQG-1:
  Antisubmarine attack-fire control
  sonar.

AN/SQQ-1:
  Directional listening sonobuoy.

AN/SQQ-2:
  Sonobuoy.

AN/SQQ-3:
  Sonobuoy.

AN/SQQ-4:
  Sonobuoy.

AN/SQQ-14:
  Mine detection and classification
  sonar.

AN/SQQ-30B:
  Shipboard active sonar with *VDS.*

AN/SQR-13:
  Sonar set.

AN/SQS-4:
  Short range shipboard, active sonar.

AN/SQS-20:
Sonar.

AN/SQS-23:
Surface ship sonar, long range, active.

AN/SQS-25:
ASW detection system.

AN/SQS-26:
Large, shipboard high-powered, low frequency sonar.

AN/SQS-29:
Intermediate range shipboard active sonar.

AN/SQS-29B:
Shipboard sonar with *VDS.*

AN/SQS-30:
Intermediate range shipboard active sonar.

AN/SQS-31:
Intermediate range shipboard active sonar.

AN/SQS-31B:
Shipboard active sonar with *VDS.*

AN/SQS-32:
Intermediate range shipboard active sonar.

AN/SQS-32B:
Shipboard active sonar with *VDS.*

AN/SQS-T3:
Sonar trainer.

AN/SRC-22:
Flight deck communication system.

AN/SRD-12:
Radio direction finder.

AN/SRN-9:
Radar navigation set for satellite communications system.

AN/SRR-13:
Receiver.

AN/SRW-4:
Target control system for QH-50C drone

AN/SSC-2:
Shipboard satellite communications set.

AN/SSQ-15:
Air drop sonobuoy.

AN/SSQ-23A:
Expendable air drop sonobuoy.

AN/SSQ-28:
Sonobuoy.

AN/SSQ-38:
Long-life, lightweight sonobuoy *JEZEBEL.*

AN/SSQ-42:
Miniature, expendable air drop sonobuoy.

AN/SSQ-45:
Advanced design sonobuoy.

AN/SSQ-46:
Air droppable detection sonobuoy, minibuoy.

AN/SXQ-1:
Mobile electronic robot manipulator and underwater TV system *MERMUT.*

AN/TCC-41:
Multiplex 48/96 channel.

AN/TPA-5:
Computer indicator group.

AN/TPA-6:
Indicator group.

AN/TPN-8:
GCA set.

AN/TPQ-10:
Radar course direction central for close support bombing.

AN/TPS-1B:
Air defense radar.

AN/TPS-1D:
Air defense radar.

AN/TPS-1G:
Search radar.

AN/TPS-15:
Air defense radar.

AN/TPS-17:
Air defense radar.

AN/TPS-21:
Portable battlefield surveillance radar.

AN/TPS-31:
Harbor surveillance radar.

AN/TPS-32:
Air defense height finder.

AN/TPS-34:
Tactical, long-range, early warning three-dimensional radar.

AN/TPS-35:
Surveillance radar.

AN/TPS-40:
Height finder radar.

AN/TRC-27:
Tactical communications.

AN/TRC-27A:
Tactical communications.

AN/TRN-14:
Ground beacon, transportable.

AN/TRN-16:
Tactical radar beacon.

AN/TRN-20:
Pathfinder radio beacon.

AN/TSA-14:
Transistorized autovoice.

AN/TSC-22:
Communications system.

AN/TSM-56:
Helicopter transportable maintenance facility.

AN/TSQ-18:
Radar surveillance central.

AN/TSQ-39:
Tracking and surveillance radar for *TERRIER.*

AN/TYQ-1:
Marine Tactical Data System.

AN/TYQ-2:
Air operations control system of *MTDS.*

AN/UAT-1:
Infra-red communications transmitter.

AN/UCC-1:
Analog integrated circuit communications system.

AN/UNH-6:
Tape recorder.

AN/UPA-3:
Mark V IFF antenna group.

AN/UPA-5:
Mark V IFF display group.

AN/UPA-6:
Mark V IFF antenna group.

AN/UPA-9:
Mark V IFF display group.

AN/UPA-38:
Mark V IFF coder-decoder.

AN/UPM-20:
Radar test set.

AN/UPM-30:
Radar test set.

AN/UPM-79:
Radar test set.

AN/UPN-8:
Radar beacon.

AN/UPX-5B:
Mark X IFF radar.

AN/UPX-T1:
Mark X IFF trainer.

AN/UQC-1:
Underwater telephone.

AN/UQN-1:
Navigation sonar.

AN/UQS-1:
High resolution submarine sonar.

AN/UQS-T1A:
Sonar trainer.

AN/UQS-T1B, 1C and 1F:
Sonar operator trainers.

AN/URC-3:
General communications set.

AN/URC-32:
General-purpose radio receiver.

AN/URD-2:
VHF direction finding system.

AN/URD-4:
UHF radio direction finder.

AN/URN-5:
Beacon transmitters for mapping.

AN/URT-14:
Medium frequency shipboard
transmitter.

AN/USC-2:
Target intercept computer.

AN/USH-5:
Facsimile recorder.

AN/USM-41:
Test set for AN/USQ-6.

AN/USM-49:
Battery test set.

AN/USM-117:
Small transistorized oscilloscope.

AN/USQ-6:
Miss-distance measuring equipment.

AN/USQ-20:
NTDS computer subsystem.

AN/UYK-1:
General purpose computer.

AN/WIC-1:
Underwater intercom system for
nuclear powered submarines.

AN/WLR-2:
Submarine sonar countermeasures
set.

AN/WLR-5:
Acoustic air intercept receiver.

AN/WPN-3A:
Loran C receiver for SSBNs.

AN/WPN-4:
Loran C surface ship receiver.

AN/WQC-1:
Underwater acoustic communication
system.

AN/WQC-2:
Sonar communication set.

AN/WRC-1:
Ship-to-shore communication set.

AN/WRR-1:
Radio receiver.

AN/WRT-1:
Medium frequency shipboard
transmitter.

AN/WRT-2:
Shipboard high frequency general
purpose radio transmitter.